SAMS Teach Yourself

Web Services

in 24 Hours

Stephen Potts

Mike Kopack

SAMS   *201 West 103rd St., Indianapolis, Indiana, 46290 USA*

Sams Teach Yourself Web Services in 24 Hours

Copyright © 2003 by Sams Publishing

International Standard Book Number: 0-672-32515-2

Library of Congress Catalog Card Number: 2002114148

Printed in the United States of America

First Printing: May 2003

06   05   04   03   4   3   2

Trademarks

All terms mentioned in this book that are known to be trademarks or service marks have been appropriately capitalized. Sams Publishing cannot attest to the accuracy of this information. Use of a term in this book should not be regarded as affecting the validity of any trademark or service mark.

Warning and Disclaimer

Every effort has been made to make this book as complete and as accurate as possible, but no warranty or fitness is implied. The information provided is on an "as is" basis. The authors and the publisher shall have neither liability nor responsibility to any person or entity with respect to any loss or damages arising from the information contained in this book or from the use of the CD or programs accompanying it.

Bulk Sales

Sams offers excellent discounts on this book when ordered in quantity for bulk purchases or special sales. For more information, please contact:

U.S. Corporate and Government Sales
1-800-382-3419
corpsales@pearsontechgroup.com

For sales outside of the U.S., please contact:

International Sales
+1-317-581-3793
international@pearsontechgroup.com

ASSOCIATE PUBLISHER
Michael Stephens

ACQUISITIONS EDITOR
Todd Green

DEVELOPMENT EDITOR
Songlin Qiu

MANAGING EDITOR
Charlotte Clapp

PROJECT EDITOR
Matthew Purcell

COPY EDITOR
Rhonda Tinch-Mize

INDEXER
Cheryl Lenser

PROOFREADER
Katie Robinson

TECHNICAL EDITORS
Craig Pfeifer
Marc Goldford

TEAM COORDINATOR
Cindy Teeters

INTERIOR DESIGNER
Gary Adair

COVER DESIGNER
Alan Clements

PAGE LAYOUT
Michelle Mitchell

GRAPHICS
Tammy Graham
Laura Robbins

Contents at a Glance

Table of Contents

PART IV Advanced Topics   325

HOUR 21 Web Services Interoperability   327

HOUR 22 Web Service Security   337

About the Authors

STEPHEN POTTS is an independent consultant, author, and Java instructor in Atlanta, Georgia (United States). Stephen received his Computer Science degree in 1982 from Georgia Tech. He has worked in a number of disciplines during his 20-year career, with manufacturing being his deepest experience. His previous books include *Java Unleashed* and *Java Primer Plus*. He can be reached via email at stevepotts@mindspring.com.

MIKE KOPACK is a graduate of the Georgia Institute of Technology, where he earned a bachelor of science degree in computer science. Mike is a Sun Certified Java Programmer with experience dating back to JDK 1.0.2. He specializes in server-side Web technologies. His prior work has involved building dynamic Web site content management systems for multibillion-dollar corporations. Currently, he works as a software engineer for ISX Corporation in Atlanta, Georgia. He can be reached via email at crazybiker_ga@yahoo.com.

Dedication

FROM STEPHEN POTTS:

I would like to dedicate this book to Suzanne, my wife of 20 years. The hours required to produce a book of this size and scope place an additional burden on her in caring for our six children.

FROM MIKE KOPACK:

To Mom and Dad—Thanks for being supportive all these years.

Acknowledgments

FROM STEPHEN POTTS:

I would like to thank all the editors on this book for their contributions. Mike Kopack, my coauthor was great to work with. Todd Green, the acquisitions editor, guided me through the phases and helped me stay on schedule. Songlin Qiu has been a big help in keeping me focused on the details. Finally, I would like to thank Craig Pfeifer and Marc Goldford, the technical reviewers, for their efforts.

FROM MIKE KOPACK:

I'd like to thank Steve for getting me involved in this project, the tech editors for checking my work and making suggestions, and Todd, Songlin, Matt and the rest of the staff at Sams for giving us the opportunity to work on this project. I'd also like to thank Simon Fell for his help with PocketSOAP, Jose Carlo Domondon for his information on The Home Depot's use of Web services, and Dan Harvey and Dougal Campbell for their help with SOAP::Lite. Finally, my family, friends, and co-workers for listening to all my complaining and helping me not get too stressed out while working on this book! Thanks, guys!

We Want to Hear from You!

As the reader of this book, *you* are our most important critic and commentator. We value your opinion and want to know what we're doing right, what we could do better, what areas you'd like to see us publish in, and any other words of wisdom you're willing to pass our way.

As an associate publisher for Sams, I welcome your comments. You can email or write me directly to let me know what you did or didn't like about this book—as well as what we can do to make our books better.

Please note that I cannot help you with technical problems related to the *topic* of this book. We do have a User Services group, however, where I will forward specific technical questions related to the book.

When you write, please be sure to include this book's title and author as well as your name, email address, and phone number. I will carefully review your comments and share them with the author and editors who worked on the book.

Email: feedback@samspublishing.com

Mail: Michael Stephens
           Sams Publishing
           201 West 103rd Street
           Indianapolis, IN 46290 USA

For more information about this book or another Sams title, visit our Web site at www. samspublishing.com. Type the ISBN (excluding hyphens) or the title of a book in the Search field to find the page you're looking for.

Introduction

Whenever a new technology comes along, the whole technical community reaches to grasp the details as well as the implications. If this technology represents a "sea change" in the way that computers are programmed, the need to comprehend becomes a matter of technical survival.

Web services represents a sea change. There have been other drastic changes in the computing environment in the past few decades. Here are a few of them:

- Stored programs replaced punch cards and paper tape.
- Online systems largely replaced batch systems.
- Graphical user interfaces replaced green screens.
- Networked computers replaced standalone computing.
- Internet-based systems replaced LAN-based systems.

In a year or two we will add the following:

- Web services–based systems replaced simple Internet-based and LAN-based systems.

One of the characteristics of a sea change is that it negatively impacts the employment prospects of everyone who gets left behind. After online CICS became popular, batch COBOL programmers had trouble finding work. DOS programmers went looking after Windows was introduced. Client-server programmers found the going tough after Internet-based systems became widespread.

This book was written to help you make the transition from the computer systems of the past. If you are a CORBA or DCOM programmer, you will likely find that Web services–based systems are trying to solve the same problems you have solved, but in a nonproprietary way.

If you are a GUI programmer, you will find that the data sources for your applications will start coming from SOAP messages. For you JSP programmers, you will soon find that you can send a lot more information over the Internet than just HTML and JavaScript code.

Scope

This book is broad. A quick perusal of the table of contents will tell you that this book contains a lot of subject matter; therefore, the number of pages available for each topic is limited. As a result, each hour's emphasis is to provide the information to jump start you in each topic.

The subject matter was chosen by answering the question, "What does a programmer or manager need to know about each topic to understand Web Services?" The answer is: this book.

The Organization of This Book

This book is organized into five parts:

- Part I—Introducing Web Services
- Part II—Working with Web Services
- Part III—Building Web Services
- Part IV—Advanced Topics
- Part V—Appendices

Each of them plays a key role helping you understand Web Services.

Part I: Introducing Web Services

Before we get into too much detail, it is critical that we create a foundation of basic understanding.

Hour 1, "Understanding Web Services," gives you a high-level understanding of what Web services are.

Hour 2, "Advantages of Web Services," provides an explanation of why Web services are better than alternative technologies.

Hour 3, "Disadvantages and Pitfalls of Web Services," helps you understand when Web services are not appropriate.

Hour 4, "Comparing Web Services to Other Technologies," shows you how Web services are different from CORBA, RMI, DCOM, and so on.

Hour 5, "Typical Web Services Designs," shows you some of the ways the Web services are being used. This will help you understand the range of problems that Web services are designed to solve.

Part II: Working with Web Services

The details of the standards that Web services are based on are provided in this section.

Hour 6, "The Web Services Architecture," talks about how the different standards that Web services is built on interact with each other to provide a complete solution.

Hour 7, "Understanding XML," provides you with an overview of XML, the metalanguage that all of the Web services standards are built with.

Hour 8, "Understanding How Web Services Communicate," shows you the different ways that a client can communicate with a Web service.

Hour 9, "Exchanging Messages with SOAP," provides an explanation of how the SOAP language is used to make method calls against a Web service.

Hour 10, "Describing a Web Service with the Web Services Description Language (WSDL)," teaches you how to create an XML document that exactly describes both the logical and physical details needed to communicate with a Web service.

Hour 11, "Advertising a Web Service," teaches you how to use the Universal Description, Discovery, and Integration (UDDI) protocol to publish the existence and capabilities of your Web service.

Hour 12, "Sending Attachments with Web Services," provides an overview of how non-textual data such as images and computer programs can be sent efficiently using Web services.

Part III: Building Web Services

Many different products have been written to help you create Web services. This part looks at each of the major products available and gives you an overview of each, along with some simple examples of how to use them.

Hour 13, "Creating Web Services with Apache Axis," introduces you to Axis, the open-source toolkit that is maintained by Apache.

Hour 14, "Creating Web Services with Java," shows you how to use option Java packages from Sun Microsystems to create Web services.

Hour 15, "Creating Web Services with .NET," introduces you to Microsoft's Web services offering.

Hour 16, "Creating .NET Web Service Clients," teaches you how to use .NET to create rich clients for accessing Web services.

Hour 17, "Creating Web Services with BEA WebLogic Workshop," shows you how create Web services using this dedicated toolkit from BEA Systems.

Hour 18, "Creating Web Services with IBM WebSphere," shows you how to use this software development suite to create Web services.

Hour 19, "Creating Web Services with Other Toolkits," introduces you to some of the alternative toolkits that have been written.

Hour 20, "Comparing the Different Web Services Tools," analyzes the different products covered in this part of the book. It covers documentation, cost, learning curves, and a host of other considerations.

Part IV: Advanced Topics

Java is a great platform for dealing with media. This section introduces you to the stars of the Java Media packages.

Hour 21, "Web Services Interoperability," teaches you about the interoperability challenges that remain and the efforts underway to solve them.

Hour 22, "Web Services Security," shows you the different approaches and proposals that are being considered for improving the security of Web services transactions.

Hour 23, "Web Services in the Real World," shows you some of the ways that Web services are being used today by pioneering companies.

Hour 24, "The Future of Web Services," tells you about the direction in which Web services standards are heading. It provides an overview of some of the more interesting proposals being considered.

Part V: Appendices

Appendix A shows you how to install Apache Tomcat and Apache Axis.

Appendix B shows you how to install the Java Web Services Developer Pack.

Appendix C shows you how to install and configure other Web services toolkits that were covered in Hour 19.

Conventions Used in This Book

Certain conventions have been followed in this book to help you digest all the material. For example, at the beginning of each hour, you'll find a list of the major topics that will be covered in that particular hour. You will also find that icons are used throughout this book. These icons either are accompanied by additional information on a subject or supply you with shortcuts or optional ways to perform a task. These icons are as follows:

Notes include additional information related to the current topic, such as asides and comments.

Tips contain shortcuts and hints on performing a particular task.

A Caution alerts you to a possible problem and gives you advice on how to avoid it.

NEW TERM   New terms are introduced using the New Term icon.   The new term appears in italic.

The following typographic conventions are used in this book:

- Code lines, commands, statements, variables, and any text you type or see onscreen appears in a `monospace` typeface.
- *Italics* highlight technical terms when they're being defined.
- The ➡ icon is used before a line of code that is really a continuation of the preceding line. Sometimes a line of code is too long to fit as a single line on the page. If you see ➡ before a line of code, remember that it's part of the line immediately above it.

At the end of each hour, you will find both a Summary section and a Q&A section. The Summary section provides a brief encapsulation of the core information covered in the hour. The Q&A section provides a series of questions and answers that help cement important facts and concepts covered in the hour.

Source Code and Updates

For updates to this book and to download the source code and examples presented in this book, visit `http://www.samspublishing.com`. From the home page, type this book's ISBN (0672325152) in to the Search window (without hyphens), and click on Search to access information about the book as well as a direct link to the source code.

PART I

Introducing Web Services

Hour

HOUR 1

Understanding Web Services

If you ask someone if they are familiar with Web services, they usually pause before answering. They know what the Web is and they certainly know what services are, but they are not sure whether you are asking a generic question or asking about a specific technology. Apart from the generic-sounding name, Web services represent a new architecture for creating applications that can be accessed from a different computer. The purpose of this hour is to improve your understanding of the topic at an executive summary level.

In this hour, you will learn

- The definition of Web services
- The promise of Web services
- The key specifications that comprise Web services
- The tools that are commonly used to create Web services

- The challenges that face Web services developers
- The organizations that manage the specifications that Web services are built upon

Understanding What Web Services Are

NEW TERM　A Web service is a software application that can be accessed remotely using different *XML*-based languages. Normally, a Web service is identified by a *URL*, just like any other Web site. What makes Web services different from ordinary Web sites is the type of interaction that they can provide.

Most Web sites are designed to provide a response to a request from a person. The person either types in the URL of the site or clicks on a hyperlink to create the request. This request takes the form of a text document that contains some fairly simple instructions for the server. These instructions are limited to the name of a document to be returned or a call to a server-side program, along with a few parameters. Figure 1.1 shows this process.

FIGURE 1.1

A browser interacts with a Web server to make requests.

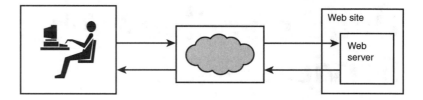

NEW TERM　A Web service is similar in that it is accessed via a URL. The difference lies in the content of what is sent in the request from the client to the service. Web service clients send an XML document formatted in a special way in accordance with the rules of the *SOAP specification*. This specification is the topic of Hour 9, "Exchanging Messages with SOAP."

A SOAP message can contain a call to a method along with any parameters that might be needed. In addition, the message can contain a number of header items that further specify the intent of the client. These header items might designate what Web services will get this method call after the current service finishes its work, or they might contain security information. In any case, the complexity of the SOAP message far exceeds the complexity that is possible using only a browser. Figure 1.2 shows this process graphically.

FIGURE 1.2
A client interacts with a Web service via a Web server such as Apache Tomcat or MS Internet Information Server.

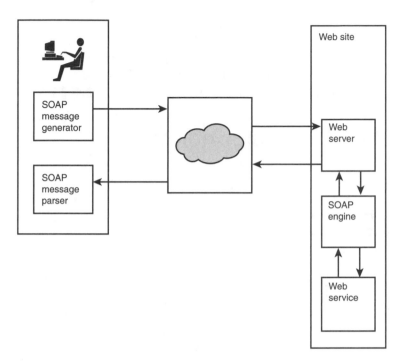

The Great Promise of Web Services

NEW TERM Most of the enthusiasm surrounding Web services is based on the promise of interoperability. The Web services architecture is based on sending XML messages in a specific SOAP format. XML can be represented as plain *ASCII* characters, which can be transferred easily from computer to computer. The implications of this are significant:

- It doesn't matter what kind of computer sends the SOAP message or on what operating system it is running.
- It doesn't matter where in the world the client is sending the message from.
- It doesn't matter what language the software that the client is running on was written in.
- There is no need for the client to know what type of SOAP processor is running on the server.

In short, Web services are the Holy Grail of computing. Every software application in the world can potentially talk to every other software application in the world. This communication can take place across all the old boundaries of location, operating system, language, protocol, and so on.

If we take off the rose-colored glasses for a minute, however, we will see that there is much work to be done before this promise is realized. Although the current specifications provide us with a solid beginning, no one believes that they are adequate for every situation. Areas such as security, transaction support, and business process execution are being addressed, but they are not yet incorporated into the SOAP specification.

The Key Components

Web services transactions take place between components. You can either program these components yourself, download them from open source software foundations such as Apache, or purchase them from commercial vendors such as Microsoft or IBM. There is no requirement that you obtain all the components that you use from a single vendor; you can write some, download others, and purchase still more.

For a Web service transaction to complete successfully, all of the components involved in processing the transaction must behave in ways that the other components expect them to. Given the differing vendors involved in the creation of the components, you might expect that they would have a lot of problems interacting. Although Web services interoperability is difficult to attain, it can be remedied by the creation of high-quality standards and a religious adherence to these standards by every programmer and vendor involved. At this writing, the following are considered the core Web services standards:

- **SOAP**—SOAP originally stood for Simple Object Access Protocol. But SOAP is now considered a specification name and not an acronym. SOAP is a specification that defines an XML grammar for both sending messages and responding to messages that you receive from other parties. The goal of SOAP is to describe a message format that is not bound to any hardware or software architecture, but one that carries a message from any platform to any other platform in an unambiguous fashion.

  The SOAP standard contains two parts: the header that carries processing instructions and the body that contains the *payload*. The payload contains the information that you want to send. The two types of SOAP messages are documents and *Remote Procedure Calls (RPCs)*. The payload of a document message is any XML document that you want moved from one computer to another. An RPC is a method call that is intended to be executed on the Web service's computer. The RPC message performs the same function as an ordinary method call in an ordinary programming language. The difference is that this call can take place over the Internet. SOAP is the subject of Hour 9.

  NEW TERM

- **Extensible Markup Language (XML)**—Extensible Markup Language (XML) is the language that all the Web services Languages are built on. XML is a tool for constructing self-describing documents. In fact, XML is more of a meta-language than a language in that it is used to create grammars. These grammars are described in XML schemas that specify the tags that are allowed and the relationships between the elements defined by these tags. SOAP, WSDL, and UDDI are all XML-based grammars. XML is the subject of Hour 7, "Understanding XML."

- **Hypertext Transport Protocol (HTTP)**—Hypertext Transport Protocol (HTTP) is a standard that precedes the advent of Web services. It was developed to facilitate the transfer of requests from a browser to a Web server. Web services takes advantage of the existence of this mature protocol to move SOAP messages and WSDL documents from one computer to another.

  Newer versions of SOAP describe how other transport mechanisms such as FTP, SMTP, and JMS can be used to perform this same function. At the time of this writing, however, the vast majority of Web services are built on HTTP.

- **Web Services Description Language (WSDL)**—Web services Description Language (WSDL) is a specification that tells us how to describe a piece of software in terms of the method calls that it responds to. These methods are described in an abstract way that is independent of what programming language the actual service is written in or what computer and operating system it runs on. In fact, you can port an application from a personal computer to a mainframe, and the abstract portion of the WSDL description will not change (assuming that the port and protocol don't change when you port them).

  The WSDL also contains a concrete section in which the various details of how to actually make a connection to the service are stored. If a Web service could be accessed using HTTP, FTP, or SMTP, you would find three entries in the concrete section—one for each service.

- **Universal Discovery Description Integration (UDDI)**—The Universal Discovery, Description, and Integration (UDDI) specification describes how a potential customer of a Web service could learn about its capabilities and obtain the basic information needed to make the initial contact with the site. Normally, this contact includes a download of the WSDL.

  UDDI registries can be public, private, or semiprivate. A public directory allows everyone on the planet to examine the information that you post in the registry. A private registry exists behind the firewall of your organization and is only accessible by members of your organization. A semiprivate registry is open only to a limited number of outsiders such as you best trading partners.

Tools and Vendors

Another aspect of Web services that is sometimes hard to grasp is what tools you need to create them. Often, the software tools that you have worked with have come from a single vendor. Microsoft sells Visual Basic and Visual C++, along with a framework and an Integrated Development Environment (IDE). Even though Sun Microsystems allows you to download Java at no cost, specific vendors such as Borland and IBM sell you an IDE.

Web services can be developed using any programming language that supports sockets. You could write a client that generated its own SOAP messages. You could then open a socket and send the message to a Web service listening on that socket. That Web service could do its own SOAP parsing, make its own method calls, write to its own logs, and prepare its own SOAP response message. Finally, it could open a response socket and send the return message to the client, who could then display the results.

Although you could do this, it would be a bit like forging your own shovels and rakes at home before going out into the garden to work. A quick trip to the local hardware store could save you a lot of time and shorten your schedule quite a bit.

Web services tools are numerous because so many software vendors have bought into its promise. In addition, a few startups have also written Web services development tools. The result is a wide variety of choices. You not only get to choose between vendors and IDEs, but you also get to determine what level of tool you want to employ.

Tools range from special Java classes that know how to create SOAP messages to full-blown development environments that remind you of a high quality Fourth generation language tool. The following is a list of the tools that we will cover in this book:

- **Apache Axis**—Apache Software Foundation coordinates the creation of open source projects. One of its projects is a SOAP engine that is normally used with its Tomcat server. Axis is the subject of Hour 13, "Creating Web Services with Apache Axis."

- **Java**—Sun Microsystems has created a set of optional packages that can access UDDI registries, generate WSDLs, and so on. These packages are the subject of Hour 14, "Creating Web Services with Java."

- **Visual Studio .NET**—Microsoft's new way to create Web services is to use this product in conjunction with any one of the Visual Studio languages such as Visual Basic, Visual C++, or C#. Hour 15, "Creating Web Services with .NET," shows an example that creates a Web service using Visual Basic .NET.

- **Web Services .NET Clients**—Clients created using .NET that can interact with any Web service. Hour 16, "Creating .NET Web Service Clients," covers this.
- **BEA WebLogic Workshop**—BEA is a leading *J2EE* vendor that has created a user-friendly way to create Web services by using an elaborate IDE. Hour 17, "Creating Web Services with BEA WebLogic Workshop," covers this tool.
- **IBM WebSphere Studio Application Developer (WSAD)**—IBM has made the creation of Web services a part of its comprehensive package called WSAD. We cover the creation of Web services with WSAD in Hour 18, "Creating Web Services with IBM WebSphere."
- **Other Important Products**—Many lesser-known companies have quality entries in the Web services development tool market. Hour 19, "Creating Web Services with Other Toolkits," covers Iona XMLbus, The Mind Electric GLUE, PocketSOAP, and SOAP::Lite.

In Hour 20, "Comparing the Different Web Services Tools," we compare the different features of these packages and talk about their strengths and weaknesses.

Who Manages the Web Services Specifications

Earlier in this hour, we covered each of the specifications that form the foundation that Web services are built on. In each instance, we mentioned what governing body was responsible for managing the decision-making process that leads to the publication of a new version of each specification. This seems like quite a confusing arrangement at first because no one authority has the final word.

This lovely confusion is a direct result of the distrust that we have for software vendors and their distrust of each other. Many of us have felt like hostages to one vendor or another. Vendors, by their very nature, are beholden to their stockholders who expect them to earn a profit. This otherwise noble goal can lead to bad behavior; however, when a vendor begins to monopolize a technology to lock in its users, decisions sometimes seem to be made on how best to restrict the user's freedom to defect to another vendor's product.

Vendors also tend to play roughly with each other. If they control one piece of the software suite, they tend to use it to expand their influence into other areas. This can perceived as "fighting dirty" by the competition. As a result, vendors often cooperate or fail to cooperate with each other based not on what is best for the industry, but what will irritate the other the most.

Having fought dozens of wars over the past two decades, users and vendors alike have been looking for an alternative to the madness of cutthroat competition. In the abstract, they all realize that a set of specifications written to be of the greatest benefit to the user would level the playing field. As a result, they have begun to cooperate with a group of nonprofit consortiums whose sole purpose is to draft and publish specifications.

The World Wide Web Consortium

The most important of these organizations is the World Wide Web Consortium (W3C). On its Web site, www.w3.org, the W3C states the following:

> The World Wide Web Consortium (W3C) develops interoperable technologies (specifications, guidelines, software, and tools) to lead the Web to its full potential. W3C is a forum for information, commerce, communication, and collective understanding.

The W3C manages the SOAP, WSDL, XML, XML Schema, and HTTP specifications, among others. In addition, the W3C manages the WS-Architecture document, which is currently in a draft status. This document is attempting to establish a formal definition of Web services.

OASIS

Another important organization in the Web services world is the Organization for the Advancement of Structured Information Standards (OASIS). The OASIS Web site, www.oasis-open.org, states the following:

> OASIS is a not-for-profit, global consortium that drives the development, convergence, and adoption of e-business standards.

OASIS manages UDDI, WS-Security, and SAML specifications, among others.

WS-I

The Web Services Interoperability Organization (WS-I) is a fairly new organization that has finally succeeded in getting the last big holdout, Sun Microsystems, to join. The WS-I Web site, www.ws-1.org, states that the mission of the WS-I is this:

> WS-I is an open industry organization chartered to promote Web services interoperability across platforms, operating systems, and programming languages. The organization works across the industry and standards organizations to respond to customer needs by providing guidance, best practices, and resources for developing Web services solutions.

1

The WS-I published profiles, testing tools, and sample applications that guarantee, as nearly as possible, that the different standards work together. The profiles are a versioned set of specifications that have been shown to be able to work together successfully.

The Specification Process

The process of creating a new specification is a bit like visiting the proverbial sausage factory—sausage is easier to eat if you don't watch it being made. Normally, a single company discovers that it needs a certain specification to go forward. It normally gets together with a couple of friendly companies and creates a draft. The industry is generally skeptical of vendor-created standards, so the creators of the draft normally try to enlist one or more of their traditional enemies to join with them in publishing the specification. They do this because enemies won't join in publishing a worthless or self-serving specification.

With an enemy on board, the growing group of supporters tries to get an established organization such as W3C or OASIS to take over the management of it. If they succeed, they get a credibility boost. If they are unsuccessful, they normally form a single specification organization to manage the feedback and publish the specification. UDDI.org was formed for this purpose. This new organization tries to get other organizations, especially more traditional enemies, to join while simultaneously working to improve the specification.

Victory is achieved when enough organizations have joined on that there is universal buy-in. Often an organization such as W3C or OASIS will agree to take over a specification after it has gained more acceptance. OASIS took over UDDI after it had proven its viability by signing up supporters. After a specification is moved into a standards organization, it is assigned to a committee.

Commercial organizations often assign internal staff to donate some of their time to these committees. Representatives of large organizations are often voted to chair the committees in order to maintain their support for the specification. Other organizations, who are interested in making sure that the resulting drafts address issues important to them, assign staffers to work on the creation of the drafts. When the committee reaches a consensus that the draft is ready for publication, the draft is published and set aside for a period of time for comment. Anyone can comment on or take issue with the published draft. The committee reviews this feedback, and changes are made if the concern is deemed valid. After the time for comments expires, the committee publishes the specification and calls it a standard (OASIS) or a recommendation (W3C).

After a standard or recommendation is published, vendors can choose to implement the changes and additions in their products. Failure to do so, however, might lead to a loss of prestige in the marketplace, which could, in turn, cause a product to be rejected by potential buyers.

Summary

The promise of Web services is great, but the obstacles are formidable. In our previous scenario, we were exchanging information about an address. If this information had been sensitive, we would have had to use SSL to encrypt the entire transaction because, at present, no security information appears in the SOAP specification.

If there had been any incompatibilities between the versions of SOAP, UDDI, HTTP, and WSDL that we were using, the transaction might not have completed successfully. Web services is also lacking a transaction model to allow for a rollback in case of failure.

Although there is much to be excited about, there is much work to be done. The good news is that we don't have to wait on any one vendor to decide the direction for us. Anyone who wants to become involved in the specification process is welcomed to join in and push.

In this hour, we looked at what a Web service is. Following that, we covered the various standards that form the foundation of Web services. We listed briefly the commercial products that have achieved some popularity in the marketplace.

Next, we looked at how all the different specifications support one another in completing a typical transaction. Finally, we looked at who controls the specifications that govern Web services and how these specifications came to be.

Q&A

Q What are the key specifications that compose Web services?

A They are XML, HTTP, SOAP, WSDL, and UDDI.

Q Who creates new or revised Web services standards?

A Anyone who wants to can create and submit draft proposals. In practice, this is normally done by groups of companies with a vested interest in the progress of Web services standards.

Workshop

The Workshop is designed to help you review what you've learned, and begin learning how to put your knowledge into practice.

Quiz

1. What is the promise of Web services?
2. What are the core standards that compose Web services?
3. What are some of the challenges that are holding back Web services?
4. Who controls the Web services specifications?

Quiz Answers

1. The promise of Web services is interoperability across hardware, operating system, geographic, and programming language boundaries.
2. The core standards are HTTP, XML, XML schema, SOAP, WSDL, and UDDI.
3. The current standards don't address issues such as security, transaction management, or business process execution. In addition, different versions of the same standard can cause transactions to fail.
4. The specifications that govern Web services are controlled by the user community through standards organizations such as W3C and OASIS.

Activities

1. Visit the W3C Web site at www.w3.org and read through the recommendations that are published such as SOAP 1.1 and drafts such as WSDL 1.2.
2. Go to the OASIS Web site at www.oasis-open.org and review the UDDI 2.4 specification.
3. Visit www.apache.org and read about Apache Axis. Download it if you plan on working the examples later in the book.

Hour **2**

Advantages of Web Services

There are many advantages to using the Web services architecture over any other. In fact, some Web services applications would be expensive or impossible to duplicate using any other technology. One of the challenges for technical leaders is to discover opportunities in which Web services can be used to solve today's problems. In addition, we need to be looking for Web services solutions to problems that are ever present, but never solved. These areas include the cost of doing business, in effect, the cost of software development, and the time that it takes to react to new market opportunities. In this hour, we will look at a fairly extensive list of the advantages that Web services provide over more traditional approaches. In addition, we will cover some concrete examples of what is happening and what can happen in the future using Web services.

In this hour, you will learn about the advantages of using Web services for

- Integrating legacy systems
- Lowering operational costs

- Lowering software development costs
- Getting systems done faster
- Interfacing with customers
- Integrating with external business partners
- Generating new revenue
- Supporting new business models

Legacy Systems

NEW TERM Many of the early adopters of Web services technology have concentrated their efforts at interconnecting *legacy* (established, reliable, operational) systems to each other. Their reasons for doing this are

- Working on internal systems entails less technical risk than working with outside entities. For this reason, companies have decided to keep the trial-and-error phase of new technology adoption out of the spotlight.
- Many firms allow their internal developers to gain experience on legacy systems before allowing them to interface with their customers' systems.
- To make a Web service useful, a client must exist. Internal projects give the developers control of both the client and the service.
- Older solutions are problematic. Many of these projects replace older programs that were written using other, often inferior approaches. Many of these approaches, like flat file transfers, are fragile. Other development projects, written in CORBA or DCOM, tend to be expensive to maintain and enhance. For this reason, they are obvious targets for replacement.

Web services wrap nicely around legacy systems, regardless of the language that they were written in. Many developers roll their eyes when they are asked to work on 25 year old COBOL or PL/1 systems. They mistake old for bad. From the standpoint of management, an older software system that has been running the company's shipping department for more than 20 years is worth its weight in gold, regardless of how uncool the technology is. Customers pay for products that get delivered properly, regardless of how stylish the program that managed the delivery process is.

The thought of writing, testing, and implementing a new system to replace one that already works well is a tough sell to a company's management. Why would they pay money to replace a solid performer with one that is certain to be buggy for the first few months, if not years?

Web services can be written in such a way that they require little or no change to the legacy code base. They can be written to interact with the older code similar to the way that a *graphical user interface (GUI)* would. The end result is a state-of-the-art distributed system that retains all the equity that a company has built up in its legacy code base.

Lower Operational Costs

Any company that is going to succeed in the long term is constantly trying to lower its costs of doing business. These cost improvement programs are focused on both internal and customer-oriented systems. Web services provides opportunities to save costs in these areas:

- **Cheaper than a LAN**—It is hard to imagine any way of interconnecting computers that is cheaper than using the Internet. Essentially, every computer that can access the Internet could serve as either a Web service, a Web services client, or both. A LAN requires that you interconnect all computers with some sort of cable. The Internet allows you to connect via each computer's existing service provider.

- **Low-cost Electronic Data Interchange (EDI)**—You might find some cost savings if you set up electronic data exchanges with your best customers and vendors. EDI has pioneered this effort, and Web services are poised to expand it in every direction.

- **Remote Status Reports**—The fact that any two computers can participate in a Web services transaction means that you can get a status report from any organization in the world at any time of the day or night. The potential savings from the elimination of paper-based reporting systems is huge.

- **Remote System Management**—There is virtually no limit to the amount of remote management that can be done using this technology. Most of the savings occurs when a technician can troubleshoot a problem from his own desk without incurring any travel overhead or expense.

- **Dynamic Routing of Service People**—Web services are being expanded onto *personal digital assistants (PDAs)* such as the Palm and Handspring models. This allows people who still have to travel from site to site to use just-in-time dispatching. Instead of planning the whole repair day in the morning, a truck can receive the next assignment when that worker is actually ready to work on the job. This can result in large increases in efficiency and less customer downtime.

Lower Software Development Cost

For the past 20 years, the Holy Grail of software development has been the concept of code reuse. The idea of code reuse is as simple as it is intuitive. Instead of reinventing the proverbial wheel a thousand times, you invent it once and use it a thousand times.

The complete promise of code reuse has remained an elusive target. One problem has always been the packaging of the code. For code to be reused, it has to be created in a way that makes it easy for a new program to find and use it. If the code existed, but you didn't know about it, you could not receive any benefit from it. If you knew about it, but it was written in Java, a Visual Basic developer probably couldn't use it. The fact that Web services can interoperate regardless of the language that each of them is written in is a tremendous development in the code reuse world.

For some time, it has been possible to create a Web service–style system by interconnecting programs written to the DCOM and CORBA standards. Practically speaking, the torment associated with doing that was so great that only the most important problems were solved in this way. To make matters worse, most company firewalls block these types of transactions, making it impossible to implement them.

With Web services, there will no longer be a need to translate DCOM objects into CORBA and vice versa. For the first time in history, all major hardware and software vendors are in agreement that Web services should exist and interoperate seamlessly. The reason for this ecumenical feeling is that Web services technology can be implemented on any computer platform using any development tools. This keeps every vendor in the game and reduces the need for professional gripers to tell us why the other company's approach is weak. Now they tell us that Web services is the future, but the competition's toolset is weak.

This ecumenical bliss is underscored by the fact that a very fair-minded organization, the *World Wide Web Consortium (W3C)*, is the official keeper of the Web services quasi-standards that they call recommendations. Most vendors have people who sit on W3C committees and steer the new proposals in the direction that they want to see them go. The end result is that everyone remains in synch with the Web services community as a whole.

The high level of vendor commitment to this technology lowers the cost of using it. Not only does competition drive down tool prices, but it also encourages innovation by pressuring the tool vendors to keep thinking outside the box.

Faster System Development

Better tools mean faster development, which in turn leads to lower development costs. Another way development costs are lowered is by allowing a wide variety of programming skill sets to play in the game. If you have an army of COBOL programmers, you can hire one Web services guru to set up the infrastructure, and then have your staff write everything else in COBOL. If you use PERL, keep your development in PERL. Web services tools are on the market that interact with almost any language. Even if the tool support is weak for your favorite language, you can create the WSDL and SOAP messages manually and communicate that way.

Many vendors provide rapid development tools that go beyond what is available for creating user interfaces. Web services are based on the creation of both a service and a formal description of the service called the *Web Services Description Language (WSDL)* document. This document contains enough information about the service to allow a client to be generated. Instead of starting with a blank sheet of paper, the programmer of a Web service client starts with a generated client that can successfully access a Web service. He can then enhance that client to interact with the other systems on the client side. The time and learning curve savings from using this approach is significant.

Many modern development tools can also generate Web service code from functional descriptions. Although these services are more limited than hand development solutions could be, they offer the advantage of speed. Even for complex requirements, the generated part of the Web service code can get the project started. From there, the programmer can hand code the unique parts that are beyond the capabilities of the tool.

Better Interfaces with Customers

Every business guru from Tony Robbins to Steven Covey will tell you that the way to succeed in business is to get close to your customers. Vendors who succeed in integrating their systems such as orders, shipping, and billing are nearly impossible for their competitors to dislodge because they are woven into the business processes of those customers.

One example of this would be an automated reordering system. If you provided an automated way of interfacing to the point-of-sale system at a major food retailer, you could know, by sales data, when to send more disposable diapers to a certain store. The competition would have trouble breaking into that account because they can provide product but not convenience. Convenience can translate into big savings for a customer because it lowers his cost of doing business. Figure 2.1 shows this business interaction.

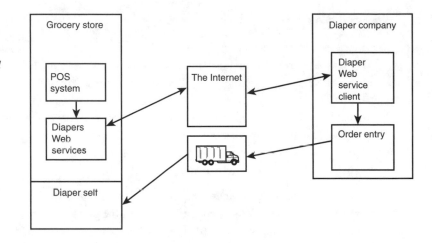

FIGURE 2.1
Web services allow tighter integration between vendors and their customers.

> Another way to endear yourself to your customers is to allow them to peek inside your systems to check on order status. For example, when I ordered a camera online and had it shipped by UPS, I would get online every day just to see where the package was. I watched with interest as it moved from warehouse to warehouse and finally onto the truck for delivery to my home.

Many companies have systems that could be opened up without much risk. Contractors could provide status reports in this way to put their customers at ease. Car companies could track the progress of custom vehicle orders so that the customer could enjoy the process of buying that special car. Baseball teams could publish their internal statistics for the rabid fans to follow.

Some Web services can provide savings to your company, while allowing your customers better access. For example, allowing customers to manage their own account data frees up your internal resources and increases the accuracy of the data. When a customer's shipping address changes, he could access and change that data via a Web service.

Better Integration with External Business Partners

Modern corporations are anything but monolithic entities. Most companies are built on the foundation of business partners—other companies that have traditionally been classified as suppliers. Forward-thinking firms have concluded that the best way to lower costs is not to beat your suppliers down to get them to cut their margins, but to help those suppliers lower their costs. It is better to find suppliers who will allow a level of integration that will benefit both companies.

One example of this is outsourced human resources. Writing paychecks to engineers is essentially the same thing as writing paychecks to the dancers in a Broadway play, even though their daily work activity is very different. For this outsourcing to be truly less expensive, however, the HR vendors' systems must be able to interact with their clients' systems well.

Web services are ideal for this type of interaction. You can interconnect two different systems without making significant alterations to either one. This can enable an outsourced company to act as a Web services client in order to collect payroll and personnel data. Figure 2.2 shows these businesses interacting.

FIGURE 2.2
Web services allow tighter integration between business partners.

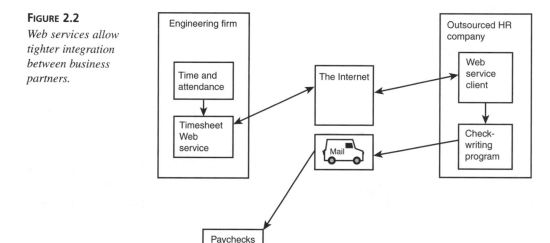

New Revenue Opportunities

NEW TERM This level of cooperation between computer systems will open up new opportunities for virtual enterprises. A *virtual enterprise* is one that is made up of several smaller enterprises. For example, if a hotel in Orlando booked your room, scheduled your flight, reserved your rental car, and sold you tickets to the theme parks, you would be doing business with a virtual company. No single company owns airplanes, cars, hotels, and theme parks. Each company owns one of these assets and offers the others through partnership agreements. In fact, you could start a company that owns none of these assets. Your sole reason for existing is to provide one-stop shopping for these types

of packages. If you have a strong advertising strategy and the proper business agreements, you could sell merchandise that you have never actually owned. Figure 2.3 shows
these businesses interacting:

FIGURE 2.3

*Web services allow
new businesses to be
assembled from
smaller businesses.*

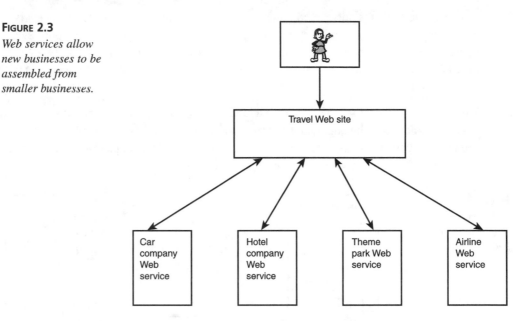

The key to making this type of virtual business work is the low-cost interconnection
between computer systems. If the cost of interconnection is too high, your enterprise will
have to pass on too much cost to the customer. If your customer feels that you are too
expensive, he will bypass your site and individually purchase services from each vendor.

Fortunately, Web services make it possible to create interconnections for far less cost
than traditional approaches. In addition, the time needed to program a new service connection is far shorter using the Web services approach.

Another new potential source of revenue can be found in charging directly for the use of
your business processes. This area is so new that we have to go into creative mode to
even think of examples. One example that comes to mind would be a cost-estimating system. It is critically important for construction companies to accurately estimate the cost
of building a certain building. Normally, these companies write internal systems that they
plug the details in to. The result is a report showing a cost breakdown for the project.

You could imagine a group of programmers breaking off from one construction company
and starting their own software company. This company could hire the best estimators in
the industry and produce a superior cost-estimating system. Every construction company

would run its own numbers internally, but it could pay our new company to run them too. The combination of the two estimates would serve to either increase confidence in the original number or to flag a potential problem if the two numbers don't agree. Figure 2.4 shows these businesses interacting.

FIGURE 2.4

Web services allow new types of businesses to exist.

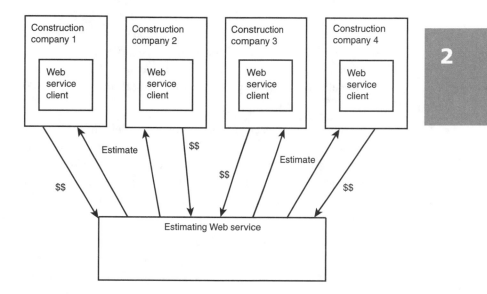

Another place where a Web service could be a revenue generator is in the field of product design. Engineering analysis software is used in the design of nearly all the physical goods we use. The automobile industry is an especially heavy user of this kind of software. Analysis is performed on the plastic in a dashboard, the beams in a chassis, the vibration in a steering column, and so on. Normally, a virtual solid model is created in the computer and submitted to one or more of these analysis programs for evaluation. The result of the evaluation might cause a design to be changed to better meet its requirements.

The software packages that perform this work are very expensive and normally only used by companies that have a lot of this work to perform. Smaller companies must either do this analysis by hand or simply do without. If the vendors of these packages could turn them into Web services, they could then charge based on the usage and not by the license. This could allow that vendor to sign up new customers easily because the initial expense would be very low. In addition, the fees paid to the vendor would come out of the customer's normal expense budget and wouldn't require a capital expenditure.

Completely New Business Models

Another opportunity for a new revenue stream would be in selling empty seats, mechanics bays, and so on. All service businesses have perishable assets. An empty bay in an automobile repair shop or an empty table in a restaurant is perishable. If it is not used this hour, it is wasted and cannot be retrieved and sold in the future. Finding a way to sell these empty seats, even at a steep discount, would improve the profitability of these businesses. A large tire and brake chain could create a Web service that prices the same procedures differently, depending on the demand. For example, a brake job performed at 10:00 a.m. on a Saturday would be charged full price, but at 8:00 a.m. on Tuesday, it might be half price.

A business with a fleet of vehicles could schedule them for maintenance based on the demand. They could write a Web service client that interacted with the brake stores whenever a maintenance procedure was required. The Web service could provide a dynamic price based on the demand at stores across town. The client would compare these prices to the cost of driving to each location and would choose the one that provided the best value.

In addition, consumers could use a Web-based version of this software. An applet might serve as the client running in a browser. The customer would enter his parameters such as the procedure needed, urgency, location of vehicle, and so on. The Web service would then provide a list of shops and prices. The customer could then choose the one that he considers to be the best value and could drive across town, if necessary, to patronize that shop.

Another type of customer-oriented Web service would be a towing system. A Web service could be written that accepts requests for a tow. Normally, this request would be created by a phone call to an operator at 1-800-tow-junk. A stranded motorist would place a high priority request at full price. If he is really desperate, he might even add a tip in the offer.

All the tow services that monitor this Web service have clients installed on Palm-sized devices. Whenever a tow is needed, it will appear on the Palm, along with the price offered. The first available tow truck will commit to do the job and accept it by clicking on the Palm device. After contacting the stranded motorist, he would get underway.

Not all tows represent emergencies, though. Car dealers, junk yards, and repair shops use towing services a lot. They are not in as big a hurry as a stranded motorist, so they would offer less for a tow. The tow truck would move these cars during slow times or even on a night shift when prices are best. Whenever an emergency comes in, he would go to it, make more money that hour, and return to the car dealer when it gets slow again.

Almost any business with excess perishable capacity is a good candidate for this type of empty-seat selling. The dynamic nature of the pricing can lead to better utilization of resources and higher profits. In low-tech businesses such as towing, a third party would be the likely Web service provider. The provider might even provide the Palm-sized devices to the trucks in exchange for a 10% fee on each tow scheduled through them.

Summary

In this hour, you learned about the advantages that might be available to you with Web services. We covered how Web services can be used to integrate legacy systems, lower operational costs, lower software development costs, and get systems done faster.

In addition, you learned how Web services can help you to interface with your customers better as well as with your business partners. Finally, you saw how Web services can help you generate new revenue and support new business models.

Q&A

Q How can Web services make legacy systems integration easier?

A Web services do this by providing a set of protocols for data exchange that can be used to move data from one legacy system to another.

Q How can Web services improve customer service?

A You can use Web services to provide your customers with better information about the status of orders, levels of inventory, and so on.

Workshop

This section is designed to help you anticipate possible questions, review what you've learned, and begin learning how to put your knowledge into practice.

Quiz

1. Why is development less expensive with Web services?
2. How can Web services be written in any language and still work?
3. What makes Web services easier to interface to a legacy system?
4. Name one new application that Web services make possible.

Quiz Answers

1. Because Web services are described precisely by a WDSL, some code on both the server and the client can be generated.

2. SOAP is written at a high enough level of abstraction that any language can implement it.

3. The fact that both the client and the server can be written as wrappers around legacy systems makes it easy to interface them.

4. Auctioning systems in which vendors of all types can sell their unused capacity at a discount holds great potential.

Activities

1. List the different categories of savings and revenue generation that are covered in this hour.

2. Choose the five types of savings or revenue that are most likely to be of interest to your organization.

3. Create at least one potential system in each of these categories. Share your ideas with others in the organization.

HOUR 3

Disadvantages and Pitfalls of Web Services

In the previous hour, we looked at what Web services are and how they can be used to solve problems. However, Web services are not a magic bullet solution for every issue; they do have limitations. In this hour, we'll discuss those issues.

In this hour, you will learn

- What pitfalls to expect with Web services
- What performance issues affect Web services
- How a lack of standards affects Web services
- How the newness of Web service technology can be a problem
- What staffing challenges exist when going with a Web services solution

Pitfalls of Web Services

No technology is perfect. Although Web services do a great job at solving certain problems, they bring along issues of their own. Some of these pitfalls are inherent to the technological foundations upon which Web services are based, and others are based on the specifications themselves. It is important to know what these issues are so that you can plan for and build around them.

Some of the biggest issues are

- **Availability**—Everyone who uses the Internet knows that no site is 100% available. It follows that Web services, which use the same infrastructure as Web sites, will not be 100% available either. Even if the server is up and running, your ISP might not be, or the ISP hosting the other side of the transaction might not be either. If you need 100% up time, do something else. Because of this situation, it is often necessary to build mechanisms that will retry the transaction or fail gracefully when this occurs. Some of the newer protocols supported by Web services (JMS, for instance) will handle this automatically, but the majority built on HTTP will not.

- **Matching Requirements**—Any time you create a general service that will handle a variety of customers, you will run into specialized requirements. Some customers might require the one extra little feature that nobody else needs. Web services are envisioned as a "one size fits many customers" technology. If your business can't fit into that model, you should consider other solutions.

- **Immutable Interfaces**—If you invest in creating a Web service for your customers, you have to avoid changing any of the methods that you provide and the parameters that your customers expect. You can create new methods and add them to the service, but if you change existing ones, your customers' programs will break. This is easy to do until you find that one of your existing methods is returning wrong answers and can't be repaired because the approach is fundamentally flawed. Early releases of Java contained methods for calculating date and time differences that could not be made to work correctly. They had no choice but to junk the first set of routines and write new ones. This caused programs to quit working, but there was no choice because the programs were getting wrong answers from the old routines. Although this sort of problem occurs in all systems, it is especially true in Web services. You might not know who is using your service, and as a result you have no way to inform those users of the change. In most other systems, because of the tight coupling, there usually is more verbal or written coordination between producers of a service and consumers of it.

- **Guaranteed Execution**—The whole idea behind having a computer program instead of doing a job by hand is that the program can run unattended. HTTP is not a reliable protocol in that it doesn't guarantee delivery or a response. If you need this kind of guarantee, either write the code to retry requests yourself or arrange to send your requests through an intermediary who will perform these retries for you. Again, newer versions of the specification allow for using protocols such as JMS to resolve this issue, but the majority of services out there still utilize HTTP, which does not.

As you can see, with such limitations, Web services might not be right for your needs. This is just the beginning of the list, however.

Performance Issues

The only performance guarantee that you have concerning the Internet is that performance will vary wildly from one time to the next. Performance-critical systems are not suited to becoming Web services.

Web services rely on HTTP—the same communication protocol upon which Web pages are requested and delivered. HTTP was designed to enable one server to handle hundreds of requests quickly by not maintaining a long-term stateful connection between the clients and the server. Instead, HTTP initiates a fresh connection with the server and maintains it only as long as it needs to transfer the data. Once complete, the connection is terminated and the server is then freed up to process a request from someone else. The server typically will not maintain any sort of concept of state to keep track of from one user's request to the next, although this can be achieved though the use of session tracking or cookies. This tends to make HTTP very transactional in nature.

Although the HTTP communication transaction enables the server side to handle many clients, it also means that a lot of time is wasted creating and terminating connections for clients that need to perform a large number of calls between the client and the server. Other technologies—such as DCOM, CORBA, and RMI—don't have this problem because they maintain the connection throughout the application lifecycle.

 See Hour 4, "Comparing Web services to Other Technologies," for more information on the differences between Web services and these other technologies.

3

The other performance consideration that must be taken into account with Web services is the conversion to and from XML during the communication process. All communication takes place as XML messages encoded in a special format (a SOAP envelope). This conversion takes time. Depending on how complex your data is and how much of it there is, this time could be a serious penalty. For instance, if you try to send a binary image as a method parameter, that data must be encoded into a format that can be represented in XML. This certainly is not as fast as transferring the image across the wire in its original format.

Although this sort of time penalty occurs with other architectures such as RMI and CORBA, it can be especially bad for Web services–based systems because data is transferred as XML text—with a large amount of extra information required in the SOAP envelope. This overhead isn't too bad when we consider a simple string or number to be encoded. Binary data, such as images, tend to be much larger though and take a lot longer to convert. XML tends to take more bytes to encode data than the equivalent binary representation.

Finally, when writing a Web service, you typically have a choice of many different languages and tools with which to build your solution. It is important that you pick ones that will scale to handle the expected loads adequately.

Lack of Standards

Another set of issues is associated with Web services that centers around incomplete or nonfinalized standards. Although there are ways to fix most of these problems, they are unique to each vendor's implementation. If the guiding principle of Web services is to create an open standardized interchange system for remote program execution, the utilization of any vendor-specific solutions should be avoided. The current Web services specifications and standards are lacking in the following areas:

- **Security and Privacy**—Anything sent over the Internet can be viewed by others. At present, the only approved option for sending sensitive information to Web services is to use a *Secure Socket Layer (SSL)* program. SSL over HTTP is sometimes called HTTPS. This technology is wonderful in that it does a good job of safeguarding information such as credit card numbers, and it is easy to set up compared to other encryption techniques. The disadvantage is that SSL is slower than unencrypted HTTP transactions and is therefore unsuited to large data transfers. In addition, SSL is much more secure than most sales statistics need. Such a transaction shouldn't ordinarily be sent as clear text though. SSL encrypts the entire data stream, not just the sensitive parts. Let's consider the case

NEW TERM

in which the data being transferred contains an item's inventory tracking number, its description, and the credit card number used to pay for it. In most cases, online thieves would not care about the inventory number or the item description, but they would want to steal the credit card number. With SSL, it's an all or nothing solution. This situation is improving, however, because the W3C has several draft proposals that hopefully will resolve this problem.

- **Authentication**—Authentication answers the question, "Who is contacting me?" At present, the standards ignore this issue and delegate it to the Web services Container. This causes proprietary solutions to be created and breaks down the promise of portability. Until a universal single sign-on solution is agreed upon, this problem will remain.

- **Nonrepudiation**—Nonrepudiation means that you have rock-solid proof that a communication took place. This is also delegated to the Web services Container.

- **Transaction**—Many activities that would be well suited to Web services are very complex. They involve dozens of smaller actions that must either all complete or all be rolled back. Closing on a new house is a good example. The last thing you need is for your financing to fall through but half the transaction (such as the escrow setup and courthouse registration of the lien) to complete anyway.

- **Billing and Contracts**—In most cases, you'll want to charge for the use of your service. As a result, a way for pricing contracts to be negotiated and maintained needs to be created. The current specifications provide for service discovery, but do not contain a mechanism for handling pricing for the service or performing automatic billing for the use of the service. This issue becomes even harder if different customers want different billing rates. This also ties into the provisioning problem because without some sort of a contract in place, secure provisioning becomes unrealistic. Contracts also need to determine service level agreements. (Who would pay for a service unless a contract stated that it would be available 99% of the time?)

Because the specifications don't have an agreed upon mechanism for handling these issues, many vendors providing Web services tools have built their own solutions. This can lead to problems when moving from one vendor's tools to another or getting two different vendor's tools to talk. As a result of this billing problem, most Web services posted to public UDDI registries are still free to use. On the other hand, companies providing Web services for their business partners typically do not post their service on public UDDI registries and can therefore control access and billing for use of the service through traditional manual billing methods.

- **Provisioning**—This is the adding of valid user accounts to a system to allow users to access the service. Currently there is no agreed upon standard way to do this. The service provider and consumer need a mechanism to exchange provisioning information, and the service provider must know who it trusts as a source of that user information.

- **Scalability**—Because it is possible to expose existing component systems such as Enterprise Java Beans as Web services, it should be possible to leverage the load-balancing and other scalability mechanisms that already exist. But are there unforeseen stumbling blocks along this path? Does there need to be a new kind of "Web service" application server? Some vendors have come up with mechanisms to provide for load balancing, but no standard for it currently exists.

- **Testing**—Because of the new structure of Web services and the decoupling of the clients from the server, testing of Web service–based solutions can be challenging. Short of adopting a "try it and see if it worked" mentality, there really are few ways to test a Web service system. This is especially true for situations in which the client applications are written by one party and the server is written by another who charges for its use. How would one test a potentially half-built client against a service that you don't control? Even more important is what happens if that client does something to break the service?

Most, if not all, of these problems will be addressed in subsequent versions of the standards. Until then, we have no choice but to implement proprietary solutions with plans to revisit them when the technology matures.

Newness of Web Service Technology

Most technologies are over hyped in their first two years because it typically takes that long for the platforms to mature to the point of fixing initial problems and the toolsets to become powerful enough to provide good solutions. During this time, you usually hear a lot of people promoting all the virtues of the new technology, but few of the issues have actually been discovered. Those issues can only be found with time and work. At the time of this publication, Web services are still in this phase of maturity.

Conversely, the same technology will usually be under recognized after the four- to five-year mark. This is unfortunate because at this point the industry would've learned how to work with the technology effectively, staff would've come up to speed, and the tools would be mature. But, because of the initial over-hype situation and the failure to live up to initial expectations, the technology in question can quite often be orphaned by the very same people who were its biggest initial champions or, worse yet, be replaced with the new solution of the week. That's not to say that the technology is totally abandoned. Rather, it is often the case that the technology has just moved beyond the "fad" phase and into the realm of being useful (sometimes extremely so), but no longer "sexy."

Figure 3.1 illustrates the typical technology adoption and maturity lifecycle.

FIGURE 3.1
The typical technology hype/usefulness life-cycle.

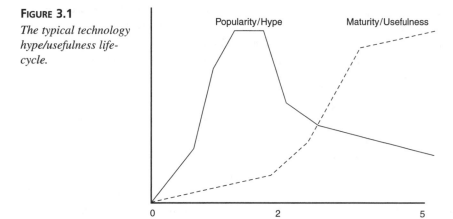

Because Web services are a relatively young technology, the standards and specifications are evolving rapidly. Applications built on one version of the specification can be quickly outdated. The specifications are also still evolving in some areas of Web services. As a result, some vendors have chosen to provide their own proprietary solutions rather than wait for a standard to emerge.

Also, because the Web service area is relatively new, a large number of vendors are fighting for market share. Although this stimulates innovation, it also means that developers who buy into the wrong vendor might be orphaned a year or two down the road and be forced to switch to another vendor's solution. This can be a big headache and cost a good deal of time and money. Even though Web services are built on standards, each vendor has its own way of implementing those standards, which could require major retooling of your system if you have to change toolsets. All markets go through a shakeout period in which the most popular (and usually powerful) products remain and the majority of the others fade away. This has not happened yet with the Web services tools market.

Staffing Issues

Staffing can be one of the most frustrating parts of implementing any new technology. Because Web services are a fairly new solution, it can be somewhat difficult to find qualified and experienced staff to implement a workable solution.

The staffing issue can be twofold. Managers and architects are not up to speed on the technology and, as such, might not trust "that new-fangled gizmo with all the hype." On the other side of the equation is the development staff who aren't familiar enough with all the ins and outs of the technology to know how to properly build solutions based on it. Hopefully, by reading this book, a lot of the problems can be resolved for both of these groups.

As with any new technology, to find qualified, experienced personnel, it might be necessary to pay a premium price. Although the recent downturn in the IT marketplace has made the available talent pool deeper, truly good developers can still be hard to find. It might be necessary to bring in an experienced contractor to help jumpstart your project. The other alternative is to train from within your organization. Both solutions have their good and bad points and must be weighed with your organization's needs in mind.

Summary

In this hour, we've discussed what issues currently affect Web services. We've looked at how some of the underlying technical foundations could be an issue for Web services.

We then discussed some of the performance problems associated with this technology. We saw how the fact that Web services rely on nonpersistent connections found in HTTP can be a performance concern and how the conversion of data into and out of XML can slow down processing.

Next, we examined some issues that exist because of present limitations of the specifications and standards. We saw how various vendors have come up with work-around solutions that are nonportable and thus should be avoided.

Finally, we discussed some of the issues regarding the young age of Web services technologies and how this relatively young solution can cause staffing problems.

By keeping these points in mind, a proper choice can be made between a Web services–based solution and other ones.

Q&A

Q If Web services have all these problems, should I use them for production-level systems?

A Although Web services do have some issues to be resolved, many of the alternatives do as well. Each technology has strengths and weaknesses. Now that you know what they are for Web services, you can make an informed decision on whether to use them for your project or not. If you're building a system to be used by many other people, Web services are probably your best bet.

Q If I go with Web services, how can I minimize the impact of the changes to the standards?

A The easiest way to reduce impact is to limit yourself to using only standards-based options from the toolkit that you choose. That way, when the standards bodies agree on a solution for, let's say, security, you can easily add it to your code once your tool vendor updates its tools. Otherwise, you might be locked into a proprietary solution that might not be supported at a later date.

Workshop

This section is designed to help you anticipate possible questions, review what you've learned, and begin learning how to put your knowledge into practice.

Quiz

1. What issues are inherent to Web services because of their underlying technologies?
2. What affects the performance of Web services?
3. What sort of staffing issues can one expect?
4. What are some of the problems found because of gaps in the specifications?

Quiz Answers

1. Immutable interfaces, unguaranteed availability and execution, and a one-size-fits-all requirement.
2. The underlying HTTP not maintaining connections long term, the conversion to XML, and the need to choose efficient server-side programming languages to build your service with.
3. As with any new technology, good people will be expensive and hard to find.
4. Billing, contract negotiation, authentication, transaction management, and security, among others.

Activity

1. You should take a look at the `w3c.org` Web site to see what emerging standards are coming down the road that are meant to address the problems we discussed in this hour. Industry and the development community have been working hard to fix some of these problems, and many of them might be resolved by the time you read this.

Hour **4**

Comparing Web Services to Other Technologies

Whenever business managers hear that a new widget is needed, they instinctively ask, "Why can't we just use the XYZ technology instead?" This is a perfectly reasonable question to ask if you are a cost-conscious manager. However, this type of thinking can often lead to the "Golden Hammer" approach. When this happens, all problems must be solved with the one magic bullet technology that is familiar to you. Usually this occurs with little thought put into the strengths and weaknesses of that technology and how well it fits the problem at hand. Good engineers always try to expand their tool chest of useful technologies. Web services are another solution to the problem, but they aren't the only solution.

The alternatives can generally be grouped into three categories:

- Stub/skeleton based remote procedure call architectures (CORBA, RMI, DCOM)
- HTTP-like transactional architectures (Servlets, JSP, ASP, PHP, CGI)
- Screen scrapers

As you read through this hour, you will see that Web services are actually an evolution of the first two methods and has many similarities to each of them—with few of the drawbacks.

Let's briefly look at each of these architectures and examine some of the solutions based on them.

Stub/Skeleton Based Architectures

Solutions in this category all work in generally the same fashion. They are meant to provide programmatic access to some form of remote service as though it was a local entity. The advantage to this sort of architecture is that it makes client program creation relatively simple because as far as the client program is concerned, the objects and their methods are local, just like every other object. The architecture itself takes care of the communications to get the data from client to server and vice versa, which frees up the client developer to worry about UI design, business logic, and everything else. Figure 4.1 illustrates the stub/skeleton architecture.

FIGURE 4.1

The stub/skeleton client-server architecture.

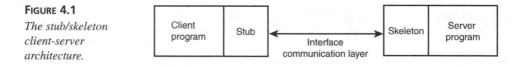

In order to make these architectures simple for the clients, developers are required to build two modules—a stub and a skeleton.

The stub is a block of code that sits on the client machine. It identifies which objects and methods are available on the server, and marshals (encodes) all calls from the client to the server into a format that the interface layer can understand. It also unmarshals (decodes) any data coming back from the server into something the client can understand.

The skeleton performs the same sort of operation as the stub, but in the opposite direction for the server side. It exposes what capabilities exist on the server that the client can call, receives the incoming requests from the clients, and returns any data back to the client.

All the solutions in this category are also denoted by the characteristic that when a new client connects with a server, it stays connected until the client is terminated. This has a tendency to reduce the number of clients that the server can handle because it must maintain those connections for long periods of time.

Finally, each of these architectures makes use of some form of directory that allows clients to look up the available services from each server. The differences are in the details because each architecture performs this process differently—hence, not allowing the solutions to be interchangeable.

The main differences between the following architectures are how the data is encoded and how the transport layer functions.

Some of the popular solutions that use this architecture are CORBA, RMI, and DCOM.

CORBA

New Term *CORBA (Common Object Request Broker Architecture)* was designed in the early 1990s to provide a mechanism for building client/server applications in heterogeneous environments.

Some of the key features of CORBA are

- **Language Neutral**—CORBA was designed to work with any language. **New Term** In order to bridge the gap between differing languages, an *Interface Definition Language (IDL)* is used to detail the structure of all objects that will be passed along the wire into a language-neutral format. Developers then take the IDL and run it through some form of code generator for the language used on each end of the transaction to get the corresponding language-specific stub or skeleton. By doing this, it's possible to write a Visual Basic client that talks to a Java server, using CORBA as the communication layer.

- **Multiple Vendors**—Multiple vendors provide *Object Request Brokers (ORBs)*. **New Term** This allows users to pick and choose between vendors for the capabilities and costs that are right for them. Some ORB vendors only support certain languages as well.

Although CORBA would seem to be an excellent solution for heterogeneous client/server systems, it has instead proven itself to be a bit of a hassle initially in practice. Initial releases of the CORBA specification left many areas open to interpretation by the vendors. As a result, many vendor's ORBs refused to work with each other, limiting the ability to mix and match.

The cross-language features of CORBA have also proven to be a bit of a curse as well because it requires developers to learn IDL and specify all their interfaces and objects that are involved in the CORBA calls. There is also the performance penalty of converting an object from one language representation into the IDL representation, and then back into some other language on the other end. This time penalty can be deadly when used in a high-volume system.

CORBA requires the use of special ports on which the ORBs communicate and transfer the data. In many network environments, network administrators are reluctant to open ports to the outside world because these represent areas for possible intrusion and attack by hackers. This can sometimes limit a developer's ability to deploy systems based on CORBA. For systems communicating entirely within a secure intranet, this isn't an issue, but for those bridging internal systems to the Internet, this is quite a security risk.

Finally, CORBA can be somewhat difficult to secure. In most cases, data transferred in CORBA-based systems is sent across the wire in clear text. This makes it rather easy for hackers to listen in on communications and steal data.

Newer versions of CORBA implementations have made great strides in overcoming many of these difficulties, but unfortunately these fixes have come too late. Most of the industry has already moved on to other solutions. CORBA is still a viable alternative in some cases though, and should not be overlooked in situations in which you need hetero-geneous capabilities and you can control and secure the network properly.

As a result, compared to Web services, CORBA solutions

- Are nearly as capable for cross-platform and cross-language development.
- Are harder to understand because CORBA relies on IDL to translate data; Web services use XML, which is much more human readable. Most toolsets also create the WSDL for you.
- Can handle higher transaction loads because they keep a persistent connection between clients and servers at the expense of servicing fewer clients per server.
- Are a much more mature technology, and many of the initial interoperability issues between vendors have been worked out already. A lot more information is currently available on CORBA as well.

Java RMI

NEW TERM Similar to CORBA, *Remote Method Invocation (RMI)* is built on top of the stub/skeleton architecture. RMI is the Java-specific mechanism for performing client/server calls. It is actually very similar to CORBA in many respects. The biggest difference is that because RMI is usually used for Java-to-Java architectures, there is no need for the IDL. Developers are working with true Java objects at all times. This has changed over the years with the addition of RMI communicating over *IIOP* (the same protocol that CORBA uses), allowing RMI to talk directly to CORBA.

Again, similar to CORBA, RMI requires that a specific port be opened for communications between the client and server. As with CORBA, this can sometimes be difficult to get network administrators to open due to security concerns.

RMI can be somewhat easier than CORBA to secure against eavesdropping as long as the various objects that are being passed are written to include code to encrypt and decrypt their binary representations during marshaling/unmarshaling. This adds a bit of additional work for the developers, but pays off in piece of mind.

In cases in which you control both the client and server and can guarantee that both will be built with Java in a trusted network environment, RMI will usually perform faster than XML-based Web services because of the reduced work in getting the data into a wire-friendly format.

Compared to Web services, RMI is the better choice if both ends are Java based, but useless in non-Java guaranteed situations.

As a result, compared to Web services, RMI solutions

- Lock you into a purely Java solution on both the client and server
- Can be somewhat more difficult to deploy because of network port considerations
- Can handle higher transaction loads because RMI keeps a persistent connection between clients and servers at the expense of servicing fewer clients per server

DCOM

4

NEW TERM *DCOM (Distributed Common Object Model)* is the Microsoft mechanism for performing remote calls. Objects are again converted into a wire-friendly format and converted back to language-specific representations at the endpoints of the communication.

Although DCOM can be built in several different languages (Visual C++, Visual Basic, C#, and so on), it only works on Microsoft platforms. As a result, if your business does not use Microsoft servers, DCOM doesn't help you. Both ends of the transaction (client and server) need to be Microsoft systems in order to use DCOM.

Although DCOM is supported by multiple languages, the strong ties to Microsoft mean that Web services still hold an edge in flexibility. Web services can be implemented with tools from many different vendors on various platforms.

Compared to Web services, DCOM solutions are nearly as capable for cross-language development, but usually lock you into a Microsoft-everywhere framework.

HTTP Transactional-based Architectures

The second category of Client/Server architectures is based on the familiar Web server paradigm. These systems operate by having some piece of code running on a server—

similar to (or extending) a Web server such as IIS or Apache. Clients communicate with
the server code through the familiar HTTP or HTTPS; the server handles the request and
performs the work, responding with whatever data was requested (typically with HTML
or XML text as the response). After the transaction is complete, the connection between
the client and the server is terminated. Figure 4.2 shows the communication process typically found in HTTP Transactional architectures.

FIGURE 4.2

*The HTTP Transaction
process.*

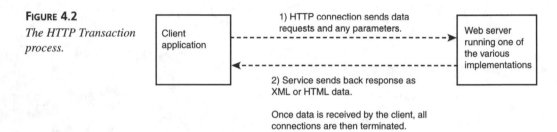

Because the connection between the clients and the server stays in place only for the
duration of the transaction, these types of systems typically have a larger client-to-server
ratio. The downside of these systems is that because the connection is not persistent, in
situations in which clients make a large number of discreet transactions with the server, a
large percentage of time is wasted creating and terminating connections. In such situations, the stub/skeleton architectures tend to be better. Some systems utilize the HTTP
1.1 keep-alive mechanism that gets around this issue by maintaining the connection
between the client and the server, but at the expense of limiting the number of clients the
server can handle.

Another strike against these types of solutions is the lack of a directory service such as
UDDI. Clients must know of the service in advance, must know what data the service
expects, and must know how the service expects to receive that data. Whereas Web services utilize WSDL to describe how to interface between the client and service, with the
HTTP-based architectures, a good deal of cooperation must take place between the developers of the service and the client-side developers in order to build a functioning system.
This limits how effective these solutions can be in an open service-type environment in
which you might want to allow anyone on the Internet to use your service.

Error handling can also be tedious on these types of systems because there is no established formal mechanism for indicating and handling problems. Where Web services
have a true fault mechanism, and the stub/skeleton systems have notions of formal exception objects, neither exists in the HTTP transaction-based architectures.

Type safety is another concern. Again, it's the lack of formalized communications that comes into play. Without such agreed upon specifications, it becomes more difficult to agree on data representations (how many digits represent an integer versus a long or a string, and so on). Also, there's no way to stop somebody from sending the wrong type of data and causing problems.

One advantage that these solutions have over their stub/skeleton counterparts is that these solutions all communicate over the familiar HTTP ports. Most networks leave the common HTTP and HTTPS ports (80 and 81, respectively) open for communications, so usually no additional work is required to get a solution based on these technologies deployed on the network.

HTTP-based solutions also send all their data across as plain text, which can be a security issue. It is rather simple, however, to use HTTPS (SSL encryption over HTTP) to secure your data. This usually incurs a slight performance penalty and should only be used in situations with sensitive data.

Let's look more closely at the more popular solutions based on this architecture.

CGI

Back in the early 1990s when the World Wide Web and HTML were new, very little interactive capability was built into the HTML and Web server specifications. Users could really only connect to a server and retrieve prebuilt, static documents with the occasional picture. There was no way to request specific data or get information tailored to the user.

NEW TERM   In order to overcome this shortfall, HTML input forms and *common gateway interface (CGI)* was created. CGI is a mechanism by which when data is sent to the server, the Web server can invoke a program (the CGI) and pass all the data that was sent along with the request to the program. The CGI program processes the data and builds up a response page that it then sends back to the user.

CGI was a great solution for the time. (In fact, it was the only solution!) Users could submit requests and get dynamically generated data returned to them. For instance, a user could go to a sports Web site, select his favorite baseball team, and get the statistics for all the players on the team for any day in the season. This added a whole new level of capabilities to the Web.

The CGI solution does have problems though. Developers quickly found that for popular sites using CGI, the Web servers needed to be rather large. Every request to the server caused a new instance of the CGI program to be instantiated, run, and then terminated.

4

All this starting and stopping put a drain on system resources. Some solutions were created to attempt to fix this issue over time, but the problem still exists. As a result, other solutions have taken the place of CGI in the mainstream.

CGI can be written in many different languages (C, Perl, Python, Shell scripts, and so on). This does allow the server-side programmer some flexibility. CGI is a mechanism supported by pretty much every Web server as well. CGI programs usually aren't cross platform capable because of language and platform differences, but they usually can be ported fairly easily from server platform to platform. For instance, a CGI program written in C for a UNIX platform will probably need at least a little modification before it can be compiled to run on a Windows platform. In some cases, the language that the CGI is written in might not even be built in to the OS and would need to be fetched as an add on (such as Perl, which is common on UNIX, but not on Windows without fetching a copy of ActivePerl and installing it). Even then, it is sometimes necessary to modify the code to tailor it to the new system. Even with these limitations, because CGIs rely on only HTTP for input and HTML/XML for output, client-side applications can be written in pretty much any language.

Web services still tend to be better than CGIs, however. CGIs really can only accept string-type data or binary attachments sent to them, not true objects. This means that a client would need to convert any data into some sort of CGI-specific data representation as a string, post the data, and then parse any data returned to it into something meaningful again. All this must be done with no mechanism to enforce the encoding mechanism or structure. Web services do all that for you. There are no real indexes of CGI services out there either. You simply need to know the URL to point your browser or client application to in order to call the CGI-based service. Finally, without knowing what the CGI is expecting to have posted to it, it becomes very difficult to write a client.

In short, compared to Web services, CGIs are

- Harder to find because of no directory service
- Harder to write clients for without a well-documented service-specific API to rely on
- Harder to interact with programmatically because there's no accepted data interchange format
- All over the place on nearly any Web server or platform

Servlets/JSP

The Java-based solution to the CGI world is the servlet.

> In this section, whenever we say servlets, we actually mean servlets and JSP. In reality, although they look very different when written by the developer, JSP code is actually compiled into a servlet by the Java servlet container. As such, a servlet and a JSP are synonymous.

Java servlets provide all the same capabilities as their CGI heritage, but without the resource penalty. Instead of running as a program, servlets are inherently multithreaded. Each request invokes a new lightweight thread instance instead of the heavyweight process instances used by CGIs.

Servlets can respond to more than just HTTP requests. It is possible to build servlets to accept nearly any protocol. In fact, many of the Java-based Web services toolkits work by placing servlet wrappers around the service code that the developer writes and executing the servlet in a servlet container.

Because servlets are written in the Java language, they gain the "write once, run anywhere" capabilities of Java. Java servlet containers are available for nearly every imaginable platform, thus allowing your servlet to be deployable anywhere. You have a multitude of vendors to choose from as well.

4

Unfortunately, even with the additional capabilities, servlets find themselves bound by the same limitations that hold back CGIs. There is no directory indicating what CGIs are available, no interface specification explaining how to communicate with them, and all data must be written into a format the servlet can understand.

The points about servlets that stand out in relation to Web services are as follows:

- Servlets can only be written in Java.
- Servlets are harder to write clients for without a well-documented service-specific API to rely on.
- Servlets are harder to interact with programmatically because there's no accepted data interchange format.
- Servlets can be found on many Web server platforms.

ASP and PHP

NEW TERM   The remaining two technologies typically used for HTTP-based services are ASP and PHP. These two systems are fundamentally similar in scope and as such will be discussed together. *Active Server Pages (ASP)* is the solution championed by Microsoft and is based on the Visual Basic language. PHP is another solution, which is championed primarily by the Open Source and Linux/Unix communities. PHP uses various shell commands and utilities such as AWK, GREP, SED, and so on.

Both of these solutions (along with JSP) require the developer to intermix code and HTML or XML to render the resulting textual data.

Unfortunately, both solutions suffer from the same limitations as CGI and servlet solutions in regards to finding services and knowing how to communicate with them. In fact, each of these solutions is no better or worse at providing remote services than servlets. All the same limitations apply for using them to build computer-to-computer linkages. They are, however, excellent for building Web systems meant for direct human consumption.

Although it is technically possible to build Web services using these technologies, to do so would require the developer to re-engineer all the same types of features that Web services use. Instead, it is more useful to use prebuilt tool libraries to provide Web service interfaces for ASP and PHP.

ASP can be run on several different vendors' Web servers (such as the ChiliSOFT ASP solution for Unix machines); however, in most cases, it is a Windows-based solution. PHP, on the other hand, runs in numerous server environments, but it really is most at home on Linux or Unix machines.

Compared with Web services, solutions using ASP or PHP are

- Harder to find because of no directory service.
- Harder to write clients for without a well-documented service-specific API to rely on.
- Harder to interact with programmatically because there's no accepted data interchange format.
- Easy to write on the server side because of the simplicity of the languages involved.
- Only portable to other servers that support those languages. Clients can be written in any language, however.

Screen Scrapers

If we consider a Web service a system by which data can be retrieved from one system and used by another, we must also consider the use of screen scrapers. Screen scrapers are client-side programs that make use of an existing interface (possibly a mainframe terminal or a Web browser), push data into the interface, and then read (or scrape) the returned data off the interface and convert it into something the client application needs.

This sort of solution actually has proven popular in some mainframe-centric shops that have legacy applications in which nobody truly understands the business rules explaining how the applications work, but they do understand how to use the applications. In these cases, it is actually easier to write a scraper to act as sort of a virtual middleman than it is to attempt to tear apart the legacy code and add a true Web service interface to it.

Screen scrapers aren't pretty. They work, but they rely on the format of the screens that they're scraping not to change. If the server-side application changes, the scraper must also be changed to handle the new format or workflow process. This can be a tedious process at best, a nightmare at worst. Still, if you have no other choice, screen scraping does work.

Summary

In this hour, we have discussed some of the alternative solutions available for building client/server systems. We've examined the strengths and weaknesses of each solution and pointed out where those solutions could be better than Web services.

We've also discussed areas where Web services have an advantage over each of these solutions. In nearly all cases, Web services do a better job of providing cross-platform, cross-language service while maintaining ease of development, more flexibility, and more vendor choices for the developer.

With the information presented here, you should be able to narrow down your selection of solution architectures and pick the one best suited to your needs.

Q&A

Q If I already have a system based on one of the technologies discussed in this hour, can I continue to leverage it while using Web services?

A Absolutely! The beauty of Web services is their capability to provide open interfaces to existing systems. Simply build a Web services wrapper interface layer around your existing system. Have the wrapper make calls to your existing system, and then take the results and send them back via SOAP.

**Q Web services looks a lot like CORBA and RMI. If this is true, why the big
deal?**

A As you've seen this hour, yes, Web services do look very much like these other
systems. That's not surprising because many of the people who created the specifications for Web services are the same engineers who grew up building systems
with CORBA and RMI. They designed Web services to take the best from those
technologies while at the same time fixing some of their problems. Some people
even like to refer to Web services as "CORBA over XML" because the architectures are so similar.

**Q Does knowing one of these existing technologies help in my understanding of
Web services?**

A Definitely! Again, Web services are an evolution, not a revolution. If you know
CORBA or RMI, and have at least a little knowledge of HTTP, Web services
should seem very straightforward to you.

Workshop

This section is designed to help you anticipate possible questions, review what you've
learned, and begin learning how to put your knowledge into practice.

Quiz

1. What are the three types of typical solutions other than Web services for building
   client/server solutions?
2. What features denote most stub/skeleton solutions?
3. What features of HTTP-based solutions limit their usefulness as compared to Web
   services?

Quiz Answers

1. Stub/skeleton based, HTTP-based, and screen scrapers.
2. Tight coupling between the client and the server throughout the client lifetime,
   some sort of directory used to find the service, stubs and skeletons to provide the
   interface between the client and server.
3. Lack of any real indexing service, mainly based around text-based data, no data
   formatting standards or interface specifications.

Activity

1. If you are unfamiliar with any of the technologies we've discussed in this hour, it is recommended that you read up on them. Knowing more about other competing technologies is always a good thing. Sams Publishing has a large line of books covering all these topics.

4

Hour **5**

Typical Web Services Designs

When a nonprogrammer asks for a quick description of how Web services are different from other distributed technologies, he normally hears a moment of silence while the programmer tries to figure out how to describe it in nontechnical terms.

In truth, many of the words that we use to describe Web services also describe other distributed computing technologies. Throughout this book, we have attempted to describe Web services directly, and through analogies. We realize, however, that sometimes a few examples are worth more than a ream of written description. This is why we have chosen to spend this hour providing examples of real-world systems. Because Web services implementations are still not yet common at the time of this writing, we will describe how you would design three different systems to use Web services.

These descriptions will be presented abstractly without referring to any one tool, language, or development environment.

In this hour, you will learn

- What types of Web service applications are possible
- The rules of thumb for determining if a system is a good candidate to be a Web service
- A basic functional design methodology

You also will examine the following systems:

- Conglomerate reporting system
- Shop floor system
- CheapestCameras.com Web site

Designing the Conglomerate Reporting System

XYZ Corporation is a traditional conglomerate. It buys companies, and it sells companies. Because of this dynamic environment, corporate management does not embark on massive Information Technology projects to integrate the systems of each company into one big system. Each company tends to keep the systems that it has traditionally used, and it makes system improvements based on the business needs of that individual company.

This "islands of technology" approach is much less expensive in the short run than massive system conversions would be. (If the companies continue to grow and if they are not going to be sold, a full conversion might be less expensive in the long term.) The basic weakness of the islands of technology approach is corporate reporting and accounting. Each of the 14 subsidiaries has an accounting team who is able to determine how that company is performing. They print reports showing this performance and mail them to corporate headquarters each quarter. These reports are formatted differently by each subsidiary's accounting department. This arrangement is shown in Figure 5.1.

Corporate accounting receives these different reports, extracts the information from them, and types it into a corporate accounting system. This system combines all the subsidiary's information and produces a corporate-level report that shows the corporation's performance for the quarter.

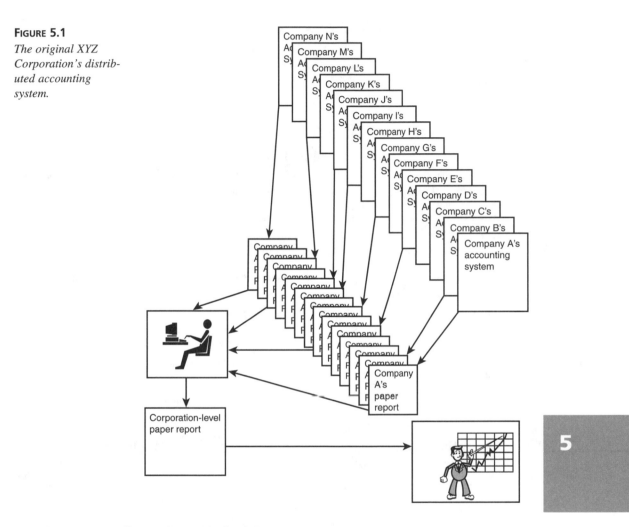

FIGURE 5.1

The original XYZ Corporation's distributed accounting system.

Reasons for Dissatisfaction

The president of the corporation is fundamentally dissatisfied with this procedure for determining profitability. His primary concern is that he only gets the information that he needs once per quarter. The board of directors asks for updates from him more often than that, however. To report to the board, the corporate president has to rely on estimates produced by the presidents of each company. These estimates are sometimes not very accurate. In addition, the corporate president has to weigh the results to reflect the size differences between companies. The end result is that his estimates are not very good. His stated goal is to receive accurate information on a monthly basis.

The corporate accounting department is not happy with the current state of affairs either. The reports are all on paper, which requires that they be entered by hand. In addition, the corporate report must be produced within the three days following the receipt of the individual company reports. This causes the accounting department to sometimes work weekends in order to make the deadline.

Past Attempts at a Solution

A proposal was made to standardize all the companies on one platform. The huge expense of performing the conversions, together with a lack of agreement as to what the standard platform should be, killed this suggestion.

CORBA was suggested, but the widely dispersed geographic locations of the different data centers made this hard. The corporate security decided against allowing direct, non-HTTP socket connections from outside the firewall.

Finally, the idea of having every subsidiary create a flat character-based file in a standard format was suggested. These files could be sent to the corporate server where they could be consolidated. Because this is basically the Web services approach, the decision was made to investigate the use of Web services instead of inventing some proprietary approach.

Basic Analysis

Several characteristics of this system make it a good candidate for a Web services–based solution:

- The volume of data to be transferred is relatively small. For this reason, performance is not an issue.
- The geographic locations involved make an Internet-based approach attractive.
- The security concerns associated with allowing HTTP through the firewall are considered manageable if they use a combination of authentication and encryption.
- All the IT departments in the individual companies can use programming languages that they are familiar with to create their servers.
- The potential acquisition of future companies (whose hardware and operating system configurations are unknown) requires that new companies be able to integrate rapidly—with a minimum of side effects to the rest of the corporation.

These considerations suggest that a Web services approach might be appropriate.

Designing the Conglomerate Web Services Solution

Web services is such a new topic that there is not yet enough experience to suggest a formal methodology for designing a solution. The approach used in this hour might serve as a starting point in this discussion, however.

Defining the Server and the Clients

We will start our discussion by considering the simple case in which there is only one client and one server. More complex Web service transactions can involve any number of Web services chained together.

NEW TERM The first step is to decide which computers will serve as the client and the servers. The client is defined as a consumer of services, and the server is defined as the provider. However, two different types of transmissions are commonly used in the type of Web service that we are designing here: *request/response* and *solicit/response*. With the request/response transmission, the client initiates the action by making a request of the server. In the solicit/response transmission, the server makes the first move by soliciting a response from the client.

Logically, we could envision this example either way. We could have 14 clients interact with one server. On the other hand, we could create 14 servers and one client. Either approach can be made to work, so this is completely dependant on what sorts of business needs we have and what problems we are trying to solve.

Normally, more expertise is required to create a Web service than is required to create a client. The Web service programmer must create, by hand or with tools, both the implementation of the service and the Web services Description Language (WSDL) document. The client, on the other hand, can use the WSDL to generate a good-sized portion of the client code. For this reason, we typically want a design in which the server is defined once and the clients are defined once for each subsidiary.

5

> When there is a one-to-many relationship in your design, make the "one" computer the server and the "many" computers the clients.

Deciding on the Transmission Primitives

The second decision that we must make is whether to require the clients to initiate communication with the Web server or to have the server solicit the responses from the client.

There is another logical reason to prefer the solicit/response transmission style. If we were using a request/response style transmission, what would the server do if no communication were received from a certain client by a certain date? It would have to send a message asking the client to provide the missing data.

Because this "pull" message must exist anyway to handle the case in which a client hasn't sent the data, it makes sense to create the system using the solicit/response transmission style.

Always begin the transmission with the party that wants the results.

Designing the Messages

The next logical step in creating a system is the design of the messages that will be exchanged. In our case, we have decided that the corporate computer is going to be our server and that the communications will follow the solicit/response transmission style. This suggests that two messages need to be sent from the server to the clients:

- Is the report ready for uploading?
- Please give me your report.

Likewise, the clients need two different response messages:

- Yes, the report is ready. (Or no, it is not ready.)
- Here is my report.

The usage of the system would be fairly simple. On a certain date each month, the server solicits the report from each client by sending out the "Is the report ready?" message. If it is ready, the client answers "Yes." Upon receiving the "Yes" response, the server sends a "Please give me your report" message. Following that, the client gathers all the data and sends the "Here is my report" message containing the report.

If the client answers "No" because the report is not ready, a time for the next retry is assigned and the server sleeps until it is time to try it again.

Figure 5.2 shows what the redesigned system will look like.

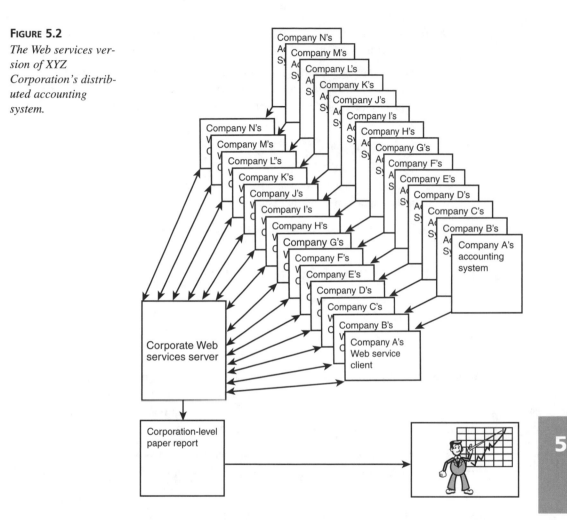

FIGURE 5.2
The Web services version of XYZ Corporation's distributed accounting system.

5

Now that all the reports are solicited and received in an electronic version that follows a specific format, the amount of work required to produce monthly reports is greatly reduced.

Designing the Project

All that is left is to actually program the parts. The details of the coding process will depend on what tools you choose to implement with. One of the big advantages of Web services is the fact that every one of the 14 different accounting systems can use a different software development tool to create its client code. In addition, the logic in each client will be different because it has to obtain its data from its own accounting system. We will create our example by following these steps:

1. The first step in the design is to write the server software. The WDSL document is then created from the server software—either by hand or automatically.

2. The WSDL is then sent to the programming staff in each subsidiary. Using this document as a guide, they create the client program either by hand or using the development tool that fits in best with their programming language background and interfaces best with their legacy system.

3. As each of the individual subsidiaries completes its work, it is run against a special test version of the Web service.

4. When all the subsidiaries complete their work, the whole system is tested and the results are compared to data that is known to be correct.

At the end of this process, the system is ready to go into production.

Redesigning the Shop Floor System

A fictitious company, MNO Corporation, is an aircraft manufacturing company. It designs and builds airframes, which are airplanes without engines. It purchases the engines from other companies and installs them on the airframes to produce a complete airplane.

The assembly of the aircraft is very complex because there are many different versions of each airplane. Each version is a set of options that the customer can specify. As a result of this, instructions for how to assemble each part of the airplane are created for each version. These documents are called the "work instructions."

The work instructions only list procedures that can vary from version to version. Procedures—such as drilling, cleaning, sealing, and so on, which are always the same—are described in other documents called "standard procedures."

Some of the work instructions and standard procedures contain steps that require the use of potentially hazardous solvents and chemicals. Federal law requires that companies make their employees aware of the safety risks associated with each substance by providing a "material safety data sheet" for each of these substances.

In addition, the work instructions have a place on them where a factory worker can use a personalized rubber stamp that indicates the completion of a step. This data is used to show progress to management and the customer. Figure 5.3 graphically shows this system.

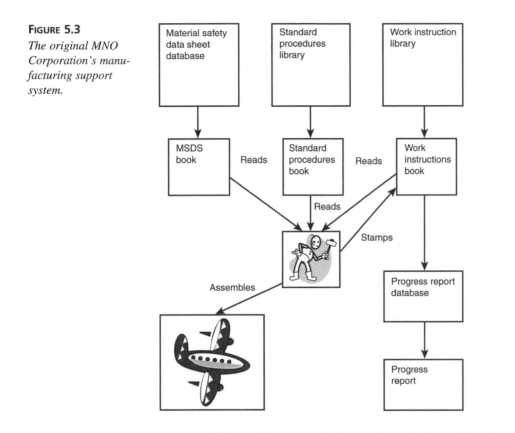

FIGURE 5.3
The original MNO Corporation's manufacturing support system.

The work instructions contain hyperlinks to standard procedures and material safety data sheets. The stamps on the work instructions provide input to the progress report.

Reasons for Dissatisfaction

The printing of the work instruction books for every procedure on every airframe is a very time-consuming, error-prone process. Last minute changes to the instructions cause the books to be broken apart and new work instructions to be inserted. The books are also heavy and cannot be carried from a desk to the work area. This causes the factory workers to under-use the instructions.

If the worker needs a standard procedure or material safety data sheet, he has to go to another book and look it up based on a number in the work instructions.

The stamping of the books is problematic also. Some of the stamps are not legible, which causes the supervisor to have to figure out who did that work and have him stamp it again.

Progress report generation is a manual process. A person goes through by hand and tabulates the percentage of completion. Finally, it takes a warehouse to store all the books that are created.

Management wants a solution that is completely paperless. The workers will view the work instructions on a terminal screen. If they want to look at a standard procedure, it will be a hyperlink that will display right on the screen. If an employee needs to carry a copy back to the work area, a nearby printer can produce that copy on request.

Updates to the instructions will be reflected immediately, so manual updating isn't necessary.

A badge reader will be attached to each terminal. The employees will swipe their employee badges to "stamp" the work as complete. If there is a read failure, they will get a message immediately to swipe the badge again. The progress report can be generated at any point in the process. The archival storage will be online.

Basic Analysis

Several characteristics of the Shop Floor system make it a good candidate for a Web services–based solution:

- The frequency of data to be transferred is relatively low. For this reason, performance is not an issue.
- All the feeder systems—such as the work instructions authoring, the standard procedure authoring, and the material safety data sheet database—are written in different programming languages and are hosted on different platforms.
- All these different systems run on separate networks in the company. The interconnections of these networks are not robust. All the platforms are capable of hosting Web servers, however.
- The Web servers in this company are connected to each other in an intranet. They are not connected to the outside Internet. This reduces security concerns and enables unencrypted data to be transferred from computer to computer.

These considerations suggest that a Web services approach might be appropriate.

Designing the Shop Floor Web Service

We will use the same design process in for the Shop Floor Web service that we used in the Conglomerate Reporting System earlier in this hour.

Defining the Shop Floor Servers and the Clients

This system has many nodes, which are shown here:

- The Work Instructions Authoring System runs on a Mainframe computer.
- The Standard Procedure Authoring System runs on a UNIX server.
- The Material Safety Data Sheet Image Database runs on a Windows NT server.
- The Shop Floor System runs under UNIX.
- The Progress Reporting System runs on a Windows NT server.

Even though there are no true one-to-many relationships between these systems, there is a quasi one-to-many relationship between the Shop Floor System and the systems that feed it: the Work Instructions Authoring System, the Standard Procedure Authoring System, and the Material Safety Data Sheet Image Database. In every one of these cases, the Shop Floor System needs to be capable of requesting a document and receiving a response that contains the requested document. This means that one set of messages could be used for all three of the feeder systems. This suggests that the Shop Floor System should operate as the Web service and the feeder systems as the clients.

The reporting system's relationship to the Shop Floor System is different, however. It requests data from the Shop Floor System, and then formats the response for management reporting. Because this is a true one-to-one relationship between systems, either could be the server. In this case, however, the developers assigned to the Shop Floor System will soon have more experience creating Web servers because of the work they will do in connecting to the feeder systems. For this reason, it makes sense to assign them the more complex role of creating the Web service and allow the reporting system to act as a client. Therefore, two Web services will be located on the server. The work instructions Web service solicits the correct work instructions and the associated documents. The reporting Web service simply provides status information whenever it receives a request from a client.

> Because more expertise is required to create a Web service than is needed to create the client, the development team with the most Web services experience should be given the task of creating the service—all other considerations being equal.

Deciding on the Transmission Primitives

The second decision we must make is whether to require the clients to initiate communication with the Web server or to have the servers solicit the responses from the client.

5

Following the rule that the party who wants the data should initiate contact would suggest that we make the communications between the Shop Floor System and the feeder systems of the solicit/response type. Whenever the Shop Floor System needs a document, it can solicit a response from the client that produces that document.

The reporting system is the one that wants to consume the data provided by the Shop Floor System. This would suggest that a request/response transmission would be the most appropriate. When the reporting system needs the data, it will issue a request to the Shop Floor System's reporting Web service. The service will respond by sending the data needed to the reporting system. The reporting system will then format and display the progress report.

Designing the Shop Floor Messages

The next logical step in creating a system is the creation of the messages that will be exchanged. In our case, we have decided that the Shop Floor System is going to host both of our Web services and that the communications with the feeder systems will follow the solicit/response pattern. The following message will be needed to do this:

- Please provide me with a document with ID=*XXXXX*.

The clients, however, need two different response messages:

- Here is the document that you requested.
- An error message indicating that the document doesn't exist.

The usage of the system would be fairly simple. The Shop Floor System would contain a menu to the different work instructions. The factory worker would choose the instructions for the work that he will do next. At that point, the Shop Floor System Web service would send a message soliciting that work instruction from the Work Instruction Authoring client. That client would return the requested instruction. This instruction could be returned in the form of an XML document, a complex data type, or as an attachment. We will explore the details of these different types of messages in Hour 12, "Sending Attachments with Web Services."

While the factory worker is looking at the instructions, she might also choose to look at a standard procedure. When she clicks the hyperlink to that procedure, the Shop Floor Web service will create a message that solicits a document from the Standard Procedure Authoring client. That client will return this document that the Shop Floor System will display or print.

The Material Safety Data Sheet client will be contacted in the same way. Its response will be different, however, because these documents are scanned in versions of the safety data provided by each vendor. This type of document will most likely be sent as an attachment.

The factory worker will perform the work, and then use the magnetic strip on his Employee ID to indicate completion of the work.

A second Web service, the Reporting Web service, must be created to respond to requests for status data. Having two Web services associated with one software application is entirely appropriate. We have chosen to create two separate Web services because the two operations are so totally different. Here is the message that the second service exchanges with its client:

- Please provide me with the status of airframe *XXXXX* as of yesterday at noon.

The server, however, needs two different response messages:

- Here is the information that you requested.
- An error message indicating that the request failed for some reason.

The reporting Web service waits for requests to come from the reporting system. When a request arrives, the Web service creates a response by examining its database and extracting the requested data. The response is then sent to the client for processing.

Figure 5.4 shows what the redesigned system will look like.

Now the system will be capable of obtaining work instructions, standard procedures, and material safety data sheets when they are needed. Any last-minute changes to these instructions will be reflected in the documents that arrive. There is no need for a person to update the books by hand because all the books are gone. Status is available at any time via the reporting system's user interface.

Writing the Web Services Code

All that is left is to actually program the parts. Once again, the details of the coding process will depend on what tools you choose to implement with. Regardless of the tools chosen, the following tasks must be performed:

1. The first step in the design is to write the software for the two Shop Floor Web services. The two WDSL documents are then created from the Web services software—either by hand or automatically.

2. The first WSDL is then sent to the programming staff for each feeder system. Using this document as a guide, they create the client programs either by hand or using the development tool that fits in best with their programming language background and interfaces best with their legacy system.

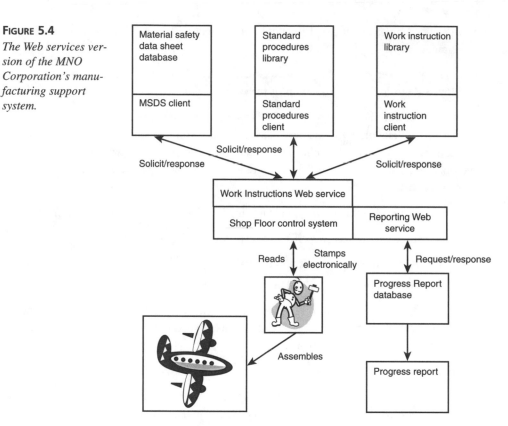

FIGURE 5.4
The Web services version of the MNO Corporation's manufacturing support system.

3. The second WSDL is sent to the reporting system where it is used to generate the Web services client that obtains messages from the shop floor.

4. As each of the individual feeder system programming teams completes its work, it is tested against a special version of the Shop Floor Web service.

5. Test data can be created to represent the progress on an airframe. The Reporting client can then make requests to the Shop Floor Progress Web service to test its functionality.

6. When all the project teams complete their work, the whole system is tested and the results are compared to data that is known to be correct.

This system demonstrates how Web services can be used to perform a variety of functions in an intranet-based system. You can mix and match the transmission types to accomplish a variety of push and pull transactions in your solution.

Designing an E-Commerce Site

The Internet has become a popular place to shop for better prices. This is especially true for items such as expensive cameras. It is theoretically possible for a single Web site to search the best camera prices available on the Internet and display them as if they were in your own warehouse. This would allow you to mark up the products a little and sell them for less than any other site. As new lower-priced wholesalers expose their price lists via Web services, our system would discover them and add their offerings to our Web site. We will call this Web site "CheapestCameras.com."

In the preceding sections, we described two high-level designs that integrated existing systems within one organization. We applied the relatively new approach of creating Web services to integrate the types of systems that have been integrated with RMI, CORBA, or DCOM in the past.

In this section, we will describe a new scenario that is very exciting, but less certain to be implemented on a large scale. This new scenario involves the discovery and interconnection of clients to Web services without human intervention. This notion is a little scary because it establishes a business relationship between parties that don't know each other.

We will use the same process in designing this system that we used in the Conglomerate Reporting System earlier in this hour.

Defining the CheapestCamera Servers and the Clients

This system has many nodes, which are shown here:

- The CheapestCameras.com Web site that is designed to allow a consumer to purchase a camera using a credit card
- A credit card server, which will be used to validate the customer's credit card
- Potentially hundreds of wholesalers' sites that have exposed their inventories as Web services

In this case, it is easy to figure out who is the client and who are the servers. All the camera wholesalers, as well as the credit card service, will be Web services. The only client will be our humble Web site. Customers will access the Web site via a browser.

In addition, our site will use the services of a commercial Web service registry to locate new vendors when they become available. The details of how these registries work can be found in Hour 11, "Advertising a Web Service."

5

Deciding on the CheapestCamera Transmission Primitives

The second decision that we must make is whether to require the potential customers to initiate communication with the Web service, or to have the service solicit the responses from the client.

A rule of thumb states that the party that wants the data should initiate contact. This would suggest that we make the communications between the client and all Web services conform to the Request/Response style. This means that the client will initiate all requests.

Designing the CheapestCamera Messages

The next logical step in creating a system is the creation of the messages that will be exchanged. In our case, we have decided that the Web site is going to be our client and that all Web services will respond to its requests. The following messages will be sent to each of the camera wholesaler Web services:

- How many cameras of model number *XXXXX* do you have for sale?
- What is the price of camera model number *XXXXX*?
- Please send one camera, model number *XXXXX* to address *YYYYY*.
- Please send the current price list.

The camera wholesaler Web services respond with these messages:

- We have *n* cameras with model number *XXXXX*.
- Camera model number *XXXXX* is $399.
- This is a confirmation that *n* cameras with model number *XXXXX* were sent to address *YYYYY*.
- Here is the current price list.
- An error message indicating that the camera is out of stock or that it doesn't exist.

The CheapestCameras.com Web site will need to send this message to the credit card validation Web site:

- Will you approve a purchase of $399 on credit card number 1111-2222-3333-4444?

In addition, the credit card validation Web service needs to be able to send these messages:

- A purchase of $399 on credit card number 1111-2222-3333-4444 is approved/not approved.
- An error message stating that the credit card number is unknown.

The operation of the system would be fairly simple. At a certain time every night, the Web site would search the Web service repository for new wholesalers to buy from. When the repository finds a new one, it adds the wholesaler to the list of current vendors.

The Web site will then send messages to each wholesaler's Web service asking for the current price list. Each wholesaler's Web service will return the latest price list. The Web site will recalculate its prices based on the information received in these price lists. The Web pages will now reflect these changes.

When a customer goes to the site, she chooses a camera to purchase. During checkout, the Web site sends a message to the credit card validation Web service. If the credit card number is approved, a message is sent to the wholesaler for that model asking if that item is still available. If it is, a message ordering that camera is sent. The wholesaler's Web service will confirm the order and ship the product directly to the customer.

If the camera is not available from this wholesaler, the next cheapest vendor's Web service is sent the same message. This continues until the requested item is located. Figure 5.5 shows what the system will look like.

Now the Web site will be able to function as an online store without carrying any inventory.

Programming the CheapestCamera Web Service

All that is left is to actually program the parts. Once again, the details of the coding process will depend on what tools you choose to implement with. Regardless of the tools chosen, the following tasks must be performed:

1. The first step in this project is to perform a search and find camera wholesalers who are Web services enabled. At the time of this writing, you would not likely find very many. The hope of Web services proponents is that these vendors will appear over time.

2. Each wholesaler Web service will provide a WSDL document. These documents need to be downloaded.

3. The Web site software will be written to act as a client and communicate with each wholesaler Web service to obtain prices and to place orders.

5

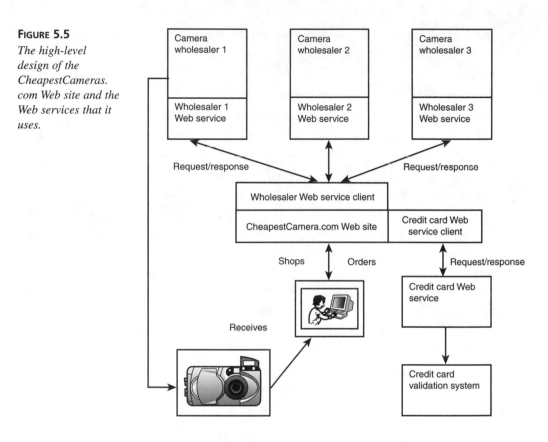

FIGURE 5.5
The high-level design of the CheapestCameras. com Web site and the Web services that it uses.

4. Part of the Web site software must also be written to process the dynamic discovery and setup of new wholesalers that it finds in the Web service registry. This will be the most difficult part to write if it is going to operate without human intervention.

5. The software that is capable of acting as a client to the credit card Web service must be written.

6. The Web site's screens (JSP, ASP, HTML, and so on) must be written.

7. When the project team completes its work, the whole system is tested.

This system demonstrates how Web services can be used to create new types of Web sites that are more dynamic than those presently available. Some hurdles must be overcome to make this practical, though. The first entrepreneur to attempt to create this type of site will have to contact the wholesalers and convince them that they want to invest the money to develop a Web service wrapper around their current systems. Another hurdle will be found in writing the dynamic discovery software. Obviously, the more similar the messages that each vendor is expecting to receive, the easier this will be to write. If a future standard emerges defining the messages that a vendor must use, the task will be easier still.

The dynamic part of the system is nice, but not strictly required to get the Web site going. If the other parts of the system can be made to work, and if the site is indeed capable of offering better prices than the competition, the business could succeed without dynamic discovery in the short term.

Uniqueness of Web Services Designs

If you have a great deal of experience in using other distributed technologies, you might notice that certain similarities exist between designing for those technologies and designing for Web services. This is certainly true. There are, however, a number of unique characteristics that you must consider when designing a Web services solution:

- **Performance**—Web services ordinarily run over the public Internet. Because the performance of the Internet varies, the response time that you can expect also varies. Systems in which timing is critical are not good candidates.

- **Rollback**—At present, there is no standard approach to rolling back part of a Web service transaction if a later step fails. If this is required, a Web service solution might not satisfy the requirements.

- **Business process execution**—There is currently no standard way to chain together set of Web services into a single transaction using logic. The only way to design multiple server systems is to send them in a single unalterable series. If...then...else logic simply isn't possible with current standards.

- **Sophisticated security**—At present, only Secure Socket Layer (SSL) can be used in Web services. If you need sophisticated encryption and decryption or digital signatures, you will have to wait for standards to emerge or use a different technology.

5

On the other hand, Web services frees you from many restrictions that exist for other technologies:

- The geographic location of each computer participating in the transaction disappears with an Internet-based approach.

- The security concerns associated with allowing HTTP through the firewall are normally easier for your Computer Security Department to approve than many of the other types of connections such as direct sockets.

- All the potential client programmers can use programming languages that they are familiar with to create their clients.

- Because of the existence of the WSDL, your clients might be able to generate the code needed to create a connection to your Web service.

If the benefits provided by Web services outweigh the current drawbacks, a Web service design might be appropriate. If not, you might eventually be able to use Web services once some of the drawbacks are lessened or eliminated by the further maturing of the core Web services specifications.

Summary

This hour shows you how Web services can be used to integrate different systems within the same organization. In these solutions, the Web services architecture is used primarily as a means of communication between heterogeneous hardware and software platforms.

You first saw a system design that gathered the same information from all of its subsidiary companies and merged them together to form a corporate financial statement.

Next, you saw a design that featured two very different Web services implemented by the same software system. These two services use two different transmission styles to communicate with their clients.

Finally, you saw a design for a Web site that takes advantage of Web services to provide products to its customers at a lower price.

Q&A

Q Generally speaking, does creating a Web service require more time and effort than creating a client?

A Yes. The designer of the service must create the messages and operations that will be described in the WSDL. The client just uses the WSDL.

Q What are the rules of thumb for deciding whether a certain node will be a Web service or a client?

A There are two rules. A one-to-many relationship suggests that the one be the server because servers are harder to write. In a one-to-one relationship, you would want to make the node with the most experienced Web service programming staff the server. If both sides are equally experienced, choose the node that makes sense to you.

Q **What is the rule of thumb governing which node should initiate the communication?**

A Normally, the node that is the consumer of the data should request it. The reason for this is that the consumer must have a way of requesting data anyway if the other node never sends it on its own.

Q **Shouldn't the client always request and the server always provide information to it?**

A No. Servers can request, or solicit, data if the design calls for it. Of course, clients can request data too.

Workshop

The Workshop is designed to help you review what you've learned, and begin learning how to put your knowledge into practice.

Quiz

1. What language are clients written in?
2. What is the best hardware platform for Web services?
3. What development tools should I purchase (or download) for developing Web services?
4. Do all the development tools on the market provide about the same functionality?

Quiz Answers

1. Clients can be written in any language that can be used to create text documents, which is any language.
2. All platforms are capable of producing Web services because Web services are abstract enough to allow any platform to implement them. The declaration of the best one will remain a subject of debate.
3. Normally, you should purchase a tool that supports your current development environment, which means that tools such as Apache Axis make sense for Java shops. Microsoft .NET makes sense for Windows programmers, and WebLogic Workshop would make sense for WebLogic shops.
4. No. The tools on the market vary greatly in the amount of automation that they provide. Some tools, such as Apache Axis, are appealing to programmers who like to work at the nuts-and-bolts level. At the other end of the spectrum, WebLogic Workshop is highly automated and generates almost all of the boilerplate code necessary for your service to function.

5

Activities

1. Using the previously outlined process, design a Web service that your organization might want to implement one day.

2. Specify which computers would host the Web services and which would act as clients.

3. If this Web service would replace an existing system or systems, create a detailed statement of reasons for dissatisfaction with the current system.

PART II

Working with Web Services

Hour

HOUR 6

The Web Services Architecture

The goal of this hour is to explain the core architecture that makes up Web services. We will concentrate on the interactions between core elements of the architecture and how this interaction provides the desired result: the successful sending of a message and receiving of a response. In addition, we will cover why this architecture is important and how it can improve the way that we program computers.

In this hour, you will learn

- The goal of the architecture
- The major software pieces that combine to create Web services
- How the major pieces work together to make Web services work

The Goal of the Web Services Architecture

At the highest level, the goal of Web services is application-to-application communication over the Internet. More specifically, this communication is performed with the idea of facilitating *enterprise application integration (EAI)* and e-commerce, specifically business-to-business e-commerce.

Web services is not the first attempt to solve this problem. In 1989, the *Object Management Group (OMG)* was formed to address this exact problem. The consortium included hundreds of member companies and organizations and produced some good results. They released CORBA 1.0 in 1991, which was used in LAN-based systems.

In 1996, OMG released the CORBA 2.0 specification, which included the *Internet Inter-ORB Protocol (IIOP)*. The IIOP allows multiple *Object Request Brokers (ORBs)* to interoperate regardless of vendor.

In that same year, Microsoft shipped software based on its *Distributed Component Object Model (DCOM)*, which was an enhanced version of its previous component architectures such as *object linking and embedding (OLE)*, *Component Object Model (COM)*, and ActiveX. In many ways, DCOM was a direct competitor of CORBA.

Given that we have had half a dozen years to perfect these technologies, the question is why we would want to use anything else. Web services is essentially a new competitor in this populated area of the computer business.

The reasons that there is still a market for a new solution is proof of dissatisfaction with the previous two approaches.

- Both CORBA and DCOM are built around the idea of making synchronous calls to methods on distributed objects. This approach leaves a gap that messaging software such as IBM's MQSeries and the *Java Message Service (JMS)* were created to fill: handling asynchronous messages. Some messages need to wait on a response, but others just want to hand data to another application.

- Both CORBA and DCOM are weak in the area of data encoding. They provide a mechanism for representing simple data types, but this data was encoded in binary formats. Binary formats cause the application logic to worry about low-level details such as whether the data is represented as big-endian or little-endian format. In addition, binary data cannot be read very easily by a person, which makes debugging harder.

- Arbitrary data is not easy to work with in CORBA or DCOM. Because they were developed before the advent of XML and the cheap computing power that makes XML practical, they send data in pure binary formats. XML makes working with arbitrary data easier.

- Data validation has to be done by the program logic in DCOM and CORBA rather than declaratively with WSDL in Web services. This increases the complexity of the endpoints because the logic to handle validation must be written for each application.

- DCOM and CORBA are two competing and rarely interoperating approaches. The promise of interoperability is a big part of both technologies' reasons for existing in the first place, but the fact that they don't talk to each other is disappointing. We don't get too excited about being able to interconnect with half the world. Interoperability is an all-or-nothing proposition.

- Vendor acrimony between those in the CORBA and DCOM camps created feelings that are not easy to heal. It is politically impossible for either camp to surrender at this point.

- The question of control held back DCOM. The smaller vendor and user community could only petition Microsoft with suggestions for changes to DCOM. This created a lack of enthusiasm for these approaches among technical leaders in the industry.

- Vendor motives are naturally self-centered, as they should be. This causes their approaches to be purposely incompatible with other vendors' approaches. The rest of us have trouble getting excited about an approach that is perceived as serving a vendor's bottom line instead of the industry as a whole.

As you might expect, Web services provides an approach that allows us to avoid many of the problems that CORBA and DCOM suffer from.

- Web services specifications have been designed from the ground up with the idea of application integration being central. This allows Web services to support message-centric asynchronous transactions as well as RPC-style synchronous transactions with equal ease.

- Data encoding is done using XML schema data types and aggregations of those types. Each endpoint in the transaction is responsible for deciding how to represent that data in its code for the duration of the application's execution. The data is reformatted into XML for the next step or the return trip.

- XML documents are human and machine readable. This makes debugging easier because each message that is transmitted over the wire can be intercepted and analyzed to discover details about the nature of the problem.

- XML is designed to represent arbitrary data. The XML schemas for complex data can be used by the WSDL in its description.

- Data validation can be added to any XML document by adding a line of text to the top of the file. This removes the need to create custom data type validation code in each application endpoint.

6

- In theory, Web services are interoperable. In reality, they are pretty interoperable, but their architecture is designed in such a way that this interoperability will increase over time.

- A surprising amount of cooperation between all vendors is the trademark of Web services. Because Web services are defined abstractly, for the most part, this allows them to be implemented using almost any software tool that you can think of.

- The question of control over the direction of Web services is easily answered. You and I control it. Certainly organizations, such as OASIS and W3C, provide direction to the specifications, but we are free to join those efforts at whatever level of interest that we have in them. Any company could join the W3C (for a fee of $15,000 U.S.), assign a few high-quality software engineers to a committee within those organizations, and exert considerable influence over the direction that the specification takes.

- Vendors are naturally self-centered, but when they cooperate in creating a specification, they tend to keep each other in line. As a result, the rest of us tend to believe that the specifications coming out of the W3C, OASIS, and other similar organizations are honest attempts to find the best solutions to problems that we all face.

The SOA

The *service-oriented architecture (SOA)* provides the theoretical model for all Web services. It is a simple model that contains three entities and three operations. Figure 6.1 shows this model.

FIGURE 6.1
The SOA provides a useful model for understanding Web services.

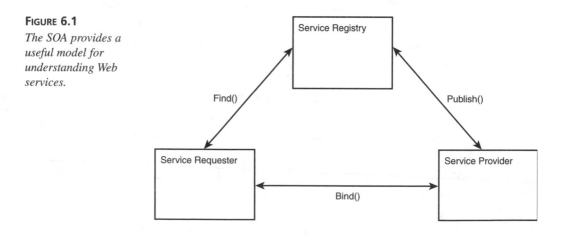

NEW TERM The *Service Requestor* is an application that wants to receive a service from another application. It doesn't know where this other application is or how to locate it, so it turns to the Service Registry and requests a `Find()` operation.

NEW TERM The *Service Registry* is a well-known application that returns information about Web services in response to search criteria that has been submitted by a Service Requestor in the `Find()` operation. This information returns the contact information for Web services based on their classifications that match the search criteria. It also includes information about how to find out the connection details.

NEW TERM The *Service Providers* `Publish()` these classification details as well as the connection details to the Service Registry. They do this for the same reason that a business would purchase a listing in the Yellow Pages of the local phone book.

The Service Requestor uses the connection details to `Bind()` to the Service Provider. Once bound, they can send messages and receive responses.

The Major Components of the Architecture

Web services are built on a foundation of different, but cooperating, specifications and standards. Some of the reasons for this are historical, but the primary reason that there are multiple standards is that no one person or group has a monopoly on the specification process. Everyone in the Web services community has a voice in determining the direction that the technology will take. At the present time, the following specifications are considered the primary software specifications that, when taken as a whole, compose what we know as Web services:

- HTTP/1.1
- RFC 2965:HTTP State Management Mechanism (cookies)
- SOAP 1.1
- UDDI version 2.04 API and the other UDDI 2.03 lesser specifications
- WSDL 1.1
- XML 1.0 (second edition)
- XML Schema Part 1: Structures
- XML Schema Part 2: Datatypes

NEW TERM The source of this list is the *Web Services Interoperability Organization (WS-I)*, but the contents are not controversial to our knowledge.

6

SOAP

NEW TERM *SOAP* used to stand for Simple Object Access Protocol, but now SOAP is considered a name and not an acronym. As we stated earlier in the hour, SOAP is a message format that enables method calls to be sent in an XML format from one computer to another. In addition, it can send an entire XML document (that contains only data) instead of a method call if you prefer.

NEW TERM The word SOAP was coined in 1998 during discussions between Microsoft, DevelopMentor, and Userland about how to best send remote procedure calls over HTTP using XML. After the usual stalls that accompany this type of discussion, Userland published a draft of the specification in the summer of 1998. After performing some updates to respond to feedback, SOAP 0.9 was submitted to the *Internet Engineering Task Force (IETC)* in September 1999. With a few changes, SOAP 1.0 was announced in December 1999.

NEW TERM IBM joined with the other companies in submitting a specification for SOAP 1.1 to the *World Wide Web Consortium (W3C)* in May 2000. This was significant because IBM is closely identified with Java and J2EE. Their joining the submission created the correct perception that this was more that a single-vendor Microsoft submission.

NEW TERM SOAP defines an *envelope* that contains a *header* and a *body*. The header provides instructions on how the message is to be processed. Sometimes this is information that the message is to be forwarded on or that the return path is to be a certain URL. Many of the draft specifications that are now circulating propose enhancements to this header. The SOAP body contains the *payload*. This payload is the method call from the originator and it is the response from the remote system.

SOAP 1.1 is commonly used today, but SOAP 1.2 is, at this writing, a candidate for release as a recommendation (the W3C equivalent of a standard).

Extensible Markup Language

Extensible Markup Language (XML) has become the common language of the computing business. It is a tag-oriented language that looks superficially like HTML, but its purpose is different. HTML describes the way a document should look when displayed in a browser. XML, on the other hand, describes what the data that you are looking at means, independent of the way that it is displayed. Hour 7, "Understanding XML," covers XML in some detail.

Briefly, XML was created to remove the ambiguity from data. Suppose that you create a string containing the following:

```
7 3 2003
```

If you send this string to my computer program, how is the program supposed to interpret it? Should we send you seven cases of books with a serial number of three and charge you $2,003 for it? If we add the following tags to the string, we can completely clear up the ambiguity:

```
<date>
    <day>3</day>
    <year>2003</year>
    <month>7</month>
</date>
```

The meaning is absolutely clear now. You are sending me a date that means "July 3, 2003." Adding these XML style tags to the data makes it easy to parse and use.

An additional feature of XML is the existence of a description of what the tag structure must look like in a document for it to be valid. The original description was called the *Document Type Description (DTD)*, but it is fast being made obsolete by the XML schema. They both serve the same purpose, but the XML schema is more powerful and allows for more precise descriptions.

The XML specification is also maintained by the W3C. This organization accepts requests for changes and enhancements to this specification and occasionally publishes a new version. The version of XML that is in common use at this writing is XML 1.0 (second edition).

Hypertext Transport Protocol

Hypertext Transport Protocol (HTTP) is the workhorse of the Web. It is managed by the W3C as well. Its current version is 1.1, and all activity has ceased on it because it is considered complete and stable.

The purpose of HTTP is to provide a protocol to move requests and responses between clients and servers. It will carry any information that is placed in it from point A to point B without regard for its data type. As a result, it is a popular way to transport SOAP messages between clients and Web services.

HTTP is not required in SOAP 1.2 because other protocols have been added. The vast majority of Web service messages will be carried by HTTP in the near term, however.

6

HTTP State Management Mechanism (Cookies)

Also known as RFC 2965, this document specifies how to create stateful sessions using HTTP requests and responses. It adds three headers to HTTP, which carry state information between participating clients and servers.

Web Services Description Language

Web Services Description Language (WSDL) is a specification that tells us how to describe a Web service. Consider the case in which you are told about a Web service that provides some information or processing that you would like to access. Your first questions would be

- What method calls does it accept?
- What parameters will it accept?
- What responses will it send back?
- What protocols can it process?
- What data format specifications can it accept?
- What are the URLs for the service?

A WSDL document is an XML document that contains all the information that you need to contact a service. In addition to being verbose, it is platform and language neutral. A programmer or program is able to read this document and create an unambiguous message that can call a method or methods in this service.

This is a marvelous achievement because now you have a specification that describes a way to describe any piece of software, including non–Web service software, in a precise way. This means that you can write software that can generate messages based on the logic in your program combined with the information in the WSDL.

Normally, a potential Web service consumer would obtain the WSDL first. Using the WSDL, this would-be client could either have a programmer create software to this WSDL or use software that is capable of generating a program to do the communications part of the client processing.

WSDL is also managed by the W3C. It is currently at version 1.1, but a version 1.2 is in draft status. In addition to the minor changes that you would expect, version 1.2 is attempting to add an abstract model to the specification. At this point, a consensus has not been reached on what that abstract model should look like.

The Structures and Data Types of XML Schema

The structures part of the XML schema specifies the schema definition language that can be used to describe the structure of XML documents. It can also be used to constrain the contents of a document.

The datatypes part of the XML schema specification defines a way for specifying datatypes in XML schemas and other XML specifications. The facilities described here are more powerful than those available in the old DTDs.

The XML schema specification is managed by the W3C also, where it has the status of a recommendation (a W3C standard).

Universal Description, Discovery, and Integration

NEW TERM The *Universal Description, Discovery, and Integration (UDDI)* specification describes a special type of registry that lists Web services that you might potentially be interested in. It contains quite a bit of information oriented toward allowing you to search its contents for a specific characteristic or feature. It uses special classification schemes called taxonomies that categorize a Web service in ways that are meaningful to potential clients.

The registries can be of various types:

- **Public**—A public registry is one that is open to the public for searching. Several major companies maintain public registries, including IBM and Microsoft. All the entries in the public registries are replicated in the other public registries so that a search performed against one registry will be able to access data about every publicly registered Web service.

- **Private**—A private registry is one that exists behind the firewall of one company. The purpose of this registry might be to provide a way to search for internal Web services. It might also contain entries to other software systems in the company that are not exposed yet as Web services. In this scenario, the UDDI registry acts as a software reuse catalog.

- **Restricted**—A restricted registry can only be accessed by certain organizations who have been granted permission to access it. Trading partners can use this information about each other's systems to find out how to interact with them better.

The industry has been slow to accept public registries because of security concerns and fear of getting out on the bleeding edge. In addition, UDDI represents a new way of doing business, and businesses are always very conservative about making drastic changes.

6

The current version of UDDI that is in popular use is version 2.04. A version 3 has been published, but it take some time for all the software vendors to bring their offerings up to the new release. Unlike many of the other Web services specifications, UDDI is not managed by the W3C. Instead, it is managed by a group called the *Organization for the Advancement of Structured Information Standards (OASIS)*.

Understanding Interactions Between Components

Sometimes it is hard to visualize the interaction between parts of a complex transaction. For this reason, we are going to walk through a scenario to show how software written to each of these standards interacts with the others in a typical transaction.

Our hypothetical Web Service (Service Provider) begins its life as a COBOL program that accepts a file of addresses. It compares the addresses against the official USPS address database, corrects the address (if needed) and adds the last four digits of the ZIP Code (if missing).

NEW TERM   The engineer in charge of creating the Web service uses Apache Axis as his SOAP engine. He creates a special piece of Java software that accepts SOAP remote procedure calls as input and makes calls to the legacy Java system. In Axis jargon, this is a special type of *handler* called a *dispatcher*.

He decides to write the WSDL by hand to gain experience. This is not too hard because the service is very simple. He describes the method calls that his Web service will accept by following a combination of the WSDL and schema specifications.

He next publishes information about the Service Provider to the Service Registry of his choice, the Microsoft public registry (which is written to the UDDI specification). There he enters in data about the Web site. Part of the information that our engineer places on the site is the URL of the WSDL for the Web service.

A potential customer performs a find operation on the Service Registry of his choice, the IBM public registry. This registry replicates the entries made on the Microsoft registry every night, so our Web service is listed in both registries. This replication is done according to the UDDI specification.

The potential customer finds the entry for our service and uses the listed URL to download a copy of the WSDL. Using the WSDL, he writes a Visual Basic program to serve as the Service Requestor to access the service. When the client-side programming is complete, he tests it by requesting that it perform a bind operation on the Web Service. After the bind operation is successful, the client passes in a version of his home address that purposely contains a misspelling and a missing ZIP Code and waits for a response.

The client software packages his request into a SOAP envelope and sends it to the URL for the site using the HTTP. The Tomcat Web server receives the HTTP message and strips off the HTTP headers. It passes the SOAP message to the Axis SOAP engine. The SOAP engine removes the header portion and processes any directives that might appear in the header.

The Axis SOAP engine calls the dispatcher program. The dispatcher calls the methods in the legacy system and passes the incorrect address to it as a parameter. The legacy address correction system fixes the address and adds the correct ZIP Code. It passes back the corrected address to the dispatcher. The SOAP engine creates the SOAP response message, adds any SOAP headers that are needed, and returns it to the Tomcat Web server. Tomcat adds the HTTP-specific data to the response and sends it back to the client.

The client program converts the SOAP message into a Visual Basic data type and returns it to the Visual Basic program. This program stores the response in a text box and displays it on the screen. The Visual Basic programmer looks at the corrected address as proof that everything worked properly. Figure 6.2 shows this process graphically.

In essence, every Web service transaction follows this same general approach with the exception of the find, which is either done the first time or omitted altogether. Sometimes the message is forwarded on to the next Web service in a chain, but even then, the basic transactions are just being chained together. In the future, the chains will become more complex as new specifications become accepted, but the basic transaction is the same.

6

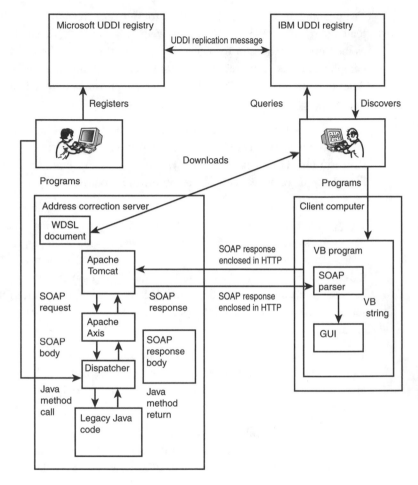

FIGURE 6.2

All the software written to the different specifications work together to produce a successful transaction.

Summary

In this hour, we looked at the Web services architecture from three angles. First, we examined the weaknesses of the DCOM and CORBA approaches and how Web services address these areas in their own architecture.

Second, we looked at the Service-Oriented Architecture (SOA) and how its components, the Service Requestor, Service Provider, and Service Registry interact. Third, we looked at the basic specifications that form the foundation of Web services. Finally, we talked through a simple example in which the SOA model and the standards were discussed in the context of the interaction between actual software components written to these specifications.

Q&A

Q What is the goal of the Web services architecture?

A The goal is to facilitate the transfer of information between computers of differing manufacture and operating system type.

Q How do the goals of Web services differ from those of CORBA and DCOM?

A The goals are virtually identical, but the details of the implementation differ in nearly every aspect.

Q Why didn't everyone just agree to use CORBA or DCOM?

A The computing world broke into two camps who couldn't find any compromise. The two systems were very difficult to make interoperable, and neither side was interested in changing.

Q Why did they agree on the Web services architecture?

A They agreed for many reasons, but the primary one might have been "battle fatigue." Both sides were tired of the contention and wanted to find something that worked.

Workshop

The Workshop is designed to help you review what you've learned and begin learning how to put your knowledge into practice.

Quiz

1. Where did CORBA and DCOM come from?
2. What are the components of the SOA model?
3. What are the methods of the SOA model?
4. What are the names of each component as they are commonly used in Web services?

Quiz Answers

1. CORBA was created by the Object Management Group (OMG). DCOM was created by Microsoft.
2. The core components are the Service Registry, Service Requestor, and Service Provider.
3. The core methods or operations are Find(), Bind(), and Publish().

6

4. The Service Registry is commonly called the UDDR Registry or the Public Registry. The Service Requestor is often called the client or service consumer. The Service Provider is normally just called the Web service, but it can be called the provider also.

Activities

1. Name the weaknesses of the CORBA and DCOM approaches.

2. Name the specifications that are considered the basic Web services specifications, along with their version number.

HOUR 7

Understanding XML

In this hour, you will learn about the need for XML. In the beginning, you will learn a little about the rules of grammar that govern XML. You will learn how XML namespaces can guarantee that there won't be any duplicate tag names in your document. Next, we will show you how you can be sure that the documents you receive are correct. In this hour, you will learn

- Why XML is needed
- The rules for creating an XML document
- Avoiding naming conflicts
- How to validate that the document is correct

Understanding Why We Need XML

Most knowledge workers like technology only when it solves a problem that is vexing them. Before launching into a discussion of the details, we should first pause and ask ourselves why we need XML anyway.

The idea of interconnecting two computers and exchanging data between them was born on the same day that the second computer was installed. We don't often scatter our data around on purpose; it happens naturally. Through mergers, acquisitions, software platform obsolescence, and new technical innovations, we end up with islands of data all over our network. Whenever we go to assemble the data that we need to support decision making, we invariably need to combine data that doesn't reside on the same computer.

NEW TERM The solution to this problem is to export the data from one computer system and import it into another. The simplicity of this statement hides a multitude of ugly details. Hardware engineers solved the problem of moving files between computers long ago. In addition, software engineers have also solved the technical problem of converting *EBCDIC* encoding into *ASCII* and converting the *byte order*. The problem is not in getting a text file from one computer to another in a readable format; the problem is how to write programs that can figure out what the data means when you get it there.

Several years ago, a major defense contractor launched an effort to place the instructions for how to assemble its airplanes online. For 40 years, these instructions had been printed and bound into a book. The mechanics who built the planes took out the book, read it, and then did the work.

The justification for the new system was based on the fact that these instructions contained many cross-references to other documents. The requirements stated that these cross-references must be changed into hyperlinks in the online system. The names of the hyperlinked files existed on the printed form and in the word-processed version of the document. They were embedded, however, in the middle of all the specifications and instructions.

There was no indication that this was a cross-reference, even in the electronic version of the paper document. Sometimes these special document references would be on the fifth line in one document but on the seventh line of another. Sometimes they started with an *x*, but other times with an *r*. Some of them were numeric, but others also contained letters. Needless to say, determining which pieces of text represented instructions and which pieces represented references to other documents was a nontrivial problem. A typical instruction looked like this:

```
"Drill hole according to procedure x151-1 and insert rivet.  Seal the top
 of the rivet using sealant 212, Material Safety Data Sheet MSDS-2324."
```

After much trial and error, a fairly sophisticated parser was written that achieved about a 98% accuracy rate. Imagine how much easier this task would have been if this document had been prepared in the following manner:

```
<instruction>
  Drill hole according to procedure
  <standard procedure> x151-1</standard procedure>
  and insert rivet
</instruction>
<instruction>
 Seal the top of the rivet using sealant 212, Material Safety Data Sheet
 <safety sheet> MSDS-2324<safety sheet>
</instruction>
```

The programmer could easily differentiate between instructions, standard procedures, and safety sheets if given a document that has been formatted in this way. This concept is at the heart of XML. An XML document is a document filled with tags telling the reader, either human or computer, what the data means.

Using XML greatly simplifies the task of preparing documents for exchange between computer systems. The XML specification contains a set of syntax rules that are fixed and inviolable. These rules govern the format that tags must obey, the special characters that are allowed and what they mean, and the format of the document as a whole.

The specification does not contain the meanings of the tags that will be used. The vocabulary is created by the XML users according to their business needs. This is somewhat analogous to the English language. English grammar rules tell us that proper names are capitalized, question sentences contain a "?" at the end, a space is needed between words, and so on. The grammar doesn't tell us what the vocabulary consists of; that is the job of the dictionary. In fact, the dictionary doesn't even define the full vocabulary; we are free to make up new words to fit our needs.

The tag <horse> can mean anything that you and I agree that it means. In fact, it can mean cow, if we so desire (and could tolerate the confusion that would ensue). As long as the programs that I write interpret the tag the same way that you expected them to, all is well.

The vocabulary of an XML document is based on an agreement between two or more parties. Automotive manufacturers can create a special set of tags that describes painting instructions. Two bakers can create a vocabulary to describe recipes and a grammar to describe the relationships between the tags in the vocabulary. These vocabularies can be thought of as mini-dictionaries. Once a vocabulary of tags is created, it can be published and used by any number of organizations to exchange data in an XML format.

7

The Components of XML

Now that we have discussed the basic purpose of XML, let's look at the major components that compose it:

- **XML document**—A file that obeys the rules of XML. It contains data and can be thought of as a data store or a mini-database. In addition, an XML document can be loaded into the memory of the computer by a program. While in memory, it can still be referred to as an XML document.

- **XML parser**—A computer program that takes XML as its input and produces a program-readable representation of its contents. Processing data in XML format would be very inefficient, so the parser transforms it into data structures that are efficient to process.

- **Document Type Definition (DTD)**—A description of the tags that are allowed to exist in a document and their relationships to each other. The DTD was made obsolete by the publication of the XML schema specification in 2001. You still see them, however.

- **XML schema**—A description of the tags that are allowed to exist in a document and their relationship to each other. You validate the document against the XML schema to ensure that it contains tags that obey the rules set forth in the schema. This validation takes place outside of your programs by an XML parser, relieving you of the burden of writing this code in every system that you work on. The XML schema is a new and much improved version of the DTD.

- **Namespaces**—A unique name can be used to avoid conflicts between tag names. Because an XML document can contain other XML documents, we must have a way to guarantee that none of the included document's tags are identical to one of the main documents. By creating a namespace for each XML document, included tags are always unique to the original document.

All these pieces work together to support your applications. They allow you to create systems that transfer data easily, and can be parsed and validated in a standard way.

The XML Grammar Rules

The purpose of covering the basics of XML grammar in this section is to permit you to understand the topic of Web services at a deeper level. The fact that you bought this book indicates that you are looking for more than a superficial understanding of how Web services work. To acquire this knowledge, it is critical that you be able to read XML files, even if you never plan on writing one yourself.

Here is the set of rules that an XML document must follow:

- Each start tag must have a corresponding end tag.

- Attribute values must be enclosed in quotes.

- Some characters in data must be represented by entity references. If they appear in text as ordinary characters, the XML parser becomes confused.

- Improperly nested tags are not permitted. If you start a tag sequence <a><b>, it must end </b></a>, not </a></b>.

- The document must have the XML prologue: <?xml version='1.0'?>.

Documents that follow these rules are considered "well formed." If a document is not well formed, it will cause errors to be thrown during parsing.

This set of rules is really pretty small when compared to the power of the XML technology. Listing 7.1 shows a sample XML document.

LISTING 7.1   The TicketRequest.XML File

```
<?xml version='1.0' encoding='utf-8' standalone='yes' ?>
<!--This XML document represents a request for a cruise ticket-->

<ticketRequest>
   <customer custID="10003" >
      <lastName>Carter</lastName>
      <firstName>Joseph</firstName>
   </customer>
   <cruise cruiseID="3004">
      <destination>Hawaii</destination>
      <port>Honolulu</port>
      <sailing>7/7/2001</sailing>
      <numberOfTickets>5</numberOfTickets>
      <isCommissionable/>
   </cruise>
</ticketRequest>
```

The first line is called the prologue:

```
<?xml version='1.0' encoding='utf-8' standalone='yes' ?>
```

The first entry contains the version of XML in which it was written. This can be important because future releases of XML might force parsers to be aware of the version. The encoding called utf-8 contains the standard Western European character set. The standalone=yes keyword tells us that an external DTD isn't used to validate this document.

7

The second line is a comment:

```
<!--This XML document represents a request for a cruise ticket-->
```

The next line is the root element of the document. There is only one root element per XML document; all other elements in the XML document must be enclosed by the root element. The `<ticketRequest>` element tells us that this is a user-defined tag with the name ticketRequest and that ticketRequest is in the default namespace. We will look at namespaccs later in this hour.

```
<ticketRequest>
```

The customer tag contains another string inside its tag. The value of this other string is custID="10003". custID is said to be an attribute of the tag customer. "10003" is called the attribute value.

```
<customer custID="10003" >
    <lastName>Carter</lastName>
    <firstName>Joseph</firstName>
</customer>
```

The `<customer>` tag can contain two other tags—the `<firstName>` and the `<lastName>` tags. These tags have values that lie outside the delimiters < and >. In reality, the document designer can place data as attributes or as tag values whenever a one-to-one relationship exists. When the relationship is one-to-many, only tag values will work. Notice the use of the corresponding `</customer>` tag to indicate the end of the `<customer>` tag.

The `<cruise>` tag follows a pattern similar to the `<customer>` tag. If an element doesn't have any nested elements, you can use the empty tag shorthand notation instead of an opening and a closing tag. Instead of having an `<isCommissionable>` and then a `</isCommissionable>` tag, we have only `<isCommissionable/>`, which means the same thing as the two tags combined. This tag is special in that it can't contain data. Its presence is sufficient to indicate that a sales commission will be paid to the agency that booked this cruise.

```
<cruise cruiseID="3004">
    <destination>Hawaii</destination>
    <port>Honolulu</port>
    <sailing>7/7/2001</sailing>
    <numberOfTickets>5</numberOfTickets>
    <isCommissionable/>
</cruise>
```

The closing tag indicates that the document is complete:

```
</ticketRequest>
```

Notice how easy it is to understand what the data in the file means. The careful selection of tag names preserves their meaning so that humans, as well as software, can understand the data. Testing XML files is easy to do using either a Netscape or IE browser. All you have to do is create a file with the XML in it, and then open the file by using the Open command on the File menu. If you have any errors in the XML document, they will show up in the browser. Figure 7.1 shows what an error message looks like in Netscape 7.0.

FIGURE 7.1

You can use a browser to validate that an XML file is well formed.

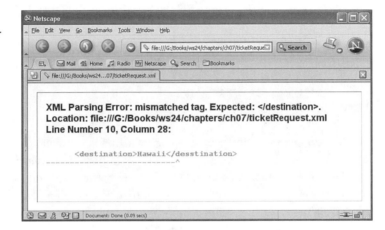

We purposely misspelled one of the tags so that we would generate an error. You will also notice that there is no designation of a DTD or schema in this code. If there had been, the parser run by the browser would have located it and used it to validate that the XML tags were created in obedience with the XML rules.

Notice also that this XML document did not contain any data that is not plain text. The reason for this is to preserve the simplicity of the document. If XML permitted the inclusion of binary data into documents, it would greatly complicate the parsing process and compromise our ability to transfer it between different computers. Integers, real numbers, dates, and times can be created from text strings within programs. By the same token, programs can convert these data types into their textual representation before putting them into XML documents.

Understanding Namespaces

7

Once you have created a vocabulary of useful elements, you will be reluctant to part with it. The principles of modularity state that you should be able to combine a number of different XML sets of tags together and use them in the same document. A problem arises, however, if you try to combine tag vocabularies with elements or attribute names that are identical. How will the program that receives your XML document differentiate between these different, but identically named elements?

The good solution to this problem would be to prefix every element with a string that is guaranteed to be unique across the whole planet. Using this scheme, two identical elements called `<captain>` could be differentiated because one of them would be called `<abc:captain>` and the other `<xyz:captain>`. Then the only problem would be to figure out a way to keep the authors of the other vocabularies that you use from using the same prefix.

If we were to use a valid URL from an organization that has registered it properly, we could be sure that no two organizations would use the same prefix. Therefore, the tag name of

```
<www.samspublishing.com/authoring:captain>
```

would work. Because this publishing organization is large and others in the same company might use the same element name, it might be more unique if I added the name of my department to the string also. Now, I can be virtually guaranteed that no one outside my own department can create a name conflict. The only problem is the size of the tag. If I have a tag name that is this long, my document will be nearly unreadable. If I could create a string variable called `wspa` and assign to it the value `www.samspublishing.com/authoring`, my tag would look like this:

```
<wspa:captain>
```

NEW TERM   This name is much more practical. In fact, this approach is exactly the one employed by XML in a feature called the *namespace*. Consider the XML in Listing 7.2.

LISTING 7.2   The TicketRequest2.xml File

```
<?xml version='1.0' encoding='utf-8' standalone='yes' ?>
<!--This XML document represents a request for a cruise ticket-->

<cust:ticketRequest xmlns:cust='www.samspublishing.com/customer'
                xmlns:boat='www.samspublishing.com/boat'>
   <cust:customer custID="10003" >
      <cust:lastName>Carter</cust:lastName>
      <cust:firstName>Joseph</cust:firstName>
   </cust:customer>
   <boat:cruise cruiseID="3004">
      <boat:destination>Hawaii</boat:destination>
```

LISTING 7.2 continued

```
        <boat:port>Honolulu</boat:port>
        <boat:sailing>7/7/2001</boat:sailing>
        <boat:numberOfTickets>5</boat:numberOfTickets>
        <boat:isCommissionable/>
    </boat:cruise>
</cust:ticketRequest>
```

We defined two namespaces—one called cust and another called boat. The xmlns string is a reserved word in XML that signifies that a namespace is being created. Using these two prefixes, we can guarantee uniqueness even if this document is combined with another. The reason for this is that the parser makes the substitution of the long name for the short whenever the document is processed. The prefix is purely for humans to look at. In fact, the name of the prefix is local to this document.

> Don't be confused by the use of a URL in the definition of the namespace. Any string can be substituted for this string, but the more unique it is, the better. URLs are the ultimate in unique strings. The parser doesn't even look at the Web site represented by the URL, even if one actually exists, when processing the document. The unique string is the goal, not a valid address on the Internet.

Understanding the XML Schema

NEW TERM Now that we have examined the topic of namespace definition, we can look at how we can create an *XML schema* for a document. Earlier, we complained that the DTD did not allow us to specify data types well and that it was not written in XML. For these reasons, the W3C has released a new way to specify the legal contents of an XML document called the XML schema.

An XML schema is an XML file that performs the same function as a DTD, but the schema does it better. XML schemas allow you to specify not only the elements and attributes, but also the range of values and the data type of an element. Listing 7.3 shows a schema for a ticket request.

7

LISTING 7.3   The TicketRequest.xsd Schema File

```xml
<?xml version='1.0' encoding='utf-8' ?>

<xsd:schema xmlns:xsd="http://www.w3.org/2001/XMLSchema"
              xmlns:cruise="http://www.samspublishing.com/"
              targetNamespace="http://www.samspublishing.com/"

<xsd:annotation>
   <xsd:documentation xml:lang="en">
    This XML Schema document represents
    a request for a cruise ticket
   </xsd:documentation>
</xsd:annotation>

<xsd:element name="cruiseTicket" type="cruise:CruiseTicketType"/>

<xsd:complexType name="CruiseTicketType">
   <xsd:sequence>
      <xsd:element name="customer" type="cruise:CustomerType"/>
      <xsd:element name="cruise" type="cruise:CruiseType"/>
   </xsd:sequence>
</xsd:complexType>

<xsd:complexType name="CustomerType">
   <xsd:sequence>
      <xsd:element name="lastName" type="xsd:string"/>
      <xsd:element name="firstName" type="xsd:string"/>
   </xsd:sequence>
   <xsd:attribute name="custID" type="xsd:positiveInteger"/>
</xsd:complexType>

<xsd:complexType name="CruiseType">
   <xsd:sequence>
      <xsd:element name="destination" type="xsd:string"/>
      <xsd:element name="port" type="xsd:string"/>
      <xsd:element name="sailing" type="xsd:date"/>
      <xsd:element name="numberOfTickets" type="xsd:positiveInteger"/>
   </xsd:sequence>
   <xsd:attribute name="cruiseID" type="xsd:positiveInteger"/>
</xsd:complexType>

</xsd:schema>
```

The first thing that you notice about a schema file is that it is a regular well-formed XML file. The tags in the file have a prefix of xsd, which means that they are part of the XML schema:

```xml
<xsd:schema xmlns:xsd="http://www.w3.org/2001/XMLSchema"
```

We define our own namespace called `cruise`:

```
xmlns:cruise="http://www.samspublishing.com/"
```

We also define a `targetNamespace`, which is the namespace that must be used in an XML file if it is going to refer to this schema. This is the namespace that will appear within the `xmlns:` tag in the header:

```
targetNamespace="http://www.samspublishing.com/"
```

The annotation and documentation allow comments to be placed in the schema to help the reader understand it:

```
<xsd:annotation>
   <xsd:documentation xml:lang="en">
```

The basic job of the schema is to define types, and then define elements of the new type that can appear in XML documents:

```
<xsd:element name="cruiseTicket" type="cruise:CruiseTicketType"/>
```

The types are defined in this file also. The complex types are those that contain other complex and simple types:

```
<xsd:complexType name="CruiseTicketType">
```

The sequence tag indicates that the order of the elements in the `complexType` must be followed:

```
   <xsd:sequence>
```

The `CruiseTicketType` is composed of two other complex types:

```
      <xsd:element name="customer" type="cruise:CustomerType"/>
      <xsd:element name="cruise" type="cruise:CruiseType"/>
```

The `CustomerType` and the `CruiseType` are complex types, but they are made up entirely of simple types. Notice that these simple types are of a variety of different data types. Notice also that the attributes are defined alongside the elements:

```
<xsd:complexType name="CustomerType">
   <xsd:sequence>
      <xsd:element name="lastName" type="xsd:string"/>
      <xsd:element name="firstName" type="xsd:string"/>
   </xsd:sequence>
   <xsd:attribute name="custID" type="xsd:positiveInteger"/>
</xsd:complexType>

<xsd:complexType name="CruiseType">
   <xsd:sequence>
      <xsd:element name="destination" type="xsd:string"/>
```

7

```
      <xsd:element name="port" type="xsd:string"/>
      <xsd:element name="sailing" type="xsd:date"/>
      <xsd:element name="numberOfTickets" type="xsd:positiveInteger"/>
   </xsd:sequence>
   <xsd:attribute name="cruiseID" type="xsd:positiveInteger"/>
</xsd:complexType>
```

Listing 7.4 shows an XML file that conforms to this schema.

LISTING 7.4   The TicketRequest3.xml File

```
<?xml version='1.0' encoding='utf-8'?>
<acruise:cruiseTicket xmlns:acruise ="http://www.samspublishing.com"
   xmlns:xsi="http://www.w3.org/2001/XMLSchema-instance"
   xsi:schemaLocation="http://www.samspublishing.com ticketRequest.xsd">

   <customer custID="10003" >
      <lastName>Carter</lastName>
      <firstName>Joseph</firstName>
   </customer>
   <cruise cruiseID="3004">
      <destination>Hawaii</destination>
      <port>Honolulu</port>
      <sailing>2001-07-07</sailing>
      <numberOfTickets>6</numberOfTickets>
   </cruise>
</acruise:cruiseTicket>
```

We first define a namespace and a prefix to identify the elements. Notice that we use the targetNamespace that was defined when we defined the CruiseTicket element:

```
<acruise:cruiseTicket xmlns:acruise ="http://www.samspublishing.com"
```

We next declare that this file conforms to an instance of the 2001 XML schema specification:

```
xmlns:xsi="http://www.w3.org/2001/XMLSchema-instance"
```

We associate the namespace string with a schema filename. The namespace string must match the one in the targetNamespace element in the schema file:

```
xsi:schemaLocation="http://www.samspublishing.com/ticketRequest.xsd">
```

We now create elements according to the complex type definitions and data types described in the schema file:

```
<customer custID="10003" >
   <lastName>Carter</lastName>
   <firstName>Joseph</firstName>
```

```
  </customer>
  <cruise cruiseID="3004">
     <destination>Hawaii</destination>
     <port>Honolulu</port>
     <sailing>2001-07-07</sailing>
     <numberOfTickets>6</numberOfTickets>
  </cruise>
```

If we submit this file to a validating parser, it will check that every rule of XML and schema conformity is followed.

Summary

This hour has introduced you to the basic concepts behind XML. You first looked at the motivation for using XML. Following that, you learned the grammar rules for creating XML documents.

Next, you learned how to use namespaces to avoid element-naming conflicts. In the final section, you learned how to validate the correctness of an XML document using XML schemas.

Q&A

Q What was the primary motivation behind the creation of XML?

A The primary goal was to create a way to transfer data in character form along with information about its meaning.

Q Why is an XML schema considered better than a DTD?

A An XML schema allows the creator to specify exactly what kind of data can appear in the document. A DTD is more limited in this area.

Q Why is XML limited to text?

A Every brand of computer can exchange text files with every other brand using software that is commonly available. Other data formats are not always easy to transfer and require special software.

Workshop

The following questions and activities will allow you to test your understanding of XML, namespaces, and XML schemas.

Quiz

1. What is the purpose of XML?
2. Why is an XML schema considered a superior way to validate a document?
3. What is the use of the URL in the definition of a namespace?

Quiz Answers

1. It allows the meaning of data to be communicated in the same document with the data.
2. An XML schema can validate an XML document as well as a DTD can; plus, it can assign more specific data types to each field. In addition, it is an XML document itself.
3. The URL that you normally see is really just a unique string. URLs are chosen because they are guaranteed to be unique. The XML parser doesn't actually access the URL.

Activities

1. Create a simple XML schema that describes a business entity in your organization.
2. Create an XML document that conforms to your schema.

HOUR **8**

Understanding How Web Services Communicate

Before we can get into the specifics on the internals of Web services, it is important to understand the communication fundamentals upon which they operate. In this hour, we'll examine the communications mechanisms upon which Web services operate. We'll examine the following topics:

- TCP/IP and how the Internet works
- HTTP
- Message queues for Web services
- SMTP as a Web service transfer protocol
- FTP
- Jabber for Web services

Although it's possible to get extremely low level in the discussion of these areas, it's not really necessary for the level of this book to do so. Instead, we'll focus more on how these protocols work from the standpoint of Web services.

One key feature of Web services is that they leave the definition of how to transmit the data over the network open ended. Although only HTTP was initially used to perform this transmission of data, newer standards have allowed for a wider range of communication protocols to be used—each with its own strengths and weaknesses in relation to the original HTTP mechanisms.

Because our focus in this hour is on the communications protocols rather than the content and structure of the messages, we'll refer to data transferred (such as the SOAP XML messages) as the payload. You'll see more about the specific payloads in later hours. For now, just consider the payload as some data that has to be transferred from one place to another in some way. This hour is about the "how it gets there" and not the "what is sent." Regardless of which transport mechanism is used, the payload is the same.

TCP/IP and How the Internet Works

Before we can talk about the various transport protocols that can be used for Web services communications, we must first establish a foundation of knowledge on how the Internet itself works. Before the Internet, computers were standalone entities. In most cases, the only way to connect and communicate from one machine to another was if both machines were identical in terms of hardware architecture and operating system. Even then, this was often a difficult endeavor.

Then in the late 1960s the U.S. military's Advanced Defense Research Agency (ARPA) was tasked to create a computer networking system that would allow for computer-to-computer communications that would be somewhat reliable even if entire nodes of the network were destroyed in a nuclear war. At the same time, there was the goal of being able to link dissimilar computer networks together. Their solution was the *TCP/IP stack*. TCP/IP stands for Transmission Control Protocol/Internet Protocol.

TCP/IP is the foundation of all communications on the Internet today. It controls how computers interconnect and how information is routed around the network, as well as the processes that take place at each node to handle the connections. In reality, TCP/IP is actually two separate protocols. TCP is considered a transport protocol (not what we mean by transport protocol in the Web services sense though), whereas IP is the network protocol. The distinction is that IP handles the actual routing of information, whereas TCP (and UDP) handles the flow of data, how the packets are arranged and sent, and so on. Each of the protocols that we will discuss in this hour run on top of TCP and make use of the services that it provides.

In reality, there are two transport layer protocols to the TCP/IP stack: TCP and UDP. TCP can be thought of as a virtual circuit, which means a connection is established from the source to the destination through various nodes. As long as the connection is maintained, all packets of data will be sent along the same path and are guaranteed to be delivered in the same sequence that they were sent out. As a result, TCP is the method of choice for streaming communications. This involves a bit of overhead, but provides for reliable transmission. UDP (User Datagram Protocol), on the other hand, has much less overhead but does not guarantee delivery or packet arrival order. It instead sends small self-contained bundles of data that match the size of the underlying IP packets. It cannot be used for large datasets or streaming applications. For this reason, TCP is the protocol used by all the Web service transports we will discuss.

How does all this fit in together? Communications on the Internet are done in a layered approach. Figure 8.1 shows this layered system of communications. This layered approach is known as the OSI model.

FIGURE 8.1
The OSI model of Internet communications provides a layered approach to network interfaces.

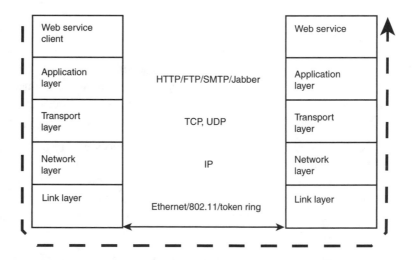

As you can see, the protocols we will discuss later in this hour sit just below the actual Web service and provide an interface down to the TCP and IP layers, respectively.

Now that you have at least a basic understanding of TCP/IP, you're ready to examine the different mechanisms for doing Web services communications.

HTTP

The most popular protocol on the Internet, and the one that most people think of when you say the word Internet, is HTTP. *HTTP* (*Hypertext Transfer Protocol*) was originally created in the early 1990s to help scientists find and share information by enabling the easy linking of information from one document to another. It quickly has grown into much more though. However, just because Web sites use HTTP as their communication mechanism, does not mean that HTTP is restricted to the World Wide Web. In fact, the Web is just an application that uses HTTP to carry its informational payload between servers and clients.

Initial versions of the Web services specifications only provided for HTTP as the means of transport and communications between clients and services. As a result, many services at this time use HTTP, and it is the most common of all the transport protocols. All the examples you will find in this book use the HTTP transport mechanism. Newer versions of the specifications have opened up the possibilities though, and as you'll see, those other transports have some advantages that HTTP doesn't.

NEW TERM   HTTP communications are established by a simple handshaking mechanism. Figure 8.2 illustrates this handshaking. In HTTP, communications are always initiated by the client machine. The client will make a connection to a server listening for HTTP requests. When the server receives the connection request, an acknowledgement is returned to the client, instructing the client which socket to communicate and send its request data through on. The client creates that new socket connection to the server and sends along some header information, as well as any parameters. This data is considered the *request*.

NEW TERM   The server reads in this request and processes it in some way. After processing has been completed, it sends back any resulting data as a *response*. While the server is processing the request, the connection between the client and server stays open, and the client is effectively blocked, waiting for the response. After the client receives the response, it signals back to the server that it has received the data. At this point, the server terminates its connection with the client.

Now that you know how HTTP works, you're probably wondering why it is used so much for Web services. HTTP provides Web services with some attractive features. The protocol is relatively simple to understand and code for. Web servers are built to handle large numbers of requests, and the software to write the server-side services is not very different from writing CGIs, servlets, or PHP/ASP/JSP scripts. Because HTTP traffic is considered relatively benign, most firewalls will allow HTTP traffic through without any special configuration. The protocol was designed to accept textual data in requests (or binary encoded as ASCII or as attachments), so it can easily handle XML on both the request and response side of the equation. Finally, HTTP is ubiquitous and standardized. The specification has been fairly stable for several years now, and its popularity in the WWW has forced vendors to stick with the standards or be cast out in the cold.

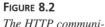

FIGURE 8.2
The HTTP communication handshake is used to establish connections and transfer data.

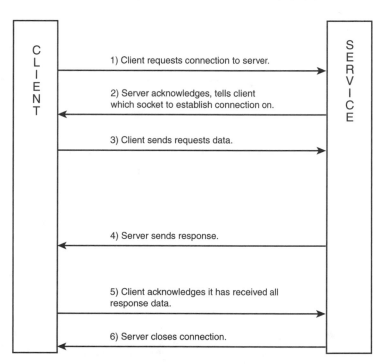

HTTP has issues though. There is no guaranteed delivery of data sent via HTTP. If you need that capability, you'll have to add it to your client and service code. As we said earlier, HTTP-based clients are forced to block until they receive a response from the service. This sort of synchronous behavior can impede scalability and is often not desirable in business systems.

Message Queues

Message queues have been a staple part of enterprise information systems for many years. They are exactly what their name implies—a queue that can contain messages. We deal with queues in computing all the time though. What makes these types of queues important is that they are used to connect systems together in a way that provides for three important facets of intersystem communications: reliable delivery, scalability, and loose coupling.

It is important to note that message queues are unidirectional. If you need communication in both directions, two separate queues are needed—one on each side of the communication process. Figure 8.3 shows how message queues fit into the Web services arena in comparison to the HTTP transport mechanism.

FIGURE 8.3

An illustration of message queue technology as opposed to HTTP for the transport of Web service communications.

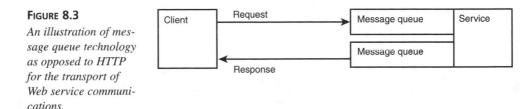

Messaging queue technology is considered reliable because the messages that enter the queue can be set to stay in the queue until they are delivered. If the intended recipient of the message happens to be disconnected or unreachable when the message enters the queue, the message will remain there until the recipient reestablishes a connection. At that time, all messages destined for that recipient will be delivered. More importantly, the messages will arrive in the order in which they entered the queue (hence the reason it's called a queue and not a pool). Unlike HTTP-based Web services, ones that use message queues as their transport protocol don't have to tack on structures to guarantee delivery or reliability; it's inherent to the transport itself.

New Term Message queues can work in one of two different modes. The first mode, called *point-to-point*, provides a communication capability from one sender to a receiver. A pair of queues are set up for that one, and only that one, pair of connections. One queue handles requests going to the server; the other handles replies coming back to the client. Only messages for that recipient are stored in the queue.

New Term The second mode is *publish-subscribe*, where multiple recipients ask (or subscribe) to listen in on the queue for messages. The producer of the messages creates (or publishes) new messages in the queue. This is analogous to subscribers of a magazine or newspaper. A single producer (the publisher of the magazine or newspaper) disseminates information to all of its subscribers.

New Term The second mode is extremely useful in Web service situations that need to operate in an event-driven mode. Clients hook into the queue and can listen for messages that are important to them. They can then trigger activities to occur on the client whenever one of those messages is encountered in the queue. In fact, once connected to the queue, the client does not have to send any other information to the service at all. It simply waits and listens. As such, the client and service are bound *asynchronously*.

NEW TERM This is very different from the HTTP approach in which all communications are performed in a strictly *request-response* mode, where a client sends a request and must sit and wait for the response from the server. Such a *synchronous* operation can impair scalability because it ties both the client and the server together for a period of time and can block access to resources from other processes.

As such, the asynchronous nature of message queues adds to their capability to scale up. Clients now can pop a request onto the service's incoming queue, and then decouple themselves and do other things. The service can process the message when it gets to it, and then respond back the same way by publishing to another queue. The client returns when the message is delivered, so no resources are tied up while waiting for processing to complete.

If message queues are so wonderful, why aren't they used by all Web services? First, setting up and managing the message queue has traditionally been much more complicated than HTTP-based packages. Second, there is an interoperability problem in that most vendor's messaging queues don't work well together. For example, a client written using Microsoft Message Queue can't communicate with a service using IBM's WebsphereMQ. As a result, this solution really only works if you control both sides of the equation: the clients and the service. However, although there is no standard wire protocol for the various message queue implementations, some abstraction API layers out there (such as Java Message service) allow the developer to write to a common API while using different underlying message queue products. Third, most message queue software requires special port numbers. One of the design goals of Web services was to enable easy communications through firewalls, and opening of ports is often not easy because of security concerns.

Even with the limitations, the use of message queues for Web services is on the rise. It is entirely reasonable to expect that the services that are the most robust (in terms of fault tolerance), most reliable, and most scalable will be written using message queues for their transport mechanism.

SMTP

Unless you've lived on another planet for the past 30 years, you've at least heard of email even if you haven't used it daily. We all know what it does, but far fewer know how it actually works. What happens after you click that Send button? How can we use email for Web services?

NEW TERM In reality, we're not using email for Web services per se. Instead, we're really using the underlying system responsible for the management and delivery of

email. That mechanism is called *Simple Mail Transport Protocol*, or *SMTP* for short.
Let's briefly look at how SMTP works.

NEW TERM   Conceptually, SMTP is the electronic equivalent to the U.S. postal system. When
you create an email message and click the Send button, several things happen.
First, the message is encoded into a special textual format. Attachments are transformed
from binary to a textual representation and labeled with an encoding type flag, referred
to as a MIME-type *(Multipurpose Internet Mail Extensions)*. All the data for the message
is then sent into a spooler on the server.

Once it's on the server, the message header is examined to see if the Send To address
corresponds to anyone on the local mail system. If so, the message is placed into a queue
for that user to read the next time he checks his email. If the intended recipient isn't
local, the server then passes the message along to some other server upstream. This passing along of the message happens over and over—with each server along the way receiving the message, storing a copy of the message, checking to see whether the message can
directly be delivered, and then forwarding it along to the next server until the message
eventually finds it's way to a server that the recipient's account is on. This type of mechanism is referred to as *store and forward*. Each server along the path of delivery stores
(either temporarily or permanently) a complete copy of the message. For this reason,
email is not considered a safe way to send unencrypted data because every machine
along the delivery path has the opportunity to intercept the message.

You'll also notice that nothing in the email designates the routing path that the message
must take to get to the recipient. When you type in a delivery address of
`johndoe@test.net`, you're not telling your server how to contact test.net, only that the
message needs to get to that server at some point. If your server has routing information
for how to directly find test.net, it will send the message directly from your server to the
destination server. In most cases, however, your mail server has no knowledge of the destination server. In these cases, your server will pass the message upstream to some other
server. In fact, it's entirely possible that two messages being sent from the same person
to the same recipient might take completely different paths, go through a different number of servers, and arrive in an order different than how they were sent. Figure 8.4 illustrates the SMTP store-and-forward and routing system.

Email (again, much like the U.S. postal system) is also considered an unreliable delivery
mechanism. There is no guarantee that your message will ever reach its destination. This
isn't as much of a problem as it used to be in the early days of the Internet when messages would sometimes be "lost in the ether." However, it does still happen on occasion.
Email has a max hop count limit embedded in its header information. If the number of
servers that the message has traveled through exceeds this limit, the server that has the

message at that time will no longer attempt to send the message on. Instead, it will attempt to send a message back to the originator of the message to indicate that the message could not be delivered. Even this message is not guaranteed to be delivered though!

FIGURE 8.4

SMTP stores the message at each server along the way. Message routing is controlled by the servers at each hop along the way, and no two messages are required to take the same path.

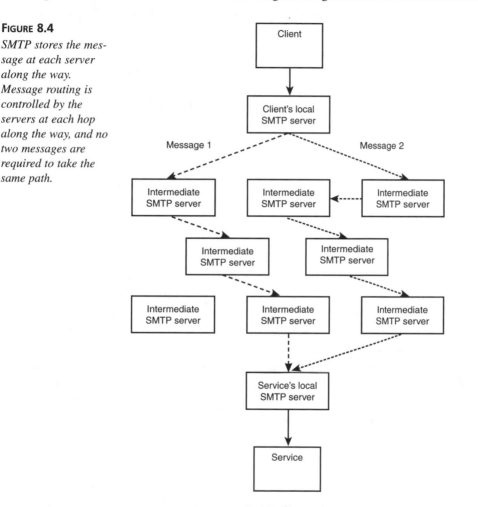

After looking at how the SMTP system works for email, you're probably wondering why you would ever want to use it for Web services. Unreliable, out of order delivery with simple eavesdropping and so on doesn't sound like a very robust system at first. However, for all its faults, SMTP has several good points in its favor.

First, similar to HTTP, SMTP traffic is usually allowed through firewalls. This means that it is often simple to get a system deployed in a corporate environment without the security folk raising a minor temper tantrum.

Second, even more so than message queues, SMTP-based systems are extremely asynchronous. It might take days before a request arrives at the destination and several more days before a response is sent back. SMTP systems also can take advantage of concepts such as mailing lists to mimic the publish-subscribe model that makes message queues so attractive.

Third, because of the nature of SMTP, with the messages being stored on server machines until they can be delivered, it is possible to send a message to a recipient that might not be available 100% of the time. With SMTP as the transport, the mail server at the service end will hold onto all the received Web service requests (spool them). Then when the service becomes active, it can process those requests and mail back out the responses. The client's mail server will then receive and likewise spool the response messages until the client checks his mail again. This is just like email. For the right system, this capability to be used for a partially connected system can be a powerful feature.

In situations in which timely, in-order response is not a necessity, you can't go wrong with SMTP. It is technology that has been around for more than 25 years and is well understood. The servers supporting SMTP are robust, scalable, and built in to or available for nearly every server operating system produced.

For Web services to work on SMTP, the payload must follow certain rules of behavior. First, the SOAP message must be processed as a MIME attachment with a content type of text/xml. The content is typically base64 encoded. Second, if the case in which a request-response type mechanism is desired, the same subject line for both the request and response should be used. The request should include a message-ID in its header information, and the response should contain the same message-ID in the In-Reply-To header field, along with a new message-ID. By using these message-IDs, a form of message ordering and pairing can be established to place some order on the apparent chaos of the SMTP delivery system for your clients and services.

FTP

NEW TERM   Another of the tried and true staple protocols of the Internet is *FTP*, which stands for File Transfer Protocol. FTP is designed to facilitate moving files from one machine to another. It can handle both text and binary data without the need for translation. One of the strengths of FTP is its capability of working with large sets of data.

FTP works slightly differently than the other protocols we've discussed here in that it makes use of two connections to transfer information. The first connection, referred to as the *command connection*, is established and remains open throughout the life of the communications. This connection is where commands associated with the sending of information and the determination of status and authentication are processed.

The second set of connections, referred to as the *data connection(s)*, are established and maintained only for the duration of a single data transfer. For instance, the command to transfer a request is sent over the command connection to inform the service that it should be waiting for data. After the server acknowledges this request, the client creates a new data connection to the service and the data is pumped through it. After the data is all received, the data connection is terminated, but the command connection remains. When the service is ready to send back the response, another data connection is established and the response message is received by the client. Figure 8.5 illustrates this sequence of events.

FIGURE 8.5

FTP maintains command connections, but only keeps data connections open for the life of a single transfer.

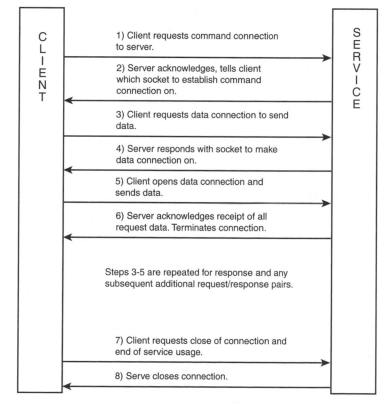

CLIENT

1) Client requests command connection to server.

2) Server acknowledges, tells client which socket to establish command connection on.

3) Client requests data connection to send data.

4) Server responds with socket to make data connection on.

5) Client opens data connection and sends data.

6) Server acknowledges receipt of all request data. Terminates connection.

Steps 3-5 are repeated for response and any subsequent additional request/response pairs.

7) Client requests close of connection and end of service usage.

8) Serve closes connection.

SERVICE

Because the data is transferred on its own connection and that connection is dedicated for that purpose, very little overhead is required. This helps FTP maintain extremely quick transfer speeds. However, it also must maintain the command connection throughout the lifecycle of the transaction. FTP usually is not fault tolerant (although some implementations do have this capability). If the connection is lost, so is the data. Connectivity must be maintained.

FTP also is considered a security risk because of its capability to drop files, as well as streaming data into another machine. As such, most network administrators restrict its use through firewalls. If you need to communicate through firewalls or be fault tolerant, usc onc of the other solutions. However, if your service and clients are all located behind the firewall, FTP is an extremely fast protocol for large-scale communications.

Jabber

One of the quickest growing applications on the Internet over the past several years has been instant messaging. A number of competing systems have evolved that provide real-time, text-based communications between users. Some of the most popular are AOL's Instant Messenger, ICQ, Yahoo! Instant Messenger, MSN Messenger, and IRC. Although all these products work in a similar manner, each has been reluctant to open its chat networks to the others. Many provide programming APIs to allow for the development of new applications, but all (except IRC) use proprietary, closed network protocols. This has been a headache for many users who end up running several clients on their machines just to chat with friends on different networks.

NEW TERM In an attempt to fix this, the Jabber project was started. Jabber's goals were not only to provide a way to communicate with users of all chat engines, but also to provide an open communication architecture upon which other software could piggy-back. Jabber refers to this as *Extensible Instant Messaging*.

The results of this effort are the Jabber system we have today. Jabber communicates using XML, provides peer-to-peer communications, and provides both API- and communication-level interfaces for developers to work with. Jabber also is capable of operating through firewalls, which gives it an advantage over transport solutions such as FTP and message queues.

Communications in Jabber typically initiate with a client making a request to send data to a recipient (in this case, the service). The request is sent to the Jabber server, where the client's account is authenticated. The server then attempts to contact the destination service node. If the connection can be made, it relays the payload message to the service. The service can reply in a similar manner. If the Jabber server can't find the recipient locally, it can automatically contact other Jabber servers to ask them to attempt to deliver the content. Once the communications are established, the Jabber server acts simply as a relay mechanism, and the client and service are linked logically as though they were communicating in a peer-to-peer fashion. Figure 8.6 shows this communication configuration.

FIGURE 8.6
The Jabber server acts as a relay between clients and services.

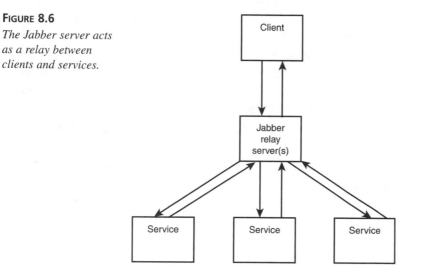

When using Jabber for Web services, communication scalability, fail-over, and load balancing are easily established through the addition of more Jabber relay servers. Jabber is the newest of the protocols we've looked at though, and as such, fewer toolsets support it for communications. Its acceptance is growing rapidly, however, and this limitation should diminish over time.

Summary

In this hour, we've looked at some of the transports available for use by Web services. We discussed how TCP/IP forms the underlying foundation of all communications on the Internet. We then saw how HTTP communicates and why it has been the predominant protocol for Web services.

Next, we examined the features and capabilities of transports such as message queues, SMTP, and FTP. We also saw how Jabber can be used to facilitate Web services.

Along the way, we examined the strengths and weaknesses of each of these protocols. With this knowledge, you should be able to choose the right protocol for your needs when building Web service solutions.

Q&A

Q Why are different transports available for doing Web services?

A Much like everything else on the Internet, there is more than one way to solve the communication problem. Each of the protocols that we have discussed has certain capabilities and limitations that should be examined to determine the correct one for your needs. In some cases, security and reliable delivery will be more important than speed or scalability. In other cases, the mixture of needs might be different. Having different protocols to call on increases the likelihood of finding one that will match the needs of your solution.

Q Is there anything that I have to do differently to use these other protocols in my Web services?

A In theory, no. The only difference would be the different transport protocol specified in your service's WSDL document. In reality though, you'll also need to make sure that any supporting infrastructure (such as message queue software, SMTP or Jabber servers, firewall ports, and so on) are configured before using these other protocols.

Q Will HTTP remain the dominant protocol for Web services?

A Only time will tell on this issue. The market will dictate which solution will prevail. Although HTTP has the biggest following now, mainly because of its two-year head start in the standards, it is very possible that message queues and technologies such as Jabber will overtake it in the next couple of years. Those two protocols in particular solve several of the problems that currently plague HTTP-based Web services.

Workshop

This section is designed to help you anticipate possible questions, review what you've learned, and begin learning how to put your knowledge into practice.

Quiz

1. What are the two transport layer protocols in the OSI model?
2. Why is asynchronous communications important?
3. What paradigm does the SMTP transport follow?
4. What are the two connections used by FTP, and what do they do?

Quiz Answers

1. TCP and UDP.

2. With asynchronous communications, the client can drop off a request, and then continue with its own operation without having to wait for the service to provide a response. This allows for greater scalability because the client is not left tying up resources while waiting for the service to process the client's request.

3. Store and forward.

4. Command connections are used for controlling the communications and remain connected throughout the life of the communications. Data connections are created for each communication and are terminated immediately following the completion of message transmission.

Activity

1. Just to prove to yourself that SMTP actually goes through multiple hops, let's examine the mail header information. Assuming that you use Microsoft Outlook Express to read your mail, open a received mail message by double-clicking the message. Next, select the File menu and choose Properties. A dialog box will appear. Select the Details tab. You will see a series of Received: from... lines. Each line indicates a server along the way that the message was sent through and stored on.

HOUR 9

Exchanging Messages with SOAP

There are times when less is really more. When asking about SOAP, programmers and programming managers often say things like, "Isn't SOAP just an alternative to DCOM or CORBA?" The correct answer to that question is, "No, it is much less than that."

Different application development platforms have various distributed computing mechanisms. Some of these mechanisms are very efficient, but limited in what operating systems and languages they support. In addition to those efficient technologies, all operating systems have a less-efficient way of exchanging data via files full of characters. At the most basic level, SOAP messages are just streams of characters. They are not just randomly created characters, though; they are carefully crafted so that programs on both sides of the transmission can understand exactly what the other side is saying.

SOAP messages are XML documents that are embedded in the transport's request and response. In this hour, you will learn how SOAP works. You will first learn what SOAP is and where it came from. Next, you will learn the anatomy of SOAP documents so that you will be able to understand them (at least in rough outline form) when you look at them.

In this hour, you will learn

- About the SOAP language
- The rules for creating a SOAP document
- What the SOAP envelope is for
- The purpose of the SOAP header
- How SOAP handles errors

What SOAP Is

Many of the standard definitions of SOAP sound like buzzwords strung together. One particularly good one is that SOAP is a specification for a ubiquitous XML-based distributed computing infrastructure. If we translate these words, we can get a better feel for what SOAP really is:

- **Specification**—SOAP is not a product that was created and sold by a vendor. Rather, it is a document that describes the characteristics of a piece of software. The basic idea is that if two parties create programs to the same specifications, these programs will be able to interoperate seamlessly.
- **Ubiquitous**—SOAP is defined at a high enough level of abstractions that any operating system and programming language combination could be used to create SOAP-compliant programs.
- **XML-based**—SOAP is built on top of XML, which means that SOAP documents are XML documents constructed to a tighter set of specifications.
- **Infrastructure**—SOAP does not specify what data can be moved or what function calls can take place over it. An analogy could be made to a railroad car. The car is capable of moving any item that will fit in it from point A to point B. In the same way, software products that are constructed to the SOAP specification can move data from computer A to computer B and hand it to another program written to the same specification. The actual real-world meaning of the data is outside the scope of the SOAP specification.

So, a SOAP message is an XML document. Using SOAP can be thought of as a set of layers, as shown in Figure 9.1.

FIGURE 9.1

Looking at the layers makes it easier to understand SOAP's multiple personalities.

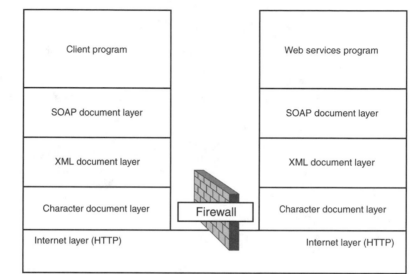

From the viewpoint of the Internet layer, computer A is sending an XML document to computer B via HTTP. Computer B's firewall policy states that XML documents are allowed to pass through via HTTP. The Web server on computer B receives the file and hands it to the SOAP processor, which uses an XML parser to read the document.

From the XML parser's point of view, the document is simply a well-formed and valid XML document. The SOAP processing engine evaluates the file against the rules of the SOAP grammar and an XML schema. It examines the SOAP vocabulary to determine if it is valid. If it is valid, the SOAP processor makes a call to the Web service described in the SOAP document and passes it any parameters that the document might contain.

When the Web service finishes its processing, it creates a response that is formatted in an application-specific way. It wraps this response in a SOAP message format, which is a valid XML document also. It stores this document in a file and hands it to the Web server for delivery back to the client computer, computer A.

On computer A, the HTTP client program receives the response file. It calls the SOAP processor to parse and to validate it. If it is a valid document, the SOAP processor passes the response back to the Web services client program that sent the original request.

A couple of details can change in the preceding scenario, but the basic thrust remains the same. Other transport protocols, such as JMS or SMTP, can be used to actually move the message from computer A to computer B. In addition, the SOAP message might not be a method call and response; it could simply be a single call or even just a document being moved.

The Origins of SOAP

SOAP has evolved from an early attempt to define a way to send method calls and parameters from one computer to another called XML-RPC, which stands for Remote Procedure Call. This early specification was defined by Dave Winer of a company called UserLand. IONA, Microsoft, and IBM became interested in improving the XML-RPC approach. This new approach became the SOAP 1.1 specification. It was submitted to the World Wide Web Consortium (W3C) in 2000. A new specification, SOAP 1.2, is moving toward recommendation status at W3C. In W3C terminology, a recommendation is the highest status for a specification. They dislike using the word "standard" because they are a consortium and not a standards body. Commercial Web services platforms and tools are incorporating parts of the SOAP 1.2 specification as of this writing.

Why SOAP Is Different

You might be wondering how this specification differs from a traditional DCOM or CORBA application. Like a CORBA application, a call is made and a response is returned. At that point, the similarity mostly ends. As we discussed in Hour 4, "Comparing Web Services to Other Technologies," a CORBA client actually makes calls to the object on the server in a tightly coupled way. The SOAP client just formats a text file and transfers it to the other machine.

Another difference is the nonchalance of the client program. After the client sends the file, he can either wait for a response or continue with other work until a response arrives. If it never arrives, the client program is responsible for deciding what to do next. It might retry the call, throw an error message, or just log the problem and go on.

Perhaps the biggest difference between the SOAP and CORBA or DCOM approach comes from the casual nature of the relationship between the two computers. You set up CORBA programs by generating special files and placing some of them on each computer. SOAP, in theory, doesn't need the name of anything. A client could use UDDI to find a service, upload the WSDL, generate the client, and make the call without knowing anything in advance.

This casual relationship between client and server mimics the relationship between a Web surfer and a Web site. Sometimes when we are surfing the Web, we visit sites that we didn't even know existed five minutes before. In theory, a Web service could publish its existence on a special type of directory called a repository. Clients could then discover it and connect to it with no human intervention. If this kind of casual relationship becomes popular, it could usher in a whole new wave of applications that are based on just-in-time peer-to-peer discovery.

The SOAP Grammar

The SOAP grammar is fairly simple to understand. Object access means calling methods. A protocol, generically speaking, is a treaty. The computer science meaning of the word "protocol" is a treaty between parties that want to exchange data between their respective computers. We can describe SOAP as a treaty that describes how to call methods on a different computer than the one that we are running on.

SOAP doesn't involve any new inventions or clever algorithms. In fact, the two strongest features of SOAP are its simplicity and the fact that everyone has agreed to use it. A SOAP message is composed of two mandatory parts—the SOAP envelope and the SOAP body—and one optional part—the SOAP header. In addition, all the XML tags associated with SOAP have the prefix SOAP-ENV. The envelope is SOAP-ENV:Envelope; the header is SOAP-ENV:Header; and the body is SOAP-ENV:Body. Figure 9.2 shows the relationship between the parts of a SOAP message.

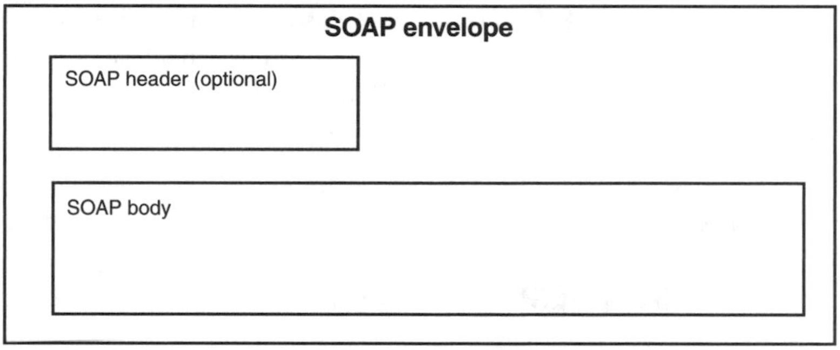

FIGURE 9.2

The SOAP envelope contains both the SOAP header and the SOAP body.

The SOAP envelope is similar to a physical envelope; we can fill it full of data and send it to someone else. The SOAP body is like the contents of the envelope. We can put any information that we want inside the envelope. The SOAP header is like a sticky note that we place inside an envelope when we are sending things to someone else. It contains data that provides special instructions such as "Send your response directly to Bill," or "My password is 12345."

The `SOAP-ENV:Envelope` Tag

A SOAP message is defined as beginning with the tag

```
<SOAP-ENV:Envelope>
```

and ending with the tag

```
</SOAP-ENV:Envelope>
```

Whenever you see the string <SOAP-ENV:Envelope>, say in your mind "beginning of the SOAP message;" and when you see </SOAP-ENV:Envelope>, you can say "end of the SOAP message." SOAP messages cannot be sent in batches, so you know that you are looking at only one message inside the envelope. There might also be a header section that can contain *n* header elements.

In SOAP 1.1, the SOAP_ENV:Envelope tag is normally constructed using the following syntax:

```
<SOAP-ENV:Envelope xmlns:SOAP-ENV="http://schemas.xmlsoap.org/soap/envelope/" >
```

The string xmlns is a keyword in XML that stands for XML namespace. The namespace is used to uniquely identify all tags in order to avoid tag name conflicts. The SOAP-ENV part is the name that SOAP requires to be used as the prefix for all the tag names that SOAP defines. The string "http://schemas.xmlsoap.org/soap/envelope/" looks like the address of an ordinary Web site. In reality, it is a unique string that serves the same purpose as a version number would. A client places a string that indicates indirectly which version of SOAP it is using. The Web service that receives the request can look at this string to determine whether it is capable of communicating using that version of SOAP. Namespaces are covered in detail in Hour 7, "Understanding XML."

Two other namespaces that are heavily used in SOAP are xsd and xsi. The xsd namespace specifies that these tags come from the XML schema definition. The xsi namespace indicates that these tags come from the XML schema–instance definition.

The SOAP-ENV:Body Tag

The body of the SOAP message begins with the tag

```
<SOAP-ENV:Body>
```

and ends with the tag

```
</SOAP-ENV:Body>
```

Whenever you see the string <SOAP-ENV:Body>, say in your mind "beginning of the SOAP body;" and when you see the string </SOAP-ENV:body>, you can say "end of the SOAP body." This is where the payload of the SOAP message is placed. Normally, that payload is a method call to a remote computer, complete with parameter values. Sometimes, however, it is simply an XML document that is being transferred.

At other times, it might be a response message containing a bank balance or a picture of the first moonwalk. The format of the body is under the control of whoever is creating a new Web service. A special XML document, called the Web services Description

Language (WSDL) document, is created to describe what a legal method call to that service would look like and what form a valid response can take. The following snippet shows a body that makes a Remote Procedure Call (RPC) to a method called `checkAccountBalance()`:

```
<SOAP-ENV:Body>
        <checkAccountBalance>
         <accountNumber xsi:type="xsd:int">123456780</accountNumber>
      </checkAccountBalance>
</SOAP-ENV:Body>
```

The first line indicates that this is the start of the body and the last line shows the end of the body. The second line,

```
<checkAccountBalance>
```

provides the name of the method to call, `checkAccountBalance`. The first element is called `accountNumber`, and it is a parameter that is being passed in with the `checkAccountBalance` method:

```
<accountNumber xsi:type="xsd:int">123456780</accountNumber>
```

The `xsi:type` is an attribute, and the `xsd:int` means that this value is an integer. `123456780` is the value of the parameter being passed. The net effect of all these characters is a method call that would look something like this in Java:

```
int balance = checkAccountBalance(123456780);
```

The `SOAP-ENV:Header` Tag

The `SOAP-ENV:Header` element is optional in a SOAP message. If a header is present, however, it must be the first child element that appears in the SOAP envelope. The format of the `SOAP-ENV:Header` element is not defined in the specification; therefore, it is available to the clients and services for their own use. Typical use would be to communicate credentials such as username and password.

Two attributes associated with the `SOAP-ENV:Header` element can be used. The first is the `SOAP-ENV:mustUnderstand` attribute. If it is set to `"1"`, an error message will be generated if the Web service is not programmed to handle the fields in this header. The client programmer has to decide whether the processing can take place on a site that can't read the header.

The second attribute is called `SOAP-ENV:actor`. This attribute is used to chain together Web services that this document must visit to be completely processed. Think about how a purchase order could be viewed by the payroll department to calculate commissions, by accounts receivable to create a bill, and by the shipping department to send the physical

9

merchandise. The chain can be created by adding `SOAP-ENV:actor` tags along with their URIs to the header.

The following snippet shows a simple `SOAP-ENV:Header`:

```
<SOAP-ENV:Header>
   <myNS:authentication xmlns:myNS="http://www.stevepotts.com/auth"
                                     SOAP-ENV:mustUnderstand="1">
      <loginID>
         admin
      </loginID>
      <password>
         rover
      </password>
   </myNS:authentication>
<SOAP-ENV:Header>
```

The header contains a made-up element called `<myNS:authentication>`. That element contains the loginID and password elements. These elements have no standard meaning in SOAP at this time. One criticism of SOAP is that it doesn't support some very needful topics such as sessions, transactions, and the authentication of users. These shortcomings don't keep us from using our own approaches to these problems; it just means that we have to communicate our approaches to our potential clients. Eventually, when these areas are added to the SOAP specification, we will have to replace our proprietary approaches with the approved ones.

Most of the growth in the SOAP standard is expected to take place in the area of headers. Expect to see many more predefined elements and attributes such as `SOAP-ENV:actor` and `SOAP-ENV:mustUnderstand` added over time to address the perceived weaknesses in the current SOAP specification.

Reporting Errors to the Client

No technology can be considered production ready until it supports error handling well. Toy systems running in a lab can defer these considerations, but production systems can't afford to be fragile. They must recover from as many errors as possible. In cases in which they can't recover, they must provide the support staff with plenty of information about what went wrong.

The SOAP approach to error handling is based on the proper use of the `SOAP-ENV:fault` tag.

The `SOAP-ENV:Body` has one child that is defined by the SOAP specification—the `SOAP-ENV:fault` tag. This tag is used to communicate that a problem has occurred in the attempted fulfillment of the request sent to the Web service.

This optional element must appear only in response messages, and it can appear only once in that message. The SOAP-ENV:fault tag has four optional tags:

- **SOAP-ENV:faultcode**—This element is required by the specification. It should contain some code indicating what the problem is.

- **SOAP-ENV:faultstring**—This required element is a human-readable version of the faultcode. It should provide details beyond the "error some place" type of message.

- **SOAP-ENV:faultactor**—This optional element tells which service generated the fault. This is important when a chain of services was used to process the request.

- **SOAP-ENV:detail**—This element should contain as much information as possible about the state of the server at the time of the crash. It often contains the values of variables at the time of the failure.

Error codes in SOAP are defined in the specification in a way that you might not have predicted. In other languages, integers are used to represent faults. In SOAP, error codes are represented as two-part strings with major and minor error codes separated by a . like this:

```
<SOAP-ENV:faultcode>
    Server.customerCreateFailed
<SOAP-ENV:faultcode>
```

Four types of generic faultcode are defined by the specification:

- **server**—An error occurred on the server, but not with the message itself. You should write your client to retry messages that fail with these codes. If the error is with the availability of the service, a subsequent retry would work. Limit the number of retries, however, because the error might be coming from the service itself and would therefore not go away with the passage of time.

- **client**—These errors indicate that something is wrong with the message itself, such as a bad message format, incomplete message, and so on.

- **versionMismatch**—This error occurs when the versions of the SOAP processors are different between the client and the server. The version is determined by the namespace URI used in the SOAP-ENV:Envelope tag.

- **mustUnderstand**—This error is generated when an element in the header cannot be processed and that element is marked as required. If an element contains a mustUnderstand attribute, it requires that the Web service be able to understand all the contents of the element. If not, you want to receive this error message.

An example of a full-blown fault tag is shown here:

```
<SOAP-ENV:Fault>
   <SOAP-ENV:faultcode>
      Client.Authentication
   </SOAP-ENV:faultcode>
   <SOAP-ENV:faultstring>
       This customer is unknown to our system.
   </SOAP-ENV:faultstring>
   <SOAP-ENV:faultactor>
      http://www.samspublishing.com/authors
   </SOAP-ENV:faultactor>
   <SOAP-ENV:detail>
       <customer custID="12345">
          <name>
             Yogi Bear
          </name>
   </SOAP-ENV:detail>
</SOAP-ENV:Fault>
```

Notice that the faultcode has a specific format and that the faultactor must contain the URI of a Web service. The other two elements accept any information that you want to provide to your user.

SOAP Data Types

One of the most difficult problems for intercomputer communication concerns the representation of data types. Declaring data to be of a certain type is fundamental to getting a computer program to work correctly.

Data typing provides three primary advantages:

- Strongly typed data is more efficient to store and process than untyped data. Untyped data processing requires additional processing to determine whether a requested action is allowed on this type of data. For typed data, this is a simple task, but for untyped data, many cycles must be consumed to make this determination.

- Typed data can be combined with other data with a higher degree of confidence than nontyped data. There is also less potential for confusion when doing conversions. The processor decides whether an operation can be performed on a piece of data. Because it is inferring the true type of the data, it sometimes behaves differently than the programmer thought it would.

- Typed data makes it easier for the language compiler to recognize and reject nonsensical operations such as multiplying your social security number, which is stored in a string variable number, by the number 3.

SOAP does allow us to pass data without data type information. If we specify no type, the default type of string is used. This default can be overridden by the inclusion of a string that indicates the type of the data along with the string version of the data itself, as shown here:

```
<accountNumber xsi:type="xsd:int">123456780</accountNumber>
```

The simplicity of this scheme is impressive. For example, different computers store integer data in different ways. Some machines store them in 16 bits, others in 32 bits, whereas still others consume 64 bits for each integer. To make matters worse, some computers store numeric data with the higher numbers in the left bytes, whereas others store them in the right bytes. But the last straw is that not all computers use the same bit patterns to represent characters; some use ASCII characters, and some use other types of encoding.

SOAP takes advantage of the one format that all computer brands and models can easily share with each other: text. All software products that can be used as transports for SOAP messages—such as HTTP, JMS, and SMTP—can take a text file that resides on one computer and transfer it to another computer without the loss of data.

SOAP delegates the data type conversion work to the programmers who create the Web service and the client software that accesses it. All Web services must have software (written in a programming language) that implements the business functionality that the service offers. All these programming languages can convert string representations of data into typed variables with accuracy if they know what data type to store it in. By requiring the inclusion of the data type information in the message, SOAP ensures that the conversion from strings to numeric and numeric to strings will be correct. Figure 9.3 graphically shows this process.

FIGURE 9.3

Data type conversion is the responsibility of the SOAP message creators and consumers.

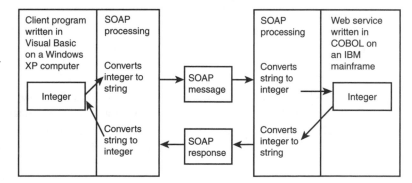

Another way to communicate the type of an element is to use an XML schema. The following is a XML schema example that contains data type declarations for the elements:

```
<xsd:schema xmlns:xsd="http://www.w3.org/2001/XMLschema"
        xmlns:xsi="http://www.w3.org/2001/XMLSchema-instance">

    <xsd:complexType name=customer content="mixed">
        <xsd:element type="custID"></element>
        <xsd:element type="lastName"></element>
        <xsd:element type="firstName"></element>
    </xsd:complexType>
    <xsd:simpleType name="custID"
        xsi:type=" xsd:integer">
    </xsd:simpleType>
    <xsd:simpleType name="lastName"
        xsi:type="xsd:string">
    </xsd:simpleType>
    <xsd:simpleType name="firstName"
        xsi:type="xsd:string">
    </xsd:simpleType>
</xsd:schema>
```

Two different categories of data types are present in this example. One category is the complexType. This type is made up of multiple simpleTypes. Each simpleType has a specific datatype, such as xsd:integer or xsd:string. The xsd: prefix indicates that this tag is a well-known member of the XML schema namespace. If you stick to the data types in this namespace, you can be certain that the Web service on the other end will be able to handle the data that you send. The data types defined by this namespace are string, normalizedString, token, byte, unsignedByte, integer, positiveInteger, negativeInteger, short, decimal, float, double, boolean, time, datetime, anyURI, language, and a number of other esoteric types.

> You can obtain a full list of the valid XML data types at http://www.w3.org/ TR/xmlschema-0/#SimpleTypeFacets.

If you include a schema definition in your SOAP document, you can skip the explicit declaration of the data types inside the document. The WSDL document normally includes this type of schema data. You will learn about the WSDL document in Hour 10, "Describing a Web Service with the Web Services Description Language (WSDL)."

Summary

This hour has introduced you to the basic concepts behind SOAP. Early in the hour, we defined what SOAP is and why it is needed. Following that, we covered how SOAP messages are used to exchange messages between Web services and their clients.

Next, we covered the SOAP grammar. You learned different parts of the SOAP document and why they exist. We also discussed how SOAP reports errors back to the client.

Finally, you saw how to specify the types of data that is being transferred between computers.

Q&A

Q What is the purpose of SOAP?

A SOAP is a specification that describes how to move data from one computer to another. Originally, SOAP was specified to make it easy to make method calls on another computer and return the result. Now, however, whole documents are commonly sent using SOAP.

Q What role does XML play in SOAP?

A SOAP is written using XML-style tags. A SOAP document is an XML document that follows a more stringent set of rules.

Workshop

The Workshop is designed to help you review what you've learned and begin learning how to put your knowledge into practice.

Quiz

1. What role does SOAP play in the creation of a Web service transaction?

2. What types of problems are well suited to this technology?

3. Why is it important to be able to specify data types in a SOAP document?

Quiz Answers

1. SOAP format is for the actual message that gets sent from the client to the service and from the service back to the client. The syntax of the SOAP grammar allows for instructions to be added to the header with the actual method call or XML document to be added to the body.

2. SOAP excels at allowing a client to make a method call on a Web service. It also does a good job of supporting the transfer of XML files from clients to servers and vice versa.

3. Values are sent in SOAP documents as strings. At times, it can be difficult for programs to determine the type of the data that is being sent unless it is provided with a hint.

Activities

1. Go to the SOAP tutorial's appendix on data types and see how many different types are supported.

2. Use a SOAP monitor to examine the messages that one of your Web services is exchanging with clients. Use one of the SOAP monitors that are provided in the commercial products that we cover in Hours 13–19 of this book.

HOUR 10

Describing a Web Service with the Web Services Description Language (WSDL)

NEW TERM One of the big advantages that Web services have over the more traditional approaches is that they can be described formally in a document called a *Web Service Description Language (WSDL) document* or just WSDL. A WSDL document is an XML document that provides all the information that you need to connect to the Web service. In addition, it contains some of the data that you need to evaluate whether this Web service can fulfill your requirements. The Universal Description, Discovery, and Integration (UDDI) document provides the rest of this information. We will cover the UDDI in Hour 11, "Advertising a Web Service."

In this hour, you will learn how to create the WSDL for a Web service. You will learn how to format it so that a client program can use it to generate the code that it needs to connect to this service.

In this hour, you will learn

- What WSDL is
- Why WSDL is needed
- What information is stored in the WSDL document
- How WSDL is used in a Web service transaction

The WSDL Document

The WSDL document is formatted to the XML specification. In addition, it is authored with a specific XML grammar that was devised to communicate metadata about a Web service in a uniform manner to all potential clients. In other words, a WSDL document is an XML document that conforms to a specification. All the metadata about the Web service is contained somewhere in this file. The structure is there to make it easy to figure out what the data means.

XML is a good choice for this type of application because it is human readable, but it is also precise enough to be machine readable. All a human has to do is learn the meaning of the WSDL element tags, and she can read the document just as you are reading this paragraph. All a programmer has to do is to use an XML parser to extract the data into local variables. The program will have all the details it needs to generate the code necessary to connect to the Web service.

We mentioned earlier that the WSDL contains some of the information needed to select a Web service that fits your requirements. It follows, then, that it also contains some of the information needed to publish your Web service's capabilities to a registry. Figure 10.1 shows how a WSDL is used to find, bind, and publish the Web service.

Any program that wants to use a Web service uses the WSDL to figure out how to bind to it. The Web service author creates the WSDL—either by hand or using a tool that generates it. He publishes it by sending it (or its URL) to a directory service, which can also be called a registry. Web service shoppers use the registry to identify a Web service that meets their needs.

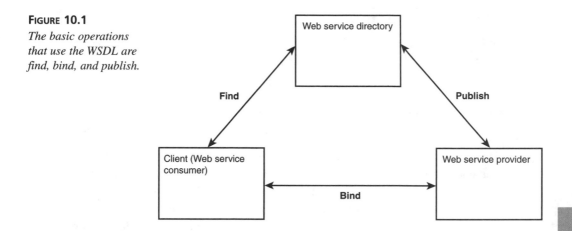

Find

Publish

Web service directory

Client (Web service consumer)

Web service provider

Bind

10

The Concrete and Abstract Description

The WSDL document is subdivided logically into two different groupings—the concrete and the abstract descriptions. These can also be called the functional and the nonfunctional descriptions. The concrete description is composed of those elements that are oriented toward binding the client to the service physically. The concrete description performs the same tasks as the Interface Definition Language (IDL) in CORBA. The abstract description is composed of those elements that are oriented toward describing the capabilities of the Web service.

The four abstract XML elements that can be defined in a WSDL are as follows:

- `<wsdl:types>`
- `<wsdl:message>`
- `<wsdl:operation>`
- `<wsdl:portType>`

In addition, there are three concrete XML elements in a WSDL:

- `<wsdl:service>`
- `<wsdl:port>`
- `<wsdl:binding>`

In addition to these, you will also see SOAP messages and XML schema definitions in the WSDL. Hour 7, "Understanding XML," discusses the special elements used for describing XML schemas. The SOAP-specific elements are covered in Hour 9, "Exchanging Messages with SOAP."

The types Element

NEW TERM The `<wsdl:types>` element is used to indicate that a WSDL type is being
declared. One of the rules of the SOAP specification is that only one input and
one output is allowed in the messages that are sent across the Internet from one computer
to another. (This one value can be a complex type such as an array, however.) The reason
for this is to maintain the simplicity of the communications by making the two computers that are communicating (the endpoints) do the work of parsing the parameters.

You can overcome this limitation by designing the messages that you send to always
send one primitive value (that is, `string` or `int`) period, which is a very limiting solution.
The best way to overcome this limitation is to create a user-defined data type by using
the `<wsdl:types>` element. A user-defined data type is a variable that is composed of
primitive data types. These types are the equivalent of C++ structs or Java classes that
contain only data and no methods.

The following snippet shows us a customer definition that we can use to illustrate how
this works:

```
<customer>
    <customerID>1001</customerID>
    <lastName>Maddox</lastName>
    <firstName>Greg</firstName>
    <address> 123 First Street</address>
    <city>Atlanta</city>
    <state>GA</state>
    <zip>30003</zip>
</customer>
```

This data is kept very simple in order to keep our focus on the process of creating the
WSDL, not on data-modeling issues. We can create an XML schema definition of this
data, which we will use later when creating the WSDL. Listing 10.1 shows this schema.

LISTING 10.1   The Customer Schema

```
<xsd:schema targetNamespace="http://www.stevepotts.com/customer.xsd"
   xmlns:xsd="http://www.w3.org/2001/XMLSchema"
   xmlns="http://www.stevepotts.com/customer.xsd">
  <xsd:element name="customer">
    <xsd:complexType >
      <xsd:sequence>
        <xsd:element name="customerID" type="xsd:string"/>
        <xsd:element name="lastName" type="xsd:string"/>
        <xsd:element name="firstName" type="xsd:string"/>
        <xsd:element name="address" type="xsd:string"/>
        <xsd:element name="city" type="xsd:string"/>
```

LISTING 10.1   continued

```
            <xsd:element name="state" type="xsd:string"/>
            <xsd:element name="zip" type="xsd:string"/>
        </xsd:sequence>
      </xsd:complexType>
    </xsd:element>
</xsd:schema>
```

The first line specifies the string that an XML document must use to specify that it must conform to this schema:

```
<xsd:schema targetNamespace="http://www.stevepotts.com/customer.xsd"
```

The namespace for the schema, xsd, is declared next:

```
xmlns:xsd="http://www.w3.org/2001/XMLSchema"
```

The root element is called "customer":

```
<xsd:element name="customer">
```

A complexType is a user-defined type. It is similar to a C++ struct.

```
<xsd:complexType name="customerType">
```

The element sequence indicates that all the elements defined next are required to be provided in exactly this sequence. Alternatively, we could have used the <xsd:all> tag if order were not important:

```
<xsd:sequence>
```

Each one of the fields that we want to include gets its own element definition. The name will be the name of the data field, and the type will be the simple data type of that field. All of these are of type xsd:string:

```
<xsd:element name="customerID" type="xsd:string"/>
<xsd:element name="lastName" type="xsd:string"/>
<xsd:element name="firstName" type="xsd:string"/>
<xsd:element name="address" type="xsd:string"/>
<xsd:element name="city" type="xsd:string"/>
<xsd:element name="state" type="xsd:string"/>
<xsd:element name="zip" type="xsd:string"/>
```

Now that we have a schema, we can create the <wsdl:types> section of the WSDL document that we are building. Listing 10.2 shows this section.

LISTING 10.2   The wsdl:types Section

```
<wsdl:types>
   <xsd:schema targetNamespace="http://www.stevepotts.com/customerType.xsd"
      xmlns:xsd="http://www.w3.org/2001/XMLSchema">
    <xsd:element name="customer">
       <xsd:complexType>
          <xsd:sequence>
             <xsd:element name="customerID" type="xsd:string"/>
             <xsd:element name="lastName" type="xsd:string"/>
             <xsd:element name="firstName" type="xsd:string"/>
             <xsd:element name="address" type="xsd:string"/>
             <xsd:element name="city" type="xsd:string"/>
             <xsd:element name="state" type="xsd:string"/>
             <xsd:element name="zip" type="xsd:string"/>
          </xsd:sequence>
       </xsd:complexType>
    </xsd:element>
   </xsd:schema>
</wsdl:types>
```

If you want to include tags from multiple schemas, you can refer to those tags by adding additional namespaces to the `<xsd:schema>` element. Hour 7 provides a detailed discussion of namespaces.

As you can see, the `wsdl:types` element is created directly by adding the `<wsdl:types>` and `</wsdl:types>` tags to the schema definition for this user-defined data type.

The reason for doing this is simple. The XML schema provides exactly the data needed to communicate the format of a data type.

The `message` Element

NEW TERM   The next important element in the WSDL is the *message*. Messages are one-way communications from one computer to another. For example, in the typical request/response scenario, one message is sent and a second message is received.

The `message` element is considered an abstract element because it describes the message logically instead of physically. By reading the message, a client or potential client can get a thumbnail sketch of what this Web service can provide in the way of processing.

If we decided to create a message called `addCustomer`, we would add a `message` element to the WSDL called `addCustomer`, as shown here:

```
<wsdl:message name="addCustomer">
   <wsdl:part name="customerInfo" element="tns:customer"/>
<wsdl:/message>
```

This message is going to add a customer to the Web service by sending it an instance of the customer element that we defined in the types element. At the detail level, the message is really going to send customer information to the Web service, and the Web service will perform the calls to the back-end system. The Web service is just an interface to the back-end system.

```
<wsdl:message name="confirmation">
  <wsdl:part name="response" element="xsd:integer"/>
<wsdl:/message>
```

This message will send an integer back that confirms that the addCustomer message successfully completed.

```
<wsdl:message name="exceptionMessage">
  <wsdl:part name="badResult" element="xsd:integer"/>
<wsdl:/message>
```

This message will send an integer back that tells the client that the addCustomer message did not successfully complete.

The operation Element

NEW TERM The operation element is analogous to a method call in Java or a subroutine call in Visual Basic. One difference is that only three messages are allowed in an operation:

- **The Input Message**—Defines the data that the Web service expects to receive.
- **The Output Message**—Defines the data that the Web service expects to send in response.
- **The Fault Message**—Defines the error messages that can be returned by the Web service.

Several types of operations can be declared in a WSDL document. They are

- **Request/Response**—A client makes a request, and the Web service responds to it.
- **Solicit/Response**—A Web service sends a message to the client, and the client responds.
- **One-way**—A client sends a message to the Web service but expects no response.
- **Notification**—A Web service sends a message to the client but expects no response.

Figure 10.2 shows these four operation types graphically.

10

FIGURE 10.2
The basic operations are request/response, solicit/response, one-way, and notification.

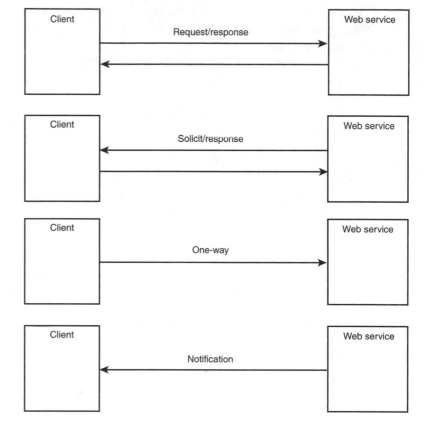

The syntax of an operation is simple. If the operation is a request/response type, the format will be as shown here:

```
<wsdl:operation name="createNewCustomer">
   <wsdl:input message="addCustomer">
   <wsdl:output message="confirmation">
   <wsdl:fault message="exceptionMessage">
<wsdl:/operation>
```

If the message is of the solicit/response type, the output element will appear before the input element. If it is a one-way message, there is no output. If it is of the notification type, there will be no input.

The portType Element

NEW TERM   The *portType* is one of the oddly named elements in the WSDL. A port, in Web services jargon, is a single Web service. The portType, then, is the set of all operations that one Web service can accept. The portType is an abstract element that doesn't provide information on how to connect directly to a Web service. It does provide a one-stop point where a client can obtain information on all the operations that a Web service provides.

The syntax for a `portType` is very simple:

```
<wsdl:portType name="newCustomerPortType">
   <wsdl:operation name="createNewCustomer">
      <wsdl:input message="addCustomer"/>
      <wsdl:output message="confirmation"/>
      <wsdl:fault message="exceptionMessage"/>
   </wsdl:operation>
</wsdl:portType>
```

As you can see, it is simply a container element for operation elements.

The `binding` Element

The elements that we have covered thus far have all been involved with specifying what a Web service is capable of providing in the way of functionality. From this point on, we will be focusing on how to obtain the information needed to physically connect to the Web service.

The *binding* element serves two purposes. First, it serves as the link between the abstract

NEW TERM elements and the concrete elements in the WSDL. One of the attributes of the `binding` tag is the name of the `portType`. The second purpose that the `binding` element serves is to provide a container for information such as the protocol and the address of the Web service. The syntax for a `binding` element is shown in Listing 10.3.

LISTING 10.3   The `newCustomerBinding` Section

```
<wsdl:binding name="newCustomerBinding" type="newCustomerPortType">
   <soap:binding style="rpc"
            transport="http://schemas.xmlsoap.org/soap/http" />
   <wsdl:operation name="createNewCustomer">
      <soap:operation
          soapAction="http://www.stevepotts.com/createNewCustomer"/>
        <wsdl:input>
          <soap:body use="encoded"
             namespace="http://www.stevepotts.com/customer"
             encodingStyle=
                  "http://schemas.xmlsoap.org/soap/encoding/"/>
        <wsdl:input>
        <wsdl:output>
          <soap:body use="encoded"
             namespace="http://www.stevepotts.com/customer"
             encodingStyle=
```

10

LISTING **10.3**   continued

```
                    "http://schemas.xmlsoap.org/soap/encoding/"/>
            </wsdl:output>
        </wsdl:operation>
    </wsdl:binding>
```

The first line connects the binding with the portType that we created earlier in this hour. The same portType can appear in more than one binding element. For example, you could have a binding for SMTP as well. A client would only use one of the bindings when communicating with the Web service.

```
<wsdl:binding name="purchaseBinding" type="newCustomerPortType">
```

This binding is designated to be a SOAP binding. In addition, it is going to use the HTTP to send the SOAP documents.

```
    <soap:binding style="document"
            transport="http://schemas.xmlsoap.org/soap/http" />
```

The soap:body element provides details about how the operation is to be encoded. This example states that it will use encoding and specifies the URI of the encodingStyle.

```
            <soap:body use="encoded"
                namespace="http://www.stevepotts.com/customer"
                encodingStyle=
                    "http://schemas.xmlsoap.org/soap/encoding/"/>
```

Notice that both the input and the output use the same encoding scheme in this example. SOAP encoding is covered in Hour 9.

The port Element

NEW TERM   The only piece of information that is now missing is the actual IP address and port of the Web service that is represented by this WSDL. The *port* element is where this information is located. The syntax of the port element is shown here:

```
<wsdl:port binding="newCustomerBinding" name="newCustomerPort">
    <soap:address
        location="http://www.stevepotts.com:1776/soap/servlet/rpcrouter">
</wsdl:port>
```

The address shown here is fictitious, but in a running example, this URL must be a real Web service handler.

The `service` Element

NEW TERM   The most bizarrely named element of all is *service*. Many Web services are gathered together and called a service! This element is a container for all ports that are represented by a WSDL document. The ports within a service can't be chained so that the output of one port is the input to another. As a result, the `service` tag is of limited value, but is required by the specification.

```
<wsdl:service name="newCustomerService">
   <wsdl:documentation>
      This is for adding new customers.
   </wsdl:documentation>
   <wsdl:port binding="newCustomerBinding" name="newCustomerPort">
   <soap:address
        location="http://www.stevepotts.com:1776/soap/servlet/rpcrouter"/>
   </wsdl:port>
</wsdl:service>
```

Through the `port` element, the `service` has access to all the information available in the rest of the document.

The `definitions` Element

NEW TERM   The root element in a WSDL document is *wsdl:definitions*. It contains elements to specify the `targetNameSpace`, as well as a number of ordinary namespaces to help keep out naming conflicts. The syntax of the `definitions` element is shown here:

```
<wsdl:definitions name="customerExample"
targetNamespace="http://www.stevepotts.com/customer.wsdl"
   xmlns:soap="http://www.schemas.xmlsoap.org/wsdl/soap/"
   xmlns:wsdl="http://www.schemas.xmlsoap.org/wsdl/"
   xmlns="http://www.stevepotts.com/customer.xsd">
```

The rest of the WSDL document appears under this element. The end of the document is indicated by

```
</wsdl:definitions>
```

The namespaces that are defined in this element are global to the WSDL document. Other namespaces can appear locally, so be aware of them. Figure 10.3 shows all these elements and their relationships.

The information in the WSDL document is adequate not only for the human reader, but also for a program to generate code to connect physically to the Web service. This automatic code generation is one of the outstanding features of the Web services architecture.

10

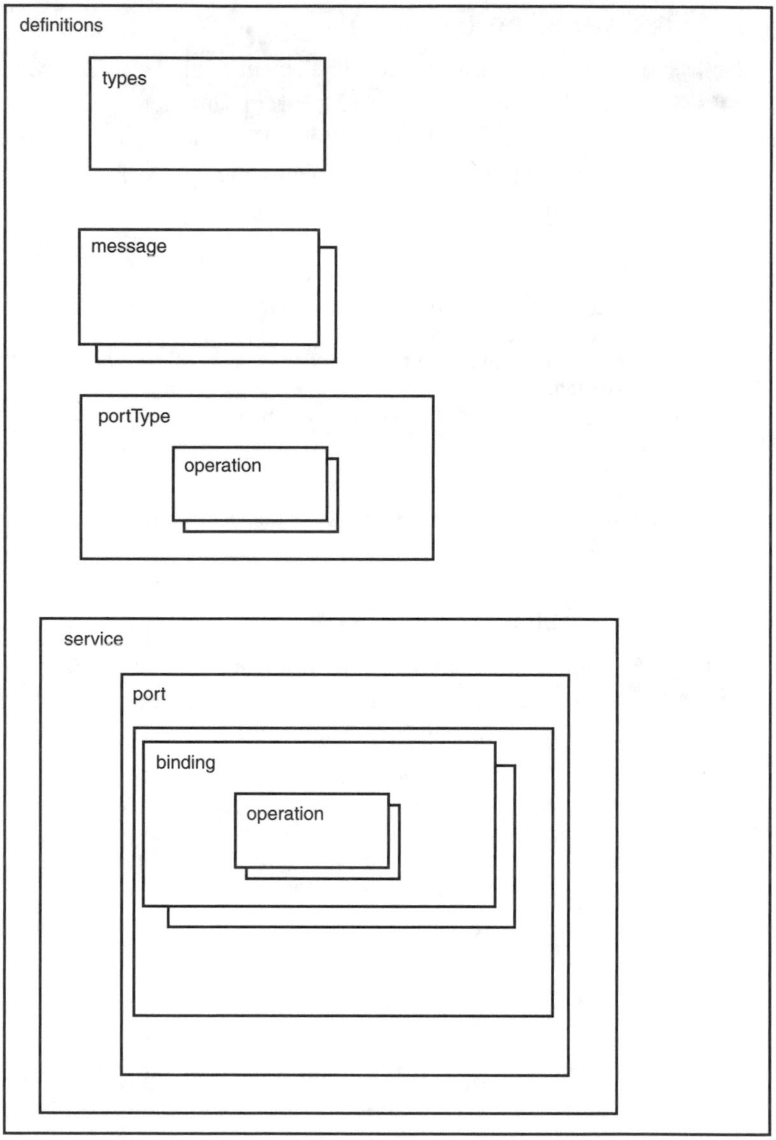

FIGURE **10.3**

The elements of the WSDL document connect together to provide a complete picture of the Web service.

FIGURE **10.3**
The elements of the WSDL document connect together to provide a complete picture of the Web service.

Listing 10.4 shows the entire customer WSDL document.

LISTING 10.4   The `customerExample` WSDL Document

```
<?xml version="1.0" encoding="UTF-8"?>
<wsdl:definitions name="customerExample"
targetNamespace="http://www.stevepotts.com/customer.wsdl"
```

LISTING 10.4   continued

```
      xmlns:soap="http://www.schemas.xmlsoap.org/wsdl/soap/"
      xmlns:wsdl="http://www.schemas.xmlsoap.org/wsdl/"
      xmlns="http://www.stevepotts.com/customer.xsd">

<wsdl:types>
   <xsd:schema targetNamespace="http://www.stevepotts.com/customerType.xsd"
      xmlns:xsd="http://www.w3.org/2001/XMLSchema">
    <xsd:element name="customer">
       <xsd:complexType>
          <xsd:sequence>
             <xsd:element name="customerID" type="xsd:string"/>
             <xsd:element name="lastName" type="xsd:string"/>
             <xsd:element name="firstName" type="xsd:string"/>
             <xsd:element name="address" type="xsd:string"/>
             <xsd:element name="city" type="xsd:string"/>
             <xsd:element name="state" type="xsd:string"/>
             <xsd:element name="zip" type="xsd:string"/>
          </xsd:sequence>
       </xsd:complexType>
    </xsd:element>
   </xsd:schema>
</wsdl:types>
<wsdl:message name="addCustomer">
   <wsdl:part name="customerInfo" element=" customer"/>
</wsdl:message>
<wsdl:message name="confirmation">
   <wsdl:part name="response" element="xsd:integer"/>
</wsdl:message>
<wsdl:message name="exceptionMessage">
   <wsdl:part name="badResult" element="xsd:integer"/>
</wsdl:message>
<wsdl:portType name="newCustomerPortType">
   <wsdl:operation name="createNewCustomer">
      <wsdl:input message="addCustomer"/>
      <wsdl:output message="confirmation"/>
      <wsdl:fault message="exceptionMessage"/>
   </wsdl:operation>
</wsdl:portType>
<wsdl:binding name="newCustomerBinding" type="newCustomerPortType">
   <soap:binding style="rpc"
              transport="http://schemas.xmlsoap.org/soap/http" />
   <wsdl:operation name="createNewCustomer">
      <soap:operation
           soapAction="http://www.stevepotts.com/createNewCustomer"/>
         <wsdl:input>
           <soap:body use="encoded"
               namespace="http://www.stevepotts.com/customer"
               encodingStyle=
```

10

LISTING 10.4   continued

```
                      "http://schemas.xmlsoap.org/soap/encoding/"/>
          </wsdl:input>
          <wsdl:output>
            <soap:body use="encoded"
                  namespace="http://www.stevepotts.com/customer"
                  encodingStyle=
                      "http://schemas.xmlsoap.org/soap/encoding/"/>
          </wsdl:output>
      </wsdl:operation>
  </wsdl:binding>

  <wsdl:service name="newCustomerService">
      <wsdl:documentation>
        This is for adding new customers.
      </wsdl:documentation>
      <wsdl:port binding="newCustomerBinding" name="newCustomerPort">
      <soap:address
          location="http://www.stevepotts.com:1776/soap/servlet/rpcrouter"/>
      </wsdl:port>
  </wsdl:service>

</wsdl:definitions>
```

When viewed in its entirety, the WSDL document represents a full-blown description of the Web service—complete with all the information needed to bind your client program to it. This information is so complete that many vendors have written software that can generate client programs from it.

Summary

This hour has shown you how Web services describe themselves. These descriptions are encoded in a special XML file called the WSDL document. You learned what the role of the WSDL document is and how it can be used.

Next, you learned about each of the elements that make up the WSDL document. You also learned how to combine them into a complete WSDL document.

Q&A

Q **What is the purpose of a WSDL document?**

A To completely describe a Web service to a client or potential client.

Q **What part of the WSDL tells what the input parameter looks like?**

A The `types` element provides a description of the input data type. This element is normally formatted using XML schema notation.

Q **What part of the WSDL provides the information about what method calls the Web service accepts and sends back to the client?**

A The `message` element defines individual messages, and the `operation` element combines messages into meaningful transactions.

Q **What part of the WSDL is concerned with the actual establishing of contact between the client and the Web service?**

A The `binding` provides information about the protocol to be used and the transport that the protocol will travel over.

10

Workshop

The Workshop is designed to help you review what you've learned and begin learning how to put your knowledge into practice.

Quiz

1. What XML grammar is used to specify the message details in a WSDL?
2. Why is the WSDL needed?
3. What are the abstract elements?
4. What are the concrete elements?

Quiz Answers

1. The XML schema is used.
2. To provide capability and connection details to clients and potential clients.
3. `portType`, `operation`, `message`, and `types` are all abstract elements because they describe the Web service in the abstract, but do not provide the details needed for a connection.
4. `service`, `port`, and `binding` are concrete elements because they provide the connection details to a Web service.

Activities

1. Print out the full `customerExample` WSDL document that is located in the code download for this hour. Take a highlighter pen and highlight each part that you understand.

2. For the parts of the `customerExample` WSDL document that you don't understand, reread the section in the hour that covers this topic, and then highlight it.

Hour 11

Advertising a Web Service

In today's sober business environment, whiz-bang technology doesn't capture the CEO's imagination the way that it did during the dot-com boom of the 1990s. However, this does not mean that they are not open to suggestions on how to improve the bottom line; pragmatic and incremental approaches mesh with the more conservative times.

NEW TERM In the world of Web services, strategies that map to the goals stated previously are being funded, whereas those that promise a "revolution" or a "paradigm shift" are falling on deaf ears. One of these paradigm-shift technologies is the concept of a *universal registry* of Web services.

The promise of the universal registry has taken quite a hit in the last 18 months. All the talk about loosely coupled pieces of software that find each other, connect automatically, and exchange data sounds like dot-com happy talk when you hear it said out loud. The idea of the universal public registry is not dead; it has just gone into hiding until both the technology and the public mood is more conducive to it.

This doesn't mean that the ideas are not valid, or that this directory will not exist some-day; it is just that it will appear incrementally in certain low-risk, high-reward situations. Over time, as both technical and business leaders gain confidence in the approach, it will become a groundswell that will have far-reaching effects. In this hour, we will look at the issue of communicating the existence of your Web service to others who might be inter-ested in it. We will also examine the opposite situation in which you learn about the ser-vices offered by other organizations.

Not all registries are public, however. Some registries can exist within the firewall of one company or in an area where only a few trading partners access it. We will look at these also.

In this hour, you will learn about

- The need to advertise a Web service
- The value of a registry
- The UDDI standard
- The UDDI architecture
- Programming the UDDI
- Creating private registries
- Using a UDDI registry

The Need to Advertise a Web Service

Some business goals are steady in spite of the business climate. Every company president believes that he pays too much for raw materials and services, has too few customers, and needs to expand into new product lines. Any strategy that maps to lowering costs, finding new customers, or identifying new sources of revenue will get a fair hearing. Lowering costs is the reason that *Enterprise Application Integration (EAI)*, supply chain management, and *Enterprise Resource Planning (ERP)* projects are so popular today. Web services projects that are mapped to making these activities easier are providing valuable experience and early success stories.

Whenever new technology appears, its first impact is often to provide an incremental improvement in old processes. The first use of the railroad was to lower the cost of trans-porting goods over a distance. As important as this was, it was surpassed by the ability to send salesmen over a distance to find new customers. The increase in sales that were generated by their activities caused factories to run day and night to meet the new demand.

As we explained in Hour 2, "Advantages of Web Services," they can be effective in lowering the cost of doing business by making it easier to get data from one computer to another. This is analogous to lowering the cost of shipping freight. The promise of getting new customers or developing new products requires more than SOAP and WSDL; it requires a registry. This registry is analogous to the traveling salesman in the age of railroads.

A registry is essentially a database of services. An analogy to today's computing environment can be found in the early days of the Internet. TCP/IP, Sockets, and HTML were in place and functioning properly in 1994 when a couple of college students at Stanford decided to create a list of Web sites that they found and store them along with keywords that allowed users to perform searches. The result was called Yahoo!, and the rest is history. Before Yahoo!, a person had to know the address of a Web site to access it, or use a search engine to locate the site. Books were published that listed some of these sites. Since the introduction of Yahoo! and its numerous competitors, most users connect to sites that they did not know existed seconds before when they entered keywords in the search engine.

A search engine is essentially a set of words linked to a URL. A registry of Web services will be much more detailed because of the difference in complexity—a Web service is far more complex than an ordinary Web site. The analogy holds though because a registry could allow customers (who didn't even know that you existed) to do business with you. This is the promise of the universal public registry.

11

Think of how most businesses get new customers today. A salesman learns about a company from reading magazines, talking to friends, or searching the Web. He contacts that business by telephone or letter and tries to set up an appointment with a decision maker. This potential customer struggles to understand what value your salesman is proposing to bring. If the salesman does a good job, you get an initial order from a new customer.

This model might never change for selling certain products such as aircraft engines, where each item is very costly and the potential customers are few. The vast majority of products and services for sale don't fit this pattern. For these products, there are customers who would order them at a good price if they only knew where to find them. Conversely, you are likely buying raw materials today from vendors who are not the best ones in the world. The same products are probably being offered for sale by vendors that you don't know about at a better price and with better terms.

Unless you have penetrated every corner of your geographic area, be it local or worldwide, you don't know about some very attractive trading partners and they don't know about you.

The Purpose of a Registry

You could solve the problem of finding new trading partners through traditional advertising. Many companies purchase television commercials or print ads to try to reach these new customers. Although this approach works well for products such as cars and personal computers, it is not such a good fit for ERP software vendors and custom metal extrusion shops—business-to-business relationships. The rule in advertising is that you pay for every pair of eyeballs that sees your ad, whether or not they are really potential customers. This is why soap is advertised during the afternoon and beer is pitched during football games. The demographics of the viewers matches the products' primary customers, thereby making the ads more effective.

Trade magazines carry this concept one step further. They tailor their articles to attract a narrow segment of the market. They then sell advertising to clients who want to reach that group of customers.

Vending Registry Entries

A registry is just an evolutionary step down that same path. The idea is that a potential customer would use the registry's search facilities in a similar fashion to the way we use Internet search engines. We type in some description of what we are looking for, and a list of potential vendors appears. You further refine your search until you have narrowed it down to the ones that are a perfect match to what you are looking for. You then make a connection to that service and send them a purchase order. They send a confirmation response and ship the goods to your loading dock.

The original vision was that all this interaction would take place without human intervention. In the near term, it appears that the vast majority of the Web services connections that will be made will involve quite a bit of telephone time between the potential vendor and customer. Figure 11.1 shows this graphically.

Rather than be discouraged by the fact that the process isn't completely automatic, we should be glad that the discovery part of the scenario worked. A new customer now knows about you and is placing orders. As the technology matures and comfort levels with it increase, this diagram will become more streamlined. You can probably remember when everyone was reluctant to enter their credit card numbers over the Internet.

Purchasing-oriented Registry Entries

Entries in the registry are not only made by vendors, but also by customers. Many vendors call on large companies because they purchase such large quantities. Normally, an organization will go through a periodic review, and then select a small number of vendors for each category of items that they purchase. This is done to reduce the amount of time that it takes talking to so many sales people.

FIGURE 11.1

*The registry allows a
customer to discover
your company.*

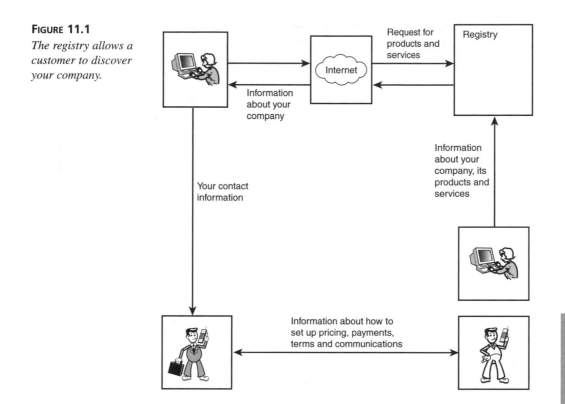

A company could write a Web service that accepts requests from vendors to compete for future purchases. The vendors could use the registry to find companies who purchase the items that they sell. They could interact with the customer's Web service to obtain approval from the company to submit bids. Whenever the customer gets ready to purchase additional quantities of items, they would send the request for pricing to all the approved vendors of that item. (This request could be sent to a vendor Web service.) Each vendor could then submit a bid based on how desperately they want to make the sale. This price could vary by the supply and demand conditions at each vendor's factories. Figure 11.2 shows this scenario.

Creating a Private Registry

Registries don't have to be public to be useful. They can be very useful behind the firewall of one company. Many companies in the Fortune 500 have dozens of divisions and subsidiaries. Many of these companies solve the same problems over and over at different locations. At times, they try to migrate an application from one part of the company to another, but much duplication remains. Software reuse has proved beneficial at the system-software level. We all purchase database management systems, networking software, and operating systems from third-party vendors. We have not had as much success in reusing our own applications. Aside from some framework software that companies use, most applications are single use.

FIGURE 11.2

The registry allows a vendor to discover your company.

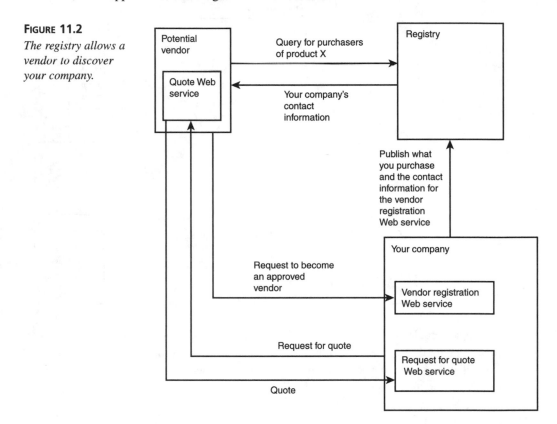

For software reuse to work, it needs to bridge operating-system and language barriers. Its interfaces also need to be described precisely. Finally, there has to be a catalog of these applications so that an employee in California can discover that the division based in Florida already has a system that he can use.

The solution to all these requirements is a Web services approach. SOAP provides the operating system and language independence. WSDL provides the precise description of the application, and a private registry provides a way for the engineer in California to find out about the service. Figure 11.3 shows this graphically.

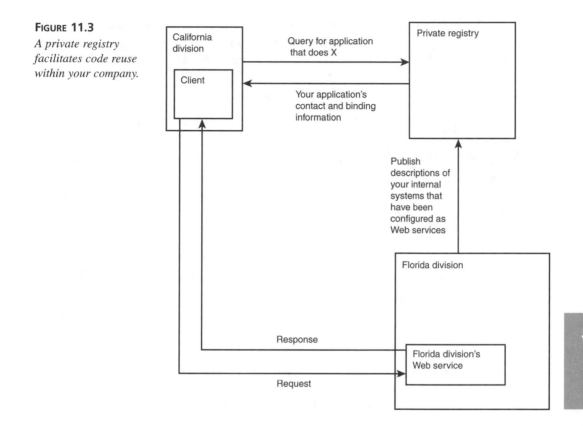

FIGURE 11.3
A private registry facilitates code reuse within your company.

Creating a Semiprivate Registry

NEW TERM One step along the evolutionary path from private to public registries is the hybrid, or *semiprivate registry*. This is a registry that can only be accessed with permission by trading partners or customers. It functions much like a public registry, but it provides its owners with some peace of mind because it is not open to every hacker on the planet—these semiprivate registries sit on a company's intranet and are protected by the company's existing IT infrastructure. Requiring proper authorization permits an organization to expose systems via Web services that are too strategic or sensitive to expose to the public.

A public registration Web service could be used in the vetting process. A company that is interested in becoming a trading partner would use the public registry to locate the "put in an application" Web service. Upon approval, trading partners would be given the keys and passwords needed to access the real Web services exposed by the company.

11

In addition, information about test versions of the company's Web services could be placed in the registry. These versions could be used by potential trading partners to prove that they are interacting with the Web services properly. Passing this test could be part of the approval process for new vendors.

Universal Description, Discovery, and Integration (UDDI)

Now that we have described why a registry is a useful thing, we need to address the issue of what the registry will look like. It would do us little good if everyone used a different format for their registry. We would just move the interoperability problem from our internal systems to the registries.

Fortunately, a consensus has emerged on how to control the process of evolving a directory standard. Whenever standardization is needed, there are always three options:

- **Standardize on one vendor's offering**—Vendors are always trying to get this approach to work, but only with their products. The problem with this is that it shuts all other vendors out, causing them to become hostile. In addition, it removes the incentive for improvement if the winning vendor becomes complacent.

- **Wait for a standards body to devise a solution**—The most relevant word is "wait." Standards bodies are notoriously slow moving. Academic types who are more interested in getting it right than in getting it done often dominate these committees.

- **Establish a vendor-sponsored standard**—The computing world is always suspicious of vendor-sponsored standards because they are often thinly veiled attempts to get the world to standardize on their offering. These bodies move quickly, though, because they are often run by industry leaders who are under orders not to dawdle.

NEW TERM   A vendor-sponsored registry standard called the *Universal Description, Discovery, and Integration (UDDI)* has emerged and taken a dominant role in this area. UDDI was the brain child of Ariba, IBM, Intel, Microsoft, and SAP. In 2002, the OASIS standards group took over UDDI from UDDI.org. BEA, Cincom, CA, E2Open, Entrust, Fujitsu, HP, IBM, Intel, IONA, Microsoft, Novell, Oracle, SAP, Sun Microsystems, and hundreds of other companies have endorsed it. The UDDI co-chairs are from IBM and Microsoft. The most notable company to sign on is Sun Microsystems. It seems that whenever Sun and Microsoft agree on a standard, the development world follows along. The reasoning seems to be that anytime those two companies agree on anything, given their rancorous past, it must be good. Additionally, no fees or licenses are required to use this technology.

UDDI is described as follows:

- It is a standardized, transparent mechanism for describing services.
- It describes simple methods for invoking the service.
- It specifies an accessible central registry of services.

An additional feature is that the registries are based on a confederated model whereby they replicate each other. If you register your Web service with one registry, the other registries will receive your information the next time they synchronize. This means that all publicly published Web services can be found by accessing any of the public registries.

The reason that UDDI is acceptable to all the vendors mentioned previously is that it is built on the same SOAP standards that ordinary Web services are. This means that a registry can be written in and accessed by any computer language running on any hardware platform running any operating system. Every vendor is able to create tools to interact with these registries.

Version 3 of the UDDI standard is now published and is being implemented by the IT community.

The UDDI Architecture

The UDDI itself is configured as a replicated collection of Web services. All the public directories replicate information posted on any of them. This ensures that you can access all the public Web services by accessing only one of them.

The information in a registry is composed of three types of entries: white, yellow, and green pages. The analogy to a telephone listing is not too subtle:

- **White pages**—Contain basic contact information such as contact names and phone numbers, plus Dun & Bradstreet D-U-N-S Number. They also contain human-readable information to assist in evaluating the Web service offering.
- **Yellow pages**—Contain classifications using various taxonomy systems. In UDDI version 1, three built-in taxonomies were provided—NAICS industry categorizations, UNSPC project and service categorizations, and ISO-3166-2 geographic taxonomies. In UDDI version 3, external taxonomy systems can be employed so that niche fields can employ their own special classification codes while maintaining the accuracy of the data by verifying all entries against lists of valid entries. Among these classifications is a geography code for situations in which proximity is important.

11

- **Green pages**—Contain the details on how to program a client that can invoke the service. You can think of the green pages as a type of data dictionary for the service.

UDDI registries work just like other Web services, as shown in Figure 11.4.

FIGURE 11.4

A UDDI registry operates as a Web service.

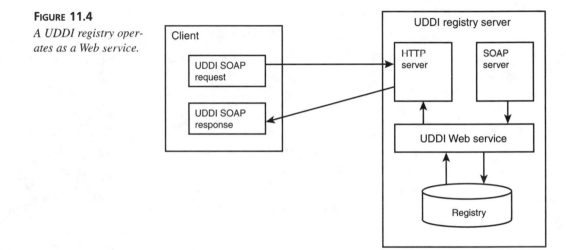

All the APIs in the UDDI specification are defined in XML, placed inside SOAP envelopes, and sent over HTTP. In addition, client requests that entail modifying data are required to be secured and authenticated.

One critical part of the whole UDDI search strategy is the technical model (tModel). If you know the Web service that you want, its URL, and that it accepts HTTP, you could, in theory, connect to it. In some instances, however, the Web service is expecting to receive an XML document in a very specific format. The tModel provides metadata about additional specifications, its name, publisher, and the URL of its schema. The tModel commits the Web service to properly process all messages that are sent in this format.

The tModel is not expected to be unique for each Web service. If two Web services are capable of processing the same messages, they would have the same tModel. This could reduce the amount of programming needed to access Web services by allowing the code written for one tModel to be used to access another.

Listing 11.1 shows a summary of the UDDI version 1 Inquiry API.

LISTING 11.1   The UDDI Inquiry Methods

```
Find_business()
Find_service()
Find_binding()
Find_tModel()
Get_businessDetail()
Get_serviceDetail()
Get_bindingDetail()
Get_tModelDetail()
Get_registeredInfo()
```

A programmer would implement these method calls to gather information from the registry about candidate Web services. Listing 11.2 shows the publishing operations in the UDDI API.

LISTING 11.2   The UDDI Publishing Methods

```
save_business()
save_service()
save_binding()
save_tModel()

delete_business()
delete_service()
delete_binding()
delete_tModel()
get_registeredInfo()
get_authToken()
discard_authToken()
```

11

You make calls to the registry using SOAP just as you would with any other Web service. You use it by downloading a WSDL and contacting the registry as a Web service.

The authToken provides an additional level of security. This token is given to a user who has identified himself to the registry's satisfaction to be the legal owner of an organization's registry information.

Programming with UDDI

Programming with the UDDI API is really the same as programming with any Web service. A client must encode messages in SOAP format and send them. When the response arrives, the client must decode the message and extract information from it.

This doesn't mean, however, that you will soon see large numbers of SOAP programmers walking around with SOAP manuals under their arms or college courses teaching

SOAP. In fact, most programmers will use their own favorite programming languages. In the Java world, UDDI4J is a popular library for accessing UDDI registries. Listing 11.3 shows a fragment of the UDDI schema that describes the businessEntity.

LISTING 11.3 The businessEntity Schema

```
<element name="businessEntity">
  <type content="elementOnly">
   <group order="seq">
     <element ref="discoveryURLs" minOccurs="0" maxOccurs="1"/>
     <element ref="name">
     <element ref="description" minOccurs="0" maxOccurs="1"/>
     <element ref="contacts" minOccurs="0" maxOccurs="1"/>
     <element ref="businessServices" minOccurs="0" maxOccurs="1"/>
     <element ref="identifierBag" minOccurs="0" maxOccurs="1"/>
     <element ref="categoryBag" minOccurs="0" maxOccurs="1"/>
   </group>
   <attribute name="businessKey" minOccurs="1" type="string"/>
   <attribute name="operator" type="string"/>
   <attribute name="authorizedName" type="string"/>
  </type>
</element>
```

The information sent in the SOAP message will be sent in accordance with this format. To make it easier to work with, UDDI4J has defined a class called com.ibm.uddi. datatype.business.BusinessEntity. Part of that class is shown in Listing 11.4.

LISTING 11.4 The BusinessEntity Class

```
public class BusinessEntity extends UDDIElement
{
  public static final String UDDI_TAG = "businessEntity";
  protected Element base = null;
  String businessKey = null;
  String operator = null;
  String authorizedName = null;
  DiscoveryURLS discoveryURLs = null;
  Name name = null;
  Contacts contacts = null;
  BusinessServices businessServices = null;
  IdentifierBag identifierBag = null;
  CategoryBag = null;
  // Vector of Description objects
  Vector description = new Vector();
  ...
}
```

You can see how a Java programmer would have an easier time populating the class in Listing 11.4 than he would generating the text, as shown in Listing 11.3. The UDDI4J provides the translation from the familiar Java class structure to the less-familiar SOAP messages.

Types of Discovery

NEW TERM There are two visions of how discovery can take place using a UDDI registry. The first, *design-time discovery*, involves quite a bit of human intervention and some programming. The second, *runtime discovery*, is much more automatic and involves quite a bit of tricky programming.

Design-time Discovery

If a company is considering using a Web service, it needs to decide which one. One way to do this is by a manual discovery process. The basic steps of this type of discovery are shown here:

1. The business analysts browse the UDDI to find candidate Web services.
2. A programmer searches the UDDI registry for a `bindingTemplate` that he wants to connect with.
3. The programmer writes a client program based on the `bindingTemplate` and the tModel that it contains. The tModel provides information about complex data (XML documents) that must be transferred to use the service.
4. The program accesses the Web service, transfers the document, and then gets the response.
5. The programmer places the client in production.

Runtime Discovery

In the future, the manual steps will be eliminated and runtime discovery will be more common. This more advanced, and futuristic, solution involves the discovery and interconnection of clients to Web services. The steps needed to perform this type of search are listed here:

1. Business analysts use the GUI to specify what kind of Web services they want.
2. A discovery program searches the UDDI registry for a `bindingTemplate` that the client can connect with, given the protocols that it already supports.
3. The discovery program searches the `bindingTemplate` for the tModel that it contains. If the client program can send requests to this tModel, it is called by the discovery program.

11

4. The client program accesses the Web service, transfers the document, and then gets the response.

The biggest problem in this scenario is trust. In a world of hackers, it is hard to see how our businesses could trust any Web service enough to allow hands-free interconnection. Keep in mind, though, that trust can be earned by applying the proper safeguards. In the 1920s, no one could have imagined that workers would one day accept a piece of paper as wages instead of an envelope of money. A doctor's board certification gives us enough confidence to allow him to operate on our child less than an hour after meeting him.

The building up of trust will take some time, but slowly, it will progress to the point at which we are able to trust more and more.

In spite of all the challenges that face this vision, UDDI has a bright future. As Brent Sleeper of the Stencil Group said, "UDDI will succeed because its technical underpinnings work for the geeks..."

Summary

In this hour, we covered the need for advertising the capabilities of your Web services. Following that, you learned why a registry is a good way to accomplish this.

Next, you learned about the Universal Description, Discovery, and Integration (UDDI) standard. We covered the origins of this standard and its current level of acceptance. Finally, we stepped through some scenarios that showed how a UDDI registry could be used to discover Web services both manually and automatically.

Q&A

Q Hasn't the whole idea of automatic discovery been rejected by the business community?

A No, it hasn't been greeted with the same enthusiasm as SOAP and WSDL, but it hasn't been rejected either. Everyone seems to put the UDDI part of Web services on the future to-do list instead on today's list.

Q Isn't the whole notion of "promiscuous e-commerce" a hacker's paradise?

A Yes. The safeguards are not really in place to allow the transfer of millions of dollars to a company found on a UDDI registry automatically. This doesn't mean that it will never be safe, however.

Q Is a private registry really useful?

A Yes, but only for companies that are large and diversified, such as GE or Lockheed-Martin. There are probably simpler ways of discovering each other's systems in smaller organizations.

Workshop

This section is designed to help you anticipate possible questions, review what you've learned, and begin learning how to put your knowledge into practice.

Quiz

1. What is a registry?
2. Why does an internal Web service need to be advertised?
3. What does UDDI stand for?
4. What is holding back the idea of automatic discovery and interconnection of Web services?

Quiz Answers

1. A registry is a kind of special-purpose database that contains information about Web services.
2. In large organizations, major systems can exist, but not every one knows about them. A private UDDI registry could keep track of all the Web services in an organization.
3. It stands for Universal Description, Discovery, and Integration.
4. Security and the fear of hackers make today's businesses prefer to have a human involved in the process of discovery and authorization.

Activities

1. List the three different types of registries and describe the different motivation behind the creation of each of them.
2. Go to Microsoft's test registry at `http://uddi.microsoft.com/` to experiment and gain experience with UDDI registries.

Hour **12**

Sending Attachments with Web Services

NEW TERM One of the earliest criticisms of XML and therefore Web services is in the area of transmitting noncharacter data. The idea of converting everything into characters is not considered practical for certain types of data such as photographs and executable code.

Because an XML document is transmitted as a set of characters, other types of *binary data*—such as images, audio files, or compiled programs (like Java class files)—are problematic.

The solution to this problem is to send these files as attachments to a SOAP message. This hour explains the different ways in which this can be done.

In this hour, you will learn how to attack this problem when using Web services. You will learn

- How to covert binary data to Base64 encoding so that it can be sent like text
- How to encode attachments with MIME

- How to encode with DIME
- How the new SOAP 1.2 Attachment Feature clarifies the issue

The Problem with Binary Data

NEW TERM   All computer data is binary, in that it is composed of 1s and 0s. Some patterns of
1s and 0s have been assigned to represent the characters in natural languages
such as English, French, Chinese, and so on. In the United States, the most commonly
used character set is called the *American Standard Code for Information Interchange
(ASCII)*. In the U.S. version of the code, US-ASCII, codes range from the 7-bit representation of the numbers 0 to 127 for a total of 128 different values. These values represent
the letters of the alphabet, the capitalized form of the letters of the alphabet, the numbers
from 0 to 9, common punctuation marks, and some special characters that are used in
data communications. Table 12.1 shows some of the common characters and their US-
ASCII codes.

TABLE 12.1   Sample ASCII Codes

Decimal	Character	Bit Pattern
32	Space	0100000
60	<	0111100
62	>	0111110
65	A	1000001
97	a	1100001
90	Z	1011010
122	z	1111010
48	0	0110000
57	9	0111001
38	&	0100110
47	/	0101111

If we wanted to encode this line (elements and data)

```
<AaZz>909090</AaZz>
```

It would be sent as these bits:

```
0111100 1000001 1100001 1011010 1111010 0111110
0111001 0110000 0111001 0110000 0111001 0110000
0111100 0101111 1000001 1100001 1011010 1111010 0111110
```

The client computer would translate the characters in the XML into the bit representations—taking special care to deal with LF, CR, and period (.)—and send them to the Web service's server. The server would translate the bits into characters and send them to the Web service. As long as all of the information in the XML document can be represented as ASCII characters, this strategy works well.

> Other character sets exist to represent languages such as French, Chinese, Arabic, and so on. With the exception of the differences in the length and composition of the binary strings that make up these characters sets, they are processed the same way as US-ASCII.

Binary data is any data representation that does not map to a character set. Although it is still composed of 1s and 0s, it does not conform to the strict rules of character encoding. If you introduce non-ASCII data into the preceding message and send it to an XML parser, confusion will be the result. Unless you find a way to represent binary data in Web services, certain types of data can't be sent.

Using Base64 Encoding

NEW TERM The conventional solution is to convert the binary data into XML friendly characters using an encoding scheme called Base64. It is popular because it is conceptually very simple. *Base64* encoding takes three bytes of binary data, which is normally grouped into *octets* (8-bit groupings), and combines them into a single 24-bit grouping. It then creates four 6-bit groupings and stores them as if they were US-ASCII. The "=" character (111101) is used as metadata. For example, consider the following set of binary values:

```
01100011 00011101 01111110
```

This string can't be treated as US-ASCII characters because there is no way to guarantee that forbidden character sequences (US-ASCII control characters) are not embedded in it. These characters are divided into four sets of 6-bits as shown here:

```
011000 110001 110101 111110
```

Special characters are added to the stream. Each of these 6-bit sets is used as an index to an array of characters that are never used as metadata. In this Base64 alphabet, the bit strings have the values shown in Table 12.2.

12

TABLE 12.2   Typical Base64 Alphabet Characters

Decimal	Character	Bit Pattern
0	A	000000
1	B	000001
2	C	000010
23	X	010111
24	Y	011000
25	Z	011001
26	a	011010
27	b	011011
28	c	011100
49	x	110001
50	y	110010
51	z	110011
52	0	110100
53	1	110101
60	8	111100
61	9	111101
62	+	111110
63	/	111111

The resulting string would be Yx1+. You could then take this data, place it in an element like this, and send it to the Web service:

```
<imageData>Yx1+</imageData>
```

You have noticed that this data is not human readable, but it will transmit without error. On the server side, the characters are retranslated:

```
Y 011000
X 010111
1 110101
+ 111110
```

A set of bits is created from these:

```
011000 110001 110101 111110
```

These bits are regrouped into octets and all metadata removed:

```
01100011 00011101 01111110
```

The Web service now has the original data in its memory where it can process it. You might think that this approach is the solution to the binary data transfer problem. The fact that the data is about 33% larger after the encoding is performed and the fact that the encoding/decoding process consumes resources at both the client and the server can cause performance problems in certain systems.

In cases in which bandwidth and processing resources are abundant, Base64 encoding works well for sending attachments inside Web services transactions. In many cases, however, bandwidth and processing resources are scarce. This is particularly true in the future wireless Web services world. In these situations, a more economical approach is needed.

Multipurpose Internet Mail Extensions

NEW TERM The problem of sending binary data from one computer to another is not new with Web services. As far back as 1992, the *Internet Engineering Task Force (IETF)* released a standard for sending attachments along with email called *Multipurpose Internet Mail Extensions (MIME)* in a document called RFC 2387. You can download this document at `http://www.ietf.org/rfc/rfc2387.txt`.

Prior to RFC 2387, the following restrictions applied to email:

- The message may contain only US-ASCII characters.
- The maximum line length allowed is 1,000 characters.
- The message must not be longer than a predefined maximum size.

After RFC 2387 email could add the following types of attachments:

- Character sets other than US-ASCII are supported.
- Image files can be sent.
- Audio files are allowed.
- Video can be sent.
- Multiple attachments are allowed in the same message.
- Messages may have more than one font.
- Messages may be of any size.
- Binary files may be sent as attachments.

MIME works by adding a Content-Type header that can be used to specify the type and subtype of the data being sent in the attachment. Seven types of attachments are specified:

12

- Type 1—**Text**—Text data in a character set
- Type 2—**Image**—Still image data
- Type 3—**Audio**—Audio or voice data
- Type 4—**Video**—Moving image data
- Type 5—**Message**—Encapsulating a mail message
- Type 6—**Multipart**—Combinations of several of the other types into one message
- Type 7—**Application**—Binary or application data

In addition to the Content-Type, a MIME header must contain a MIME-Version and a Content-Transfer-Encoding field. It may also contain a Content-ID to allow references from one attachment to another, and a Content-Description, which allows the sender to add a descriptive message to the attachment. Listing 12.1 shows a sample multipart message.

LISTING 12.1   A MIME Multipart Message

```
From ranl@ecitele.com Sun Aug 6 18:32:49 1995
Return-Path: ranl@ecitele.com
Received: from elf.ecitele.com ([147.234.56.1]) by taurus.math.tau.ac.il
(8.6.10/math) with ESMTP id SAA03892 for <sdascal@math.tau.ac.il>;
Sun, 6 Aug 1995 18:31:14 +0300
From: ranl@ecitele.com
Received: from pc-ranlahat.ecitele.com (pc-ranlahat.ecitele.com
[147.234.18.108]) by elf.ecitele.com (8.6.12/8.6.12) with
SMTP id SAA23658; Sun, 6 Aug 1995 18:27:18 +0300
Date: Sun, 6 Aug 95 18:14:51 IST
Subject: sending gifs
To: shlomit <sdascal@math.tau.ac.il>
X-Mailer: Chameleon V0.05, TCP/IP for Windows, NetManage Inc.
Message-ID: <Chameleon.950806182312.ranl@pc-ranlahat.ecitele.com>
MIME-Version: 1.0
Content-Type: MULTIPART/MIXED; BOUNDARY="pc-
ranlahat.ecitele.com:807722592:1402405494:1451687977:1917059072"
Status: R

--pc-ranlahat.ecitele.com:807722592:1402405494:1451687977:1917059072
Content-Type: TEXT/PLAIN; charset=US-ASCII


Hi Shlomit,

I'm sending you some GIF files

Bye
```

LISTING 12.1 continued

```
Ran
--pc-ranlahat.ecitele.com:807722592:1402405494:1451687977:1917059072
Content-Type: IMAGE/gif; SizeOnDisk=658; name="FINGERAC.GIF"
Content-Transfer-Encoding: BASE64
Content-Description: FINGERAC.GIF
```

```
R0lGODdhJAAkAPYPAAAAAIAAAACAAICAAAAAgIAAgACAgMDAwICAgP8AAAD/
AP//AAAA//8A/wD//////wAAAIAAAACAAICAAAAAgIAAgACAgMDAwICAgP8A
AAD/AP//AAAA//8A/wD//////wAAAIAAAACAAICAAAAAgIAAgACAgMDAwICA
gP8AAAD/AP//AAAA//8A/wD//////wAAAIAAAACAAICAAAAAgIAAgACAgMDA
.
.
.
CNELhsvE2KnSg9vdq9O2q6W0p6LfyrXmmcLpB4WwnvC2uAD0msLFqPm3/9Lt
U8TOVzF02QK6ozSJ3MEH/oihWniJYKJ/hIpRnPWoWUJEEy1xajSNHQB5GkUq
enQAgbxB+EIRc6myUkuXxMYRW8mQJymMNWUB3URw3UVyhaSt+wYRIrWntpqi
YmoR49FDSgcxJXnKp65dXr/2FDvwqtmLgQAAOw==
```

```
--pc-ranlahat.ecitele.com:807722592:1402405494:1451687977:1917059072
Content-Type: IMAGE/gif; SizeOnDisk=787; name="GOPHRACT.GIF"
Content-Transfer-Encoding: BASE64
Content-Description: GOPHRACT.GIF
```

```
R0lGODdhJAAkAPYPAAAAAIAAAACAAICAAAAAgIAAgACAgMDAwICAgP8AAAD/
AP//AAAA//8A/wD//////wAAAIAAAACAAICAAAAAgIAAgACAgMDAwICAgP8A
AAD/AP//AAAA//8A/wD//////wAAAIAAAACAAICAAAAAgIAAgACAgMDAwICA
.
.
.
3Inq3k8AQZ8WXZTT4strJp3aRNiLX0iq9hrKBCqUaMp9U3grumzHlBHWmlAn
ThXZkqTapm1RfkQ6F6C7q2LzmpVLEkAAxG0jRuw17xC1dQEQZAsgc+zbxf/q
OUbwWFMAzolSF8rMGdfp17Bjy57N2jEu1bgPZcZFmrbv37udfeo9vLjx48Q/
2V374DTy58Wda15Oqjqk3NhTBwIAOw==
```

```
--pc-ranlahat.ecitele.com:807722592:1402405494:1451687977:1917059072
Content-Type: AUDIO/wav; SizeOnDisk=22230; name="PHONE.WAV"
Content-Transfer-Encoding: BASE64
Content-Description: PHONE.WAV
```

```
UklGRs5WAABXQVZFZm10IBAAAAABAAEAESsAABErAAABAAgAZGF0YalWAABd
an+RiHhreI2hi3RsfpGReFtrgZSIdmp5kaSLcWp/kpB1V2uDlId0aXqUpYpw
a4CVj3NWa4aVhnFme5alimxqgpmNcFVsiJWGb2Z9mqWIa2uFmo1uU2uKloVs
Zn+epYdpa4Wbi2pRbIyXhWtlgJ+mhmdrhpyLaVBsjJeDamWBo6aHZ2uHn4tn
UG6PmYVqZoKkpoZla4igi2ZObpGXg2dlgqamhmVriqGKZE5ukZeDZmWDqKWF
.
.
.
```

12

LISTING 12.1 continued

```
g29sgpyag2xxhpaDaWB1jI+Bbm+GnpWAbHSIloJmYnaNjH9ucYaekn5sdoqU
gGVmeY+Mf2xzh5+PfWt2ipR/ZGl6j4t+bHSHno15a3mLkn5ha32RintsdYqe
i3hse4yQe2Fsf5CIemx2i56IdGx9jY96YG6BkYd4bnmNnIh0bn6PjHhgb4KQ
hnZue4+bh3Nvf5CLdmFxg4+FdW5+kZmFcHCBkYh1ZHSGj4V0b36SloNwc4KR
h3NldYiPg3RwgZWUgnB0g5GFcGZ2ioyCc3GGClZGAb3SDkIFuaXmLi4FzdIOW
j39wdoWPgGtqeYuKgHN1hZeNfnB4ho1/amx6i4h/cHWFlop6b3qHjX5pbn6M
iH1xeIeXiHlwe4iMfWdvf4yGe3F5iJaGeHF9iop6ZnCAjIV6cXuLlYV2c36K
iHlnc4GLg3Z0g5SLe3N5goeBeXl6eH9/gX+CgH17go2Ge3V9gYOAfn57eHsA
```

```
--pc-ranlahat.ecitele.com:807722592:1402405494:1451687977:1917059072--
```

The first MIME headers in this email appear just before the first message.

```
MIME-Version: 1.0
Content-Type: MULTIPART/MIXED; BOUNDARY="pc-
ranlahat.ecitele.com:807722592:1402405494:1451687977:1917059072"
```

This tells the server that the content of this message is MULTIPART and that its subtype is MIXED, meaning that this message has multiple attachments that are of different types. It also defines a unique string as a boundary between message parts.

The boundary is repeated, and the first content type and subtype are shown:

```
--pc-ranlahat.ecitele.com:807722592:1402405494:1451687977:1917059072
Content-Type: TEXT/PLAIN; charset=US-ASCII
```

After the text message, another boundary appears followed by another header. This header says that this is a GIF image that is being sent using BASE64 encoding.

```
Content-Type: IMAGE/gif; SizeOnDisk=658; name="FINGERAC.GIF"
Content-Transfer-Encoding: BASE64
Content-Description: FINGERAC.GIF
```

```
R0lGODdhJAAkAPYPAAAAAIAAAACAAICAAAAAgIAAgACAgMDAwICAgP8AAAD/
AP//AAAA//8A/wD//////wAAAIAAAACAAICAAAAAgIAAgACAgMDAwICAgP8A
```

This is followed by another GIF file:

```
Content-Type: IMAGE/gif; SizeOnDisk=787; name="GOPHRACT.GIF"
Content-Transfer-Encoding: BASE64
Content-Description: GOPHRACT.GIF
```

```
R0lGODdhJAAkAPYPAAAAAIAAAACAAICAAAAAgIAAgACAgMDAwICAgP8AAAD/
```

And is finally followed by a WAV file:

```
Content-Type: AUDIO/wav; SizeOnDisk=22230; name="PHONE.WAV"
Content-Transfer-Encoding: BASE64
Content-Description: PHONE.WAV
```

```
UklGRs5WAABXQVZFZm10IBAAAAABAAEAESsAABErAAABAAgAZGF0YalWAABd
```

Later in the hour, you will learn how MIME can be used to send attachments to SOAP messages.

Direct Internet Message Encapsulation

NEW TERM In the world of standards, it seems as if there are always several to choose from in the early stages. An alternative standard, *Direct Internet Message Encapsulation (DIME)*, has been proposed to the IETF to be used instead of MIME.

DIME is less flexible than MIME because it is based on a simpler message format. DIME is written from the ground up to be used in conjunction with SOAP for the specific purpose of adding attachments to Web services messages. As a result, the DIME header contains very little information about the attachments, deferring most of the details to the body of the SOAP message.

DIME could be thought of as a new version of MIME that is designed for Web services. It uses the existing MIME Content-types and subtypes to identify the encoding of the records.

A DIME message consists of one or more DIME records. Each record contains information about its own contents.

```
00001 1 0 0 0010 00000000000000000000
0000000000000000 0000000000101000
00000000000000000000000110110101
http://schemas.xmlsoap.org/soap/envelope
<soap-env:Envelope
 xmlns:soap-env="http://schemas.xmlsoap.org/soap/envelope/"
 xmlns:msg="http://example.com/DimeExample/Messages/"
 xmlns:ref= "http://schemas.xmlsoap.org/ws/2002/04/reference/"
>
 <soap-env:Body>
  <msg:GetMediaFile>
   <msg:fileName>myMediaFile.mpg
   </msg:fileName>
   <msg:file ref:location=
     "uuid:F2DA3C9C-74D3-4A46-B925-B150D62D9483" />
  </msg:GetMediaFile>
 </soap-env:Body>
</soap-env:Envelope>
-------------------------------------------------------------------
00001 0 0 1 0001 00000000000000000000
0000000000101001 0000000000001010
00000000000101011010101011100000
uuid:F2DA3C9C-74D3-4A46-B925-B150D62D9483
video/mpeg
```

12

```
<<First 1.42 MB of binary data for myMediaFile.mpg>>
- - - - - - - - - - - - - - - - - - - - - - - - - - - - - - - - - - - - - - - - -
00001 0 1 0 0000 0000000000000000000
0000000000000000 0000000000000000
000000000000100001101100010000000
<<Remaining 552 KB of binary data for myMediaFile.mpg>>
```

The bits that you see at the top of each record are in a fixed format and are used to specify the following data about the record:

- Version (5 bits)—Version of the DIME message.
- MB (1 bit)—First record indicator.
- ME (1 bit)—Last record indicator.
- CF (1 bit)—Chunked Flag—Indicates whether a record has been chopped into pieces for convenience in transmitting the document.
- TYPE_T (4 bits)—Structure and format information of the TYPE field.
- OPTIONS_LENGTH (16 bits)—The length of the OPTIONS field.
- ID_LENGTH (16 bits)—The length of the ID field.
- TYPE_LENGTH (16 bits)—The length of the TYPE field.
- DATA_LENGTH (32 bits)—The length of the data.
- OPTIONS—Any information sent by the DIME encoder.
- ID—A URI to identify the payload.
- TYPE—The type reference URI or MIME type and subtype of the payload.
- DATA—The actual data.

By using the data in the header, a parser can determine exactly what the data in the record is, where it starts, and where it ends.

```
00001 1 0 0 0010 0000000000000000000
0000000000000000 0000000000101000
0000000000000000000000110110101
```

The first record contains the SOAP message itself. It might seem strange to have another object type encapsulating the SOAP message, but from a practical standpoint it makes sense. When the DIME parser gets the message, it can send the SOAP message on to the SOAP parser and store the attachments in some type of cache. When the SOAP message refers to the attachment, the Web service can retrieve and process the attachment.

```
<soap-env:Body>
 <msg:GetMediaFile>
  <msg:fileName>myMediaFile.mpg
  </msg:fileName>
```

```
    <msg:file ref:location=
        "uuid:F2DA3C9C-74D3-4A46-B925-B150D62D9483" />
  </msg:GetMediaFile>
</soap-env:Body>
```

Notice that the `uuid` in the SOAP message is identical to the one in the next DIME record.

```
uuid:F2DA3C9C-74D3-4A46-B925-B150D62D9483
```

This makes it easy for the Web service to be certain about the identity of the attachment.

The fixed format of the header makes processing it much faster than the freer format of the MIME standard.

> Microsoft and IBM submitted a document called WS-Attachments to the Internet Engineering Task Force in an attempt to start it down the road to becoming a standard or recommendation. This document formalized the format that was described in the earlier DIME section of this hour.

Understanding the New SOAP 1.2 Attachment Feature

NEW TERM On August 14, 2002, the *World Wide Web Consortium (W3C)* published a working draft of what it calls the *SOAP 1.2 Attachment Feature*. It states that this draft is "based in part on the *WS-Attachments* proposal" mentioned in the previous section of this hour. The URL for this draft is `http://www.w3.org/TR/2002/WD-soap12-af-20020814/`.

This draft proposal doesn't require that a SOAP receiver process any of the secondary parts of a compound document. The receiver determines, based on the primary SOAP message, whether to process the attachments.

In addition, the draft proposal does not specify that either DIME or MIME be used to specify the document, but it mentions them both in the context of how a message might actually be sent. As examples, it lists the following three ways to handle the compound message:

- The primary SOAP message part and the attachment can be encapsulated in a single DIME message and sent using a protocol such as TCP or HTTP. This means that your software can send attachments using DIME.

12

- The primary SOAP message part and the attachment can be encapsulated in a single MIME message and transmitted using a protocol such as HTTP. This means that you can send attachments using MIME encapsulation if you choose to.
- The primary SOAP message part can be exchanged using the HTTP binding without any encapsulation, and the attachment can be transmitted using a separate request. This makes it legal to send only the data describing the attachment along with instructions on how to perform the transfer.

As a caution, the draft mentions the potential security problems associated with attachments. This document makes particular mention of using the "application/postscript" and the "message/external-body" media type. Therefore, you should avoid sending these types of attachments because they can contain viruses.

Summary

In this hour, you learned about the difficulties associated with attaching noncharacter data to XML and SOAP messages. These difficulties include data corruption and bloated message size. In particular, you saw how attachments can be included using Base64 encoding.

Following that, you learned about the potential use of MIME and DIME to format SOAP messages that contain attachments. Finally, you learned about the SOAP 1.2 Attachment Feature that is currently being circulated by the W3C as a draft as of this writing.

By using these technologies, you can send binary data along with your XML documents in your Web services transactions.

Q&A

Q Why do we need additional standards beyond MIME?

A MIME was originally designed for use in email messages. DIME was designed to be used in Web services. DIME is easier to parse and therefore consumes fewer resources than MIME.

Q Why didn't the SOAP 1.2 Attachment Feature specify either MIME or DIME?

A The decision appears to be a compromise. The draft proposal left the door open to please both sides.

Q **Why don't we just place the binary data in the middle of an XML document?**

A XML parsers expect character data and control characters to compose 100% of the transmission. Binary data can contain bit patterns that cause errors in these parsers.

Workshop

The Workshop is designed to help you review what you've learned and begin learning how to put your knowledge into practice.

Quiz

1. How does MIME define a boundary between messages?
2. What is the role of the WS-Attachment proposal now that the W3C has issued the SOAP 1.2 Attachment Feature?
3. What type of encapsulation is specified by the SOAP 1.2 Attachment Feature?

Quiz Answers

1. The message creator defines the boundary in the header.
2. The WS-Attachment proposal provided input to the SOAP 1.2 Attachment Feature. Now that the SOAP draft has been published, it will become the focal point.
3. The draft doesn't specify an encapsulation, but it allows for any encapsulation including MIME or DIME (or neither) to be used.

Activities

1. Using Java classes, create a Web service that consumes an attachment.
2. Create a client program that sends a message with an attachment to the Web service that you wrote in Activity 1.

12

PART III
Building Web Services

Hour

HOUR 13

Creating Web Services with Apache Axis

In order to create a Web service, you will need some tools. At a minimum, you will need some type of SOAP processing engine to parse the messages that are received and to call the functions or methods that the message indicates.

Many products are on the market that provide this processing. In addition, many of them provide other tools to help the developer write the code needed to do this work. In this hour, we will look at one such product—Apache Software Foundation's Axis product. We will cover its architectural approach. Following that, we will work an example to illustrate the process that you use to create Web services with this tool.

In this hour, you will learn

- What Apache Axis is
- The architecture of Axis
- How to create a Web service with Axis
- How to create clients that use Axis

Understanding Apache Axis

Apache Axis is an *open-source project* of the Apache Software Foundation. Axis stands for *Apache Extensible Interaction System*, which could mean anything. You can think of Axis as Apache's latest version of its legacy SOAP processor, Apache SOAP V2.

> Apache Software Foundation was created to manage open-source software projects. Open-source projects are staffed by volunteers who contribute code to collaborative, consensus-based development projects. There are many reasons that developers cite for their interest in working on open-source projects. Some engineers are graduate students and professors of computer science who work on these projects as part of their academic tasks. Other programmers are employees of companies who value open-source tools and want to have a say in their direction. Still others are just programmers who are interested in one of the projects that is being developed. All open-source projects are free for the public to download and use. The most successful open-source software projects to date have been the Apache HTTP server and the Tomcat servlet engine.

The primary attraction of open-source projects is the fact that they can be freely downloaded. They are also valuable to the self-taught developer who needs software to learn with. This is also important for anyone who wants to experiment with Web services without making a big investment.

On the other hand, established companies realize that the lowest life-cycle cost is not always associated with the lowest-cost product. In the world of software development, the cost of hiring a staff can far outweigh the cost of acquiring a piece of software. For this reason, it is important to select tools that best fit the mission and budget of your organization.

Toolsets range from bare-boned implementations that expect you to code almost everything by hand, to wizard-laden development environments that can generate many different types of software modules for you.

Axis is closer to the bare-boned model, but that doesn't mean that it is lacking in functionality. The engineers on the Axis team just spend their energy on creating tools for programmers like themselves.

The Axis Architecture

The goal of every Web services development tool is to build a bridge between the SOAP processor and the business logic that is running on the server. Normally, this business logic is kept separate from the SOAP processing logic. Figure 13.1 shows this arrangement.

FIGURE 13.1
The Web service architecture forms a bridge between the incoming SOAP messages and your business logic.

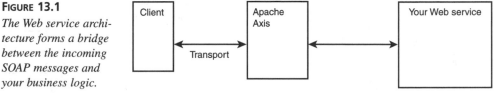

The Apache Axis architecture is built on the foundation of a SOAP engine. This engine accepts SOAP messages, parses them, and calls the appropriate methods and functions in the Web service. At this level of detail, Axis is just like every other Web services engine. The uniqueness of this product, and every other product, lies in how a developer would go about organizing the processing so that the message can be responded to properly.

Apache Axis is organized in a fairly unique way. The following sections introduce you to the most important features of this organization.

Handlers

NEW TERM Axis is built upon the concept of *handlers*. A handler is a piece of code that performs a specific function. One handler may log the message, another may decrypt it, another may make the calls to the legacy system, and so on. These handlers must be written in Java currently, but a C++ version of Axis is in development and might be available by the time you read this. You can think of handlers as method calls, and you would be mostly on target. Be aware, though, that handlers are not called by a `main()` method. They are called by Axis directly.

Chains

NEW TERM Axis *chains* are a special type of handler that can contain other handlers. The handlers that they contain can also be chains, so the concept is very powerful. The execution of these contained chains is ordered, so chains represent a type of Axis control language, but without parameter passing.

NEW TERM A *targeted chain* is a special type of chain that contains more than one entry point. *Transport handlers* are handlers that have both a request side and a response side, which enables a single HTTP handler to both receive and send messages.

13

A targeted chain can act in both roles, however. Figure 13.2 shows how handlers can be used to subdivide the tasks associated with consuming SOAP messages.

FIGURE 13.2

The Axis engine uses chains of handlers to process its messages.

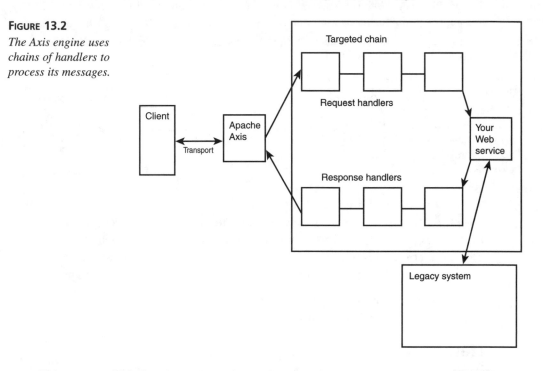

Thus, we could define the Web service as the sum of all the handlers defined to process the incoming messages, combined with the legacy system that does the heavy lifting.

Transport

NEW TERM A *transport* is the communications mechanism that brings messages to and from the Axis engine. Originally, HTTP was the only transport supported by any Web services engine, but support for SMTP, FTP, and JMS has recently begun to appear. Because a SOAP message can be thought of as a stream of characters, it is easy to see how any transport can be used. If you want to send a picture of the new baby to your mother, you could put it on a Web site that travels over HTTP. Alternately, you could put it in a file and ask her to run FTP to retrieve it. Or, you could attach it to an email with SMTP. All these transports have a way to transfer data from one computer to another, but with varying degrees of reliability and speed.

The SOAP Engine

The main entry point into a Web service is the Axis engine. This engine parses the messages and calls the appropriate handlers and chains according to instructions provided by the deployment engineer.

Dispatcher

NEW TERM A *dispatcher* is a special type of handler that is used to separate business logic from handler logic. A special dispatcher, the RPCDispatcher converts SOAP messages to Java objects, and then makes calls to the Web service. This removes all business logic from the handlers, which is a nice design approach. Figure 13.3 shows the relationship between a dispatcher and a Web service.

FIGURE 13.3

The dispatcher separates the business logic from the handlers.

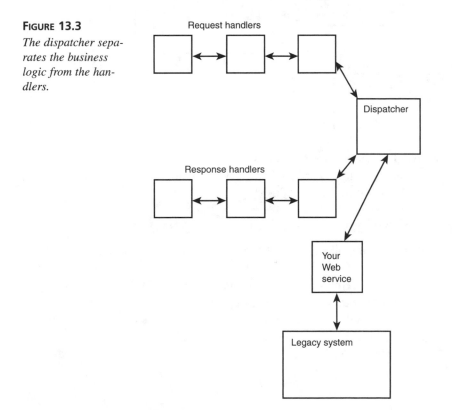

Transport Listeners

NEW TERM A *transport listener* is a servlet that waits for a SOAP message. It is responsible for creating an instance of Axis (or finding an existing instance) and passing the

SOAP message to it. It also tells the Axis engine what transport this message came in over. It is used to return the response to the client. A system that supports three transports would have three transport listeners as shown in Figure 13.4.

FIGURE 13.4

Each supported transport must have a transport listener installed.

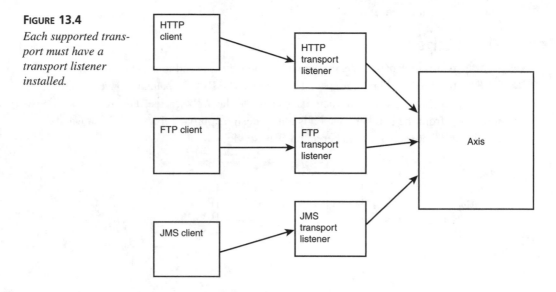

After the transport listener processes the message, it becomes a generic SOAP message. This allows the processing to proceed in the same way for all messages regardless of the transport mechanism employed to send them.

Transport Senders

NEW TERM   When Axis is acting like a client, it needs a way to send the requested SOAP message to a SOAP server. The Axis handlers for doing this are called *transport senders*. If you have a SOAP message that you want to send to a Web service via HTTP, you would use the HTTP transport sender that ships with Axis. This sender opens an HTTP connection to the Web server on the computer that hosts the Web service. It then formats the message with the appropriate HTTP headers, sends it, and waits for a response. Figure 13.5 shows this arrangement.

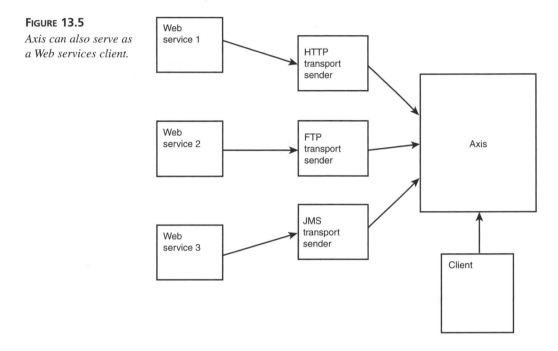

FIGURE 13.5
Axis can also serve as a Web services client.

Other handlers are also allowed to be invoked when sending a message using Axis.

Creating Web Services with Axis

Now that you are familiar with the basic architecture of Axis, you are ready to learn how to use it. It is beyond the scope of this book to teach you how to program with Axis, but a few simple examples can be worth the proverbial thousand words. Our first example illustrates how to create a Web service automatically by taking advantage of a special Axis facility. Listing 13.1 shows a Java class for doing math.

LISTING 13.1   The ArithmeticProcessor.java File

```
public class ArithmeticProcessor
{
    public int add(int input1, int input2)
    {
        return input1 + input2;
    }

    public int subtract(int input1, int input2)
    {
```

13

LISTING 13.1   continued

```
      return input1 - input2;
   }

   public int multiply(int input1, int input2)
   {
      return input1 * input2;
   }

   public int divide(int input1, int input2)
   {
      if (input2 != 0)
      {
         return input1/input2;
      }else
      {
         return -1000;
      }
   }
}
```

Our sample class is called ArithmeticProcessor.

```
public class ArithmeticProcessor
```

The first Web service method is called add. It returns an integer value when it completes. In this case, the add() method will need two integer parameters. It will add them together and return them as an int value:

```
public int add(int input1, int input2)
{
   return input1 + input2;
}
```

The subtract() and multiply() methods are similar to the add() method; except the math operations are different:

```
public int subtract(int input1, int input2)
{
   return input1 - input2;
}

public int multiply(int input1, int input2)
{
   return input1 * input2;
}
```

The divide() method is also different in that it checks for a divide-by-zero situation before proceeding:

```
public int divide(int input1, int input2)
{
   if (input2 != 0)
   {
     return input1/input2;
   }else
   {
     return -1000;
   }
}
```

Now that we have a class, let's turn it into a Web service. The easiest way to do that is by renaming it and storing it in a special directory under Axis.

> You might want to run these programs for yourself. If so, you will need to install Apache Tomcat and Apache Axis on your computer before you can run them. Appendix A, "Installing Apache Tomcat and Axis," provides step-by-step instructions on how to download and install this software.

Axis provides a really simple way to turn this class into a Web service by changing its name and storing it in a special directory. The following procedure does this:

1. Rename the file ArithmeticProcessor.java to ArithmeticProcessor.jws; jws stands for Java Web service.

2. Move the file into <axis-installation-directory>. (On our test machine running Windows XP, this directory is C:\Program Files\Apache Tomcat 4.0\webapps\axis.)

That's it! For simple Web services, this is all you have to do to make your Web service available to the world.

Creating a Client for an Axis Web Service

13

Now that we have a server, we need a client to test it. Unfortunately, there is no two-step method for creating clients in Axis. If you are a programmer, however, the Axis approach only requires that you learn a few new classes and methods. Listing 13.2 shows a client that can access our ArithmeticProcessor Web service.

LISTING 13.2   The ArithmeticClient.java File

```
//Use the import statement to tell what packages these classes
//can be found in

import org.apache.axis.client.Call;
import org.apache.axis.client.Service;
import org.apache.axis.encoding.XMLType;
import org.apache.axis.utils.Options;
import javax.xml.rpc.ParameterMode;
import java.net.URL;

public class ArithmeticClient
{
  //A main method is the entry point for this program

  public static void main(String[] args) throws Exception
  {
    //The Options class is a container for the
    // inputs on the command line
    Options options = new Options(args);

    //An endpoint is the URL of the web service
    String endpointString = "http://localhost:" +
     options.getPort() + "/axis/ArithmeticProcessor.jws";

    //The args are the command line arguments
    args = options.getRemainingArgs();

    //check to see if the right number of args were passed in
    if (args == null || args.length != 3 )
    {
      System.err.println("Wrong number of args");
      return;
    }

    //The first arg is the name of the method to call
    String methodName = args[0];

    //The other two args are the values to be combined
    Integer i1 = new Integer(args[1]);
    Integer i2 = new Integer(args[2]);


    //The Service object will contain a handle
    //to the web service
    Service service1 = new Service();

    //The Call object will contain a handle to one call
    // to the web service
```

LISTING 13.2   continued

```
        Call  callOne  =  (Call)service1.createCall();

        //The endpoint is really a URL
        URL endpoint = new URL(endpointString);

        //tell the Call object what endpoint to access
        callOne.setTargetEndpointAddress(endpoint);

        //tell the Call object what method to call
        callOne.setOperationName(methodName);

        //Set up the parameter types and the return type
        callOne.addParameter("op1", XMLType.XSD_INT,
                                ParameterMode.IN);
        callOne.addParameter("op2", XMLType.XSD_INT,
                                ParameterMode.IN);
        callOne.setReturnType( XMLType.XSD_INT );

        //make the call with the invoke() method
        Integer ret = (Integer)callOne.invoke(
                            new Object[] { i1, i2 });

        //Print the result on the screen
        System.out.println("The result is : " + ret);
    }
}
```

NEW TERM   In Java, import statements clear up any possible name conflicts by stating clearly what *packages* each imported class comes from:

```
import org.apache.axis.client.Call;
import org.apache.axis.client.Service;
import org.apache.axis.encoding.XMLType;
import org.apache.axis.utils.Options;
import javax.xml.rpc.ParameterMode;
import java.net.URL;
```

The `main()` method is the entry point into a Java program:

```
public static void main(String[] args) throws Exception
```

The `Options` class is a container for the inputs on the command line:

```
Options options = new Options(args);
```

13

The endpointString is a string version of the Internet address of the Web service:

```
String endpointString = "http://localhost:" +
    options.getPort() + "/axis/ArithmeticProcessor.jws";
```

The first argument is the name of the method to call:

```
String methodName = args[0];
```

The other two arguments are the values to be combined:

```
Integer i1 = new Integer(args[1]);
Integer i2 = new Integer(args[2]);
```

The Service object will contain a handle to the Web service. The Service and Call objects are always present:

```
Service service1 = new Service();
```

The Call object represents one call to the Web service:

```
Call  callOne  = (Call)service1.createCall();
```

The endpoint is really a URL object that points to the Web service:

```
URL endpoint = new URL(endpointString);
```

We have to tell the Call object what endpoint to access:

```
callOne.setTargetEndpointAddress(endpoint);
```

Next, we tell the Call object what method to call:

```
callOne.setOperationName(methodName);
```

We have to set the parameter types and the return type so that our program will not be confused as to what types they are intended to be:

```
callOne.addParameter("op1", XMLType.XSD_INT, ParameterMode.IN);
callOne.addParameter("op2", XMLType.XSD_INT, ParameterMode.IN);
callOne.setReturnType( XMLType.XSD_INT );
```

Next, we make the call with the invoke() method:

```
Integer ret = (Integer)callOne.invoke(new Object[] { i1, i2 });
```

Finally, we print the result on the screen:

```
System.out.println("The result is : " + ret);
```

To run this program, you must first compile it by issuing the following command:

```
javac ArithmeticClient.java
```

To run the program, you type in the following:

```
java ArithmeticClient -p8080 add 2 5
```

The java command means to run the program. ArithmeticClient is the name of the class containing the main() method. -p1880 is the port number of your Tomcat server. (The default is 8080.) add is the name of the method to run. 2 and 5 are the two numbers that you want added.

The result of running this command with Tomcat listening on port 1880 is shown here:

```
java ArithmeticClient -p1880 add 2 5
```

A session that runs all these methods is shown here:

```
C:\projects>java ArithmeticClient -p1880 add 2 5
The result is : 7

C:\projects>java ArithmeticClient -p1880 subtract 6 3
The result is : 3

C:\projects>java ArithmeticClient -p1880 multiply 7 4
The result is : 28

C:\projects>java ArithmeticClient -p1880 divide 8 4
The result is : 2
```

Notice that the same service is run each time, but with a different method called.

Summary

This hour has introduced you to the architecture of one popular Web services engine, Apache Axis. You learned the basic concepts of how Axis handles Web service requests. Following that, you learned how to create a simple Web service and deploy it in Axis.

Finally, you learned how to create a client in Java that can call the methods in the service and receive a response.

13

Q&A

Q If open-source products are available for no cost, how can other vendors charge money for theirs?

A Open-source software tends to be programmer oriented. Vendors that charge money for their products normally offer more of a wizard-style interface with more generated code.

Q Is Apache Axis ready for production development, or is it just for lab demos?

A Axis is a serious product. IBM's WebSphere Application Developer product is built on the Apache SOAP/AXIS foundation.

Workshop

This section is designed to help you anticipate possible questions, review what you've learned, and begin learning how to put your knowledge into practice.

Quiz

1. What is an open-source product?
2. What do the letters in Axis stand for?
3. What is a SOAP engine?
4. What is a handler?

Quiz Answers

1. Open-source products are the result of software projects that are staffed by volunteers. These products are free to use.
2. It stands for Apache Extensible Interaction System.
3. A SOAP engine sends and receives messages in SOAP format. Normally, a program calls the engine's API via methods. The engine translates the programming language calls into SOAP.
4. Handlers are pieces of Java code that are called by Axis.

Activities

1. Download and install Apache Tomcat and Axis according to the instructions that you find in Appendix A.
2. Type in the `ArithmeticProcessor` class, rename it, and store it in the file structure of Axis.
3. Type in the `ArithemticClient` class and compile it.
4. Run the `ArithmeticClient` program and prove to yourself that it works.

Hour **14**

Creating Web Services with Java

The Java Web Services Developer Pack is a toolkit provided by Sun to demonstrate how to build Web services solutions using Java. The toolkit is meant for teaching purposes, not production use. Sun is in the process of rolling many of this pack's API's and features into an upcoming release of the J2EE toolkit. It is useful to see how Sun's toolset works as many of the other vendor's tools build on the principles found in this tool suite. In this hour, you will see

- What is included in the Java Web services Developer Pack
- How to build Web services solutions by utilizing the Java Web Services Developer Pack
- How to deploy and register your service with the provided Tomcat server so that it can be used by clients
- How to write a simple client that can interact with your new service

What's Included in the Java Web Services Developer Pack

As you've seen in previous hours, Web services can be built using a variety of languages on both the server side where the service resides and on the client side. In an effort to help jump-start the adoption of Web services, Sun has created the Java Web Services Developer Pack. This toolkit provides everything needed to build and deploy Java-based Web services solutions. It is meant to serve as the reference implementation for all other Java-based Web services. As such, it is not meant to replace a full-on commercial implementation, only to provide a basis for learning and a pure implementation of the Web services specifications.

See Appendix B, "Installing the Java Web Services Developer Pack," for information on how to download and install the Java Web services Developer Pack.

The Java Web Services Developer Pack contains a number of tools for building Web services. These include the Apache Tomcat servlet engine (upon which your Web service will run) and the Jakarta-ant tool (which is a tool similar to the Unix "make" tool). Because ant is packaged, we'll use that to handle all of the build and deployment process in this hour.

The toolkit also packages together a number of Java extension libraries that are used to process various pieces of the Web services suite. It's not really important to know too much about these APIs because the tools found in the toolkit will abstract away much of their use. Instead, just know that they're there, and what they do at a high level. These APIs include

- **Java API for XML Processing (JAXP)**—Provides a standardized interface for different types of XML parsers. By writing to this API, the underlying XML parser can be switched out for ones with different performance and memory characteristics without forcing a change in user code.

- **Java API for XML-based RPC (JAX-RPC)**—Gives developers the hooks needed to build Web applications and Web services incorporating XML-based RPC functionality according to the Simple Object Access Protocol (SOAP) 1.1 specification. Typically, this is the API that you'll use the most for building Web services.

- **The Java API for XML Messaging (JAXM)**—Provides much of the underlying code needed to create SOAP messages and perform the communication between systems.

- **The SOAP with Attachments API for Java (SAAJ)**—Enables developers to produce and consume messages conforming to the SOAP 1.1 specification and SOAP with Attachments note.

- **The Java API for XML Registries (JAXR)**—Gives a standard Java API for accessing different kinds of XML registries. We'll use this API when communicating with a UDDI or an ebXML registry.

- **The Java Architecture for XML Binding (JAXB)**—Makes XML easy to use by compiling an XML schema into one or more Java classes.

In addition to these APIs, the toolkit includes the Java servlet and Java Server Pages (JSP) APIs. These are not directly needed for building Web services, but are supported by the Tomcat engine.

> If you'd like to dig deeper into the Java Web Services Developer Pack, a tutorial is available at `http://java.sun.com/webservices/docs/1.0/ tutorial/index.html`.

The Java Web Services Developer Pack also includes several support tools that are used to help with the creation of the interface code. Sun refers to these pieces of code as ties (the Service side module) and stubs (the client side modules). Figure 14.1 shows how the system is structured.

FIGURE 14.1

The Java Web Services Developer Pack structure for JAX-RPC service communications.

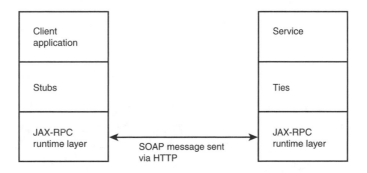

NEW TERM The ties and stubs are generated by a packaged set of tools called wsdeploy and wscompile, respectively. wsdeploy examines the methods found in your service and creates a series of classes that handle the unmarshaling of the passed in SOAP

14

message, and the marshaling of the return data. The WSDL file is created by this tool as well. It also builds a wrapper servlet that your service runs within. This servlet, along with your service code, composes a *Web Application Archive (WAR)* file that will be deployed to the Tomcat server.

The wscompile tool works by looking at the WSDL file for the specified service. It examines the XML descriptors in that file to generate a set of proxy classes that will handle the communications to the service and the marshaling of all method calls. In essence, wsdeploy and wscompile are conjugates of each other. Together, these tools take a lot of the manual labor out of building the Web service interconnects. Without them, you'd have to write all the code to build up the XML SOAP envelopes, consume them, and convert the data to and from Java objects. This would require much more intimate knowledge of the API's included in the pack and adds a lot more complexity to the development process.

The pack directly supports arguments of the data types shown in Table 14.1.

TABLE 14.1   Supported Types

Group of Types	Types That Are Supported
Primitives	Boolean, Byte, Double, Float, Int, Long, Short.
Class versions of the primitives	Boolean, Byte, Double, Float, Integer, Long, Short, String, BigDecimal, BigInteger, Calendar, Date.
Collections	ArrayList, LinkedList, Stack, Vector, HashMap, HashTable, Properties, TreeMap, HashSet, TreeSet.
User-created classes as long as they conform to the following rules	It must have a public default constructor. It must not implement (either directly or indirectly) the java.rmi.Remote interface. Its fields must be supported JAX-RPC types. The class can contain public, private, or protected fields. For its value to be passed (or returned) during a remote call, a field must meet these requirements: A public field cannot be final or transient. A nonpublic field must have corresponding getter and setter methods.
JavaBeans	Must conform to the same rules as user classes. Must also have getter and setter methods for every bean property, and the properties must be supported types from the previous lists.
Arrays of any of the preceding types	Single or multidimensional.

Now that you've seen what's included in the pack, let's start looking at how to build a Web service with it.

Building a Simple Web Service

Building a Web service with the Java Web Services Developer Pack is actually quite easy. Only two files must be built. The first is an interface that lists the methods that can be called by clients. The second is a class that implements that interface.

We'll use the following example to demonstrate the procedure involved. Let's say that you want to write a service that will process credit card approvals. To keep things simple, we'll say that any credit card ending in an even number is considered valid and any card with an odd number is invalid. (This obviously isn't true in real life; we're just simplifying the problem for demonstration purposes.) In order to process the card, we'll need to know the card number. We'll send back a true if it's valid—false if it's invalid. In such a system, our interface class would look like Listing 14.1.

LISTING 14.1   Credit Card Validation Web Service Interface

```
package ch14;

import java.rmi.Remote;
import java.rmi.RemoteException;

public interface CreditValidatorInterface extends Remote
{
  public boolean validateCard(String cardnumber)
        throws RemoteException;
}
```

You might notice that we make use of the RMI packages. This is actually fairly typical in Java systems that perform remote method calls—regardless of the underlying communication protocols.

You'll also notice that our method has to throw a RemoteException. This (or a subclass of it) must be used in order to communicate problems back to the client.

Once we're done building the interface, we then need to build a class that implements the interface. We'll do that using the code in Listing 14.2.

14

LISTING 14.2   Credit Card Validation Web Service Implementation Class

---

```
package ch14;

import java.rmi.Remote;
import java.rmi.RemoteException;

public class CreditValidator implements CreditValidatorInterface
{
  public boolean validateCard(String cardnumber)
        throws RemoteException
  {
    long cardnum = (new Long(cardnumber)).longValue();
    if(cardnum %2 ==0)
        return true;
    else
        return false;
  }
}
```

As you can see, we kept the Web service's code very simple. We read in the card number, divide it by 2, and see if there's any remainder. If there isn't, it's valid.

To compile this code and build the directory structure we need for the project, open a command prompt and navigate to the ch14 directory. Then run the following command:

```
ant compile-server
```

Provided that there are no compile errors, the code will be turned into Java .class byte-code files and placed into the build/shared subdirectory.

Now that we have our service, we need to make use of the tool that comes with the pack to create tie classes that will perform the conversion to and from SOAP for us.

Deploying and Registering the Service

Now that we have the code for our service, we next need to package and deploy it so that it can be used by clients. In order to do this, we must provide a couple of additional files and place our compiled code into a package.

First, we'll need to create the following directory structure inside our ch14 directory:

```
WEB-INF\
        classes\
                ch14\
```

Don't bother doing this yet because we have an ant command to take care of this for us, which we'll use in a moment.

Next, we need to create two files that will describe how to find and work with our service. Both of these files will need to be placed into the WEB-INF directory.

First, create a file called web.xml. This file is used by the container to identify the service and set up some properties such as the session timeout information. This file mainly is used by the servlet container for application management. The web.xml file can be seen in Listing 14.3.

LISTING 14.3 The Web.xml File

```
<?xml version="1.0" encoding="UTF-8"?>
<!DOCTYPE web-app PUBLIC
"-//Sun Microsystems, Inc.//DTD Web Application 2.3//EN"
    "http://java.sun.com/j2ee/dtds/web-app_2_3.dtd">
<web-app>
   <display-name>Credit Card Validation Application</display-name>
   <description>A web application containing a simple
JAX-RPC endpoint</description>
   <session-config>
      <session-timeout>60</session-timeout>
   </session-config>
</web-app>
```

The second file we need to create is specific to the Java Web Services Development Pack. This file details which file contains the interface and which is the implementation. It links this data to the Web service that we described in the web.xml file. You can see the jaxrpc-ri.xml file in Listing 14.4.

LISTING 14.4 The Jaxrpc-ri.xml File Links the Class Files to the Service

```
<?xml version="1.0" encoding="UTF-8"?>
<webServices
    xmlns="http://java.sun.com/xml/ns/jax-rpc/ri/dd"
    version="1.0"
    targetNamespaceBase="http://com.test/wsdl"
    typeNamespaceBase="http://com.test/types"
    urlPatternBase="/ws">

    <endpoint
        name="MyCreditValidator"
        displayName="Credit Card Validator"
```

14

LISTING 14.4   continued

```
          description="A simple web service"
          interface="ch14.CreditValidatorInterface"
          implementation="ch14.CreditValidator"/>

      <endpointMapping
          endpointName="MyCreditValidator"
          urlPattern="/creditcard"/>

</webServices>
```

The important lines are the interface and implementation ones. Notice that we listed the fully qualified names of our interface and service implementation classes here.

You'll notice that we named the endpoint value "MyCreditValidator". It is very important that you don't try to name it CreditValidator. Doing that will cause problems because when the ties and proxy classes are created by the automated tools later, they will be named the same as our class files, which will confuse the system. For the sake of simplicity, we'll just put "My" at the front of our endpoint names. You can really call the endpoint anything that you want. As long as the endpoint isn't the same as the name of an existing class, you'll be safe. If you don't, you'll end up with two .class files with the same name, which will confuse the Java runtime engine.

To build the directory structure and get the two .xml files into the correct spot, run the following command:

```
ant setup-web-inf
```

This will build the directory structure and copy in the compiled bytecode files, as well as the web.xml and jaxrpc-ri.xml files, into the proper places.

Now that we have all the files that compose our Web service, we next need to package it into a WAR file. To do this, we execute the following command from the ch14 directory:

```
ant package
```

This will create a new file named credit-portable.war that contains our server code and the two XML files and places it into the dist subdirectory.

Now that we have our service, we need to create the WSDL listing that will explain to clients how to communicate with it. To simplify this process, Sun has provided a tool called wsdeploy. This tool reads the information in the javarpc-ri.xml file. wsdeploy examines information in the javarpc-ri.xml file and generates the needed interfaces and tie classes. The following ant command will call wsdeploy, which creates the ties and places them, as well as the contents of our WAR file, into a new WAR file (which is the one we will eventually deploy). To perform this step, type the following:

```
ant process-war
```

After running this command, you will find that a new file named credit-deployable.war has been created in the dist directory. If you open that file using a tool such as WinZip, you'll see that a large number of other files have been created and added to the archive, including a CreditValidator.wsdl file. These files are the tie interface files.

Now that we have a deployable WAR file, we can go ahead and deploy it and confirm that it's correct. Make sure that you have Tomcat running. Then use the following command:

```
ant deploy
```

This will copy the credit-deployable.war file to the <jwsdp_home>\work\Standard Engine\localhost directory (where <jwsdp_home> is the directory in which the Java Web Services Developer Pack is installed) and will register the new service with the Tomcat server.

Let's confirm that everything is good so far. Start up the Tomcat Application server. (On Windows machines, this can be done through the Start menu.) Once Tomcat is running, open a new browser window and point it to

```
http://localhost:8080/credit-deployable/creditcard
```

If everything is working correctly, you should get a screen that looks like the one in Figure 14.2.

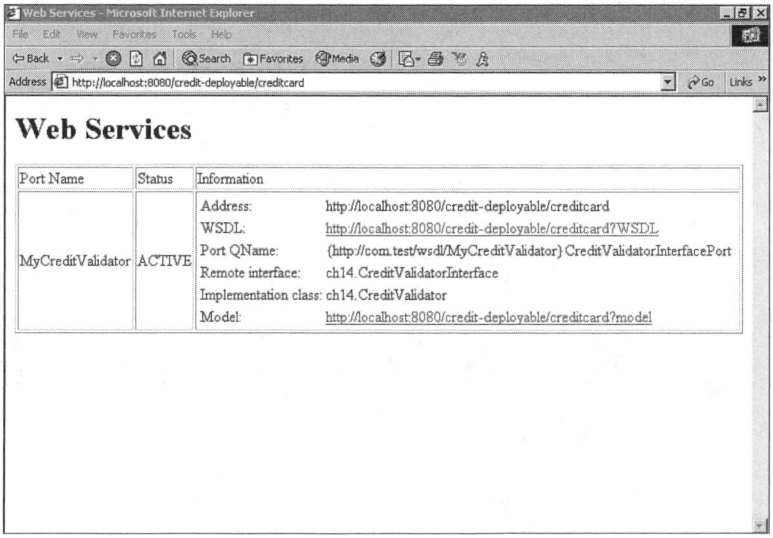

FIGURE 14.2

The deployed Credit Card Web service.

14

Creating a Client to Attach to the Service

Now that we have built what we need for the service, let's concern ourselves with the client side. Before we can do that though, we need to build the necessary stubs so that we can communicate with the service in the expected manner. We'll need one more XML file to do this. In the ch14 directory, create a new file named config.xml. It needs to look like Listing 14.5.

LISTING 14.5   The Config.xml File Details Where the Wscompile Tool Can Find the WSDL File

```
<?xml version="1.0" encoding="UTF-8"?>
<configuration
    xmlns="http://java.sun.com/xml/ns/jax-rpc/ri/config">
  <wsdl location="http://localhost:8080/credit-deployable/creditcard?WSDL"
    packageName="ch14"/>
</configuration>
```

Now that we've got the config file, we'll make use of another tool provided for us called wscompile. Again, we have this process automated for us in the ant build script.

```
ant generate-stubs
```

You'll notice that a number of new .class files are now created in the build\client\ch14 directory. These are the stubs generated by the wscompile program. Wscompile used the WSDL file specified in the config.xml file to determine what interface classes would be needed and created them. We can now use those in our client program to perform the communication for us. If we were building a client to talk to some other service, we'd need to list it in the config.xml file and perform a similar action to get the stubs to talk to that service.

Next we'll build a simple client that will take a credit card number, pass it to the service, and then report the results from the service. In a real system, you'd probably make this part of a shopping cart transaction system, but for simplicity's sake, we'll just hard code a number in. Listing 14.6 shows the client.

LISTING 14.6   A Client That Uses the Credit Card Processing Service

```
package ch14;
import javax.xml.rpc.Stub;

public class ShoppingClient
{
```

LISTING 14.6 continued

```java
public static void main(String[] args)
{
    try
    {
        String cardnumber = "123456";
        Stub stub = createProxy();
        CreditValidatorInterface cardvalidator =
            (CreditValidatorInterface) stub;
        boolean results = cardvalidator.validateCard(cardnumber);
        if(results)
            System.out.println("Card was valid...");
        else
            System.out.println("Card was rejected!");
    }
    catch (Exception ex)
    {
        ex.printStackTrace();
    }
}

private static Stub createProxy()
{
    return (Stub)(new
     MyCreditValidator_Impl().getCreditValidatorInterfacePort());
}
}
```

Before we compile this example, let's discuss the structure of the code a bit.

```java
import javax.xml.rpc.Stub;
```

This line tells the java compiler that we're going to be using a class called Stub from the RPC package.

```java
Stub stub = createProxy()
```

This line calls a private method responsible for setting up the linkage between our client and the stub that will handle communication to the server for us. The guts of that method are shown here:

```java
return (Stub)(new MyCreditValidator_Impl().getCreditValidatorInterfacePort());
```

Here we create a new Stub called MyCreditValidator_Impl (which the wscompile tool built for us) and tell it to make a linkage to the server. How this works really isn't important. Just follow the template in your own code, replacing CreditValidator and CreditValidatorInterface with the names of your own implementation class and interface.

14

Back in the `main()` of our client, we then see

```
CreditValidatorInterface cardvalidator = (CreditValidatorInterface) stub;
```

This line takes the stub and converts it into a reference for a `CardValidatorInterface` so that we can work with it pretty much as though it were a local class. Finally, we make our method call to the service to find out whether the card is valid:

```
boolean results = cardvalidator.validateCard(cardnumber);
```

As you can see, this looks no different than it would if we were referencing a local object and making a call to it. That's the beauty of Web services. With just a little extra work, we get a distributed system!

To compile this code, run the following `ant` command from the ch14 root directory:

```
ant compile-client
```

We then need to package the client into a usable (and easier to distribute) package. Type the following command:

```
ant jar-client
```

If everything worked correctly, you'll find a new jar file in the dist directory called ch14-client.jar.

Okay, now is the time to try out our client. Make sure that you have Tomcat running, and you might want to reconfirm that your service is deployed (see earlier in this hour on how to do that). To run the code, just type

```
ant run
```

You should get the following output if everything worked correctly:

```
[echo] Running the ch14.ShoppingClient program...
[java] Card was valid...
```

There you are! You've just built and deployed a Web service and hooked into it. You'll notice that it took what seemed like a long period of time (several seconds) for our simple little test to run even though both the client and the server were on the same machine. Although the `CardValidator` object might appear to be local to the client, it still had to go through the XML conversion process, a network connection, and so on. These steps take time.

Summary

This hour walks you through the Java Web Services Developer Pack. We examined what Java packages are in the pack and briefly discussed their purposes.

Next we stepped through a simple Web service example that validated credit card numbers. We saw how the Web Services Developer Pack takes care of building the tie and stubs for you, leaving you to worry more about the business logic. We then deployed our service to the Tomcat App Server that came packaged in the pack.

Finally, we built a client to interface with our service. We saw that with very few changes, we can reference a remote class as though it were local. We also saw that there are performance considerations when accessing remote objects through Web services.

Q&A

Q Does the Java Web Service Developer Pack support message mode SOAP calls?

A Yes, but it requires the direct manipulation of the SOAP envelope and familiarity of the JAXM API. With the JAXM API, the developer must manually build up the SOAP envelope request, make connections, and handle exceptions. This can be a powerful capability, but also requires much more work on the developer's part. In general, if you can use the RPC format, do so, and take advantage of the tools provided in the kit for building ties, stubs, and WSDL.

Q Is a UDDI server provided in the pack?

A There is a demonstration UDDI server in the pack. It is referred to as the Registry Server. You can write clients that will query this registry server by using the JAXR API. The included registry is not meant for production scale use though.

Workshop

This section is designed to help you anticipate possible questions, review what you've learned, and begin learning how to put your knowledge into practice.

Quiz

1. What tool builds the WSDL file for you?
2. What is your Web service run within on the Tomcat server?
3. What WSDP-specific file is used by the wsdeploy tool to generate the ties and WSDL file?

14

4. What type of exception must all service methods throw?

5. What is contained in the Java Web Services Developer Pack?

6. What's the difference between a stub and a tie?

Quiz Answers

1. Wsdeploy.

2. A servlet generated during the wsdeploy process.

3. Javarpc-ri.xml.

4. RemoteException or a subclass of it.

5. A number of API libraries used to work with XML and create SOAP messages, as well as Tomcat, ant, and several other tools for the creation of WSDL files and stubs and ties.

6. A stub is the client-side component that is built from the service's WSDL. A tie is the server-side interface that accepts SOAP messages and converts them for use by the service.

Activity

1. Modify the Web service we built in this hour to make a more realistic credit card transaction processing engine. Make the service track the transactions in a file. Make the client pass not only the card number, but also the cardholder's name and the expiration date. Be sure to verify that the date is past the current date on the server.

Hour **15**

Creating Web Services with .NET

Microsoft, one of the early backers of the Web services concepts and standards, is also one of the vendors who is betting the future on the success of Web services. The .NET platform is designed from the ground up to support the efforts of Web services developers and consumers.

NEW TERM The conversion of almost the entire Microsoft software development toolset to create .NET applications is proof of this commitment. As of this writing, of all the tools in the Visual Studio IDE, only Visual C++ contains an option to generate traditionally compiled executables, which are called *unmanaged applications*.

Visual Studio .NET is a full-featured Integrated Development Environment (IDE). As such, it contains tools to create a large number of different types of Windows and Web applications. In this hour, we will look at the .NET platform and tools from a Web services developer's point of view. You will learn

- About the .NET architecture
- What .NET is and how it is different
- How to create Web services using Visual Basic
- How to create a .NET Web service that passes parameters

Understanding the .NET Architecture

The .NET architecture is a completely new direction in software development for the Microsoft Windows platform. Microsoft has abandoned the traditional DLL approach in favor of a runtime-based system that resembles the approach Sun used when creating Java. In this section, we will look at some of the unique features of this new architecture.

Visual Studio .NET

A Web services development tool must do more than just support standards to be useful. It must facilitate the creation, deployment, scaling, and maintenance of programs written to the Web services standards. One complication that arises from comparing different Web service development tools is that no two tools have exactly the same mission. One might be a bare-boned SOAP engine, whereas another is a full-featured IDE that can produce any number of types of programs in addition to Web services.

NEW TERM One development tool might be free to download, and the other could cost hundreds of dollars. The Visual Studio .NET Integrated Development Environment (VS .NET IDE) contains so many features and software products that it seems unfair to discuss only the aspects of it that pertain to Web services. In addition to Web services projects, the VS .NET IDE allows a programmer to create a C++ program, a Web application, a Web service, a class library, a Windows control library, a Web control library, a console application, or a Windows service. In addition, every one of these projects, except for the compiled (nonmanaged) C++ project, can be created in C++, Visual Basic, or C#.

> C# is a Microsoft platform programming language that has an almost identical syntax to Java. Because it only runs on Windows platforms, it has not made many converts among Java programmers.

The thrust of this hour, however, is the use of Visual Studio to create Web services. In Hour 16, "Creating .NET Web Service Clients," you will learn how to write a Visual Basic program that calls a Web service.

Pros and Cons of Microsoft Tools

15

Microsoft's storied past has divided the developer world into two factions. One faction is composed of developers who have never given any thought to using a Microsoft programming language or product to create Web services. The other faction is composed of developers who have never considered using anything else.

Microsoft detractors offer several reasons for their attitudes—some rational and some emotional. Among the emotional reasons are memories of the wars that Microsoft has participated in with IBM over Windows, with Sun Microsystems over Java, with Netscape over browsers, with WordPerfect over word processing, and so on. The job of a technical author is not to editorialize or to take sides in these issues. Rather, our job is to evaluate product offerings based on their merits, leaving the nonquantifiable parts of the decision making process to the reader.

Ignoring the emotional reasons for not using Microsoft development tools, there have been, in our opinion, real reasons to use them and real reasons to avoid them. Among the many reasons to use them are

- **Ease of use**—Until recently, few other tools in the marketplace provided as nice an IDE as Visual Studio.
- **Cost**—Many developers could afford to purchase their own PC and a copy of Visual Studio. This allowed them to enhance their skill sets in the evenings.
- **Jobs**—Before Java became all the rage, so many more opportunities were available for developers who knew Visual C++ and Visual Basic than for any other language.
- **Documentation**—Microsoft provides reams of documentation on every one of its products.
- **Support**—Microsoft answers the phone.

For these reasons, hordes of developers have become proficient with Microsoft software development. There are also valid reasons for not choosing Microsoft tools:

- **Windows architecture**—Windows has been considered unstable and complicated by developers. Some of this springs from the *Dynamic Link Library (DLL)* architecture. A DLL is a library of function calls loaded into the memory of the computer and shared by multiple applications. Whenever a new software product is installed on a machine, it normally installs the DLL versions that it needs. As a result, the installation of a new product might cause an old product to stop working. In extreme cases, hard drives have been reformatted to get rid of DLL conflicts.

- **Over-engineered tools**—Visual Basic provides so much handholding that developers sometimes felt like they were fighting with the tool in order to get certain tasks accomplished.

- **Strangely engineered tools**—Some tools, like Visual C++, require the use of macros in their Windows application code. The existence of anything mysterious in a program drives software engineers crazy.

- **Unnecessary complication**—Many GUI developers considered the Windows API to be a nightmare. The MFC helped this a little, but only a little.

- **Hardware and operating system monopoly**—Microsoft tools produced code that only ran under Microsoft Windows on X86 machines.

- **Proprietary mindset**—Many developers interpreted Microsoft's opposition to Netscape and Java as being against open standards. The truth of this point is of little importance because the developer community believed it to be true.

This being said, Microsoft has made great strides—both with regard to technology and people's perceptions—in the past few years. Most companies have been known to "throw sharp elbows" at the competition from time to time. In recent years, Microsoft has actively participated in countless efforts to create standards that are truly open and developer driven. The short list includes XML, SOAP, WSDL, and UDDI. On the longer list are many of the emerging specifications for dealing with Web service security, encryption, transactions, business process support, and so on.

Microsoft has also established polite relationships with former enemies. IBM and Microsoft have worked together to write an impressive number of emerging Web service specifications. Recently, Sun Microsystems joined the Web Services Interoperability Organization that Microsoft helped found.

The .NET Runtime

The .NET platform represents a radical departure from the traditional Microsoft approach to software development. In the past, Visual C++ was used to do most of the heavy lifting on Windows machines. Visual C++ is a traditional, compiled language in which machine-level instructions are emitted from the compiler. Although this option is still available in Visual Studio .NET, the preferred approach to writing applications in C++, C#, and Visual Basic is to use the features of the .NET platform. The .NET platform is organized in a way that is similar to the Java platform.

NEW TERM   At the top level, each programmer uses the language that she prefers (for example C#, VB.NET, or managed C++). When the code is compiled, however, it is compiled into a byte-code called *Microsoft Intermediate Language (MSIL)*. Regardless of the language used, the MSIL code generated will be identical if the same functionality is created. This MSIL code is compiled at runtime into CPU instructions and run. Figure 15.1 shows this process.

FIGURE 15.1

Your code is compiled into MSIL code. At runtime, the MSIL code is interpreted into CPU instructions.

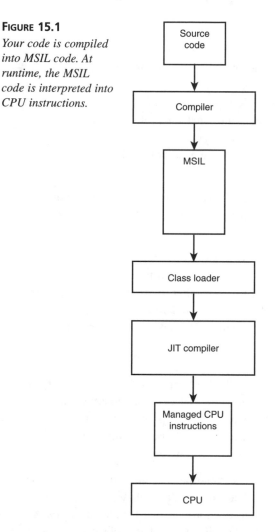

Many of you might notice how similar this approach is to the Java approach. In some ways, this serves as a ratification of the Java architecture. This is good news for the development community.

15

Although it is useful to think of the .NET runtime as similar to the Java Virtual Machine, it would be a mistake to carry the analogy too far. .NET is composed of quite a number of features—some of them have a Java counterpart, whereas others don't.

Common Language Runtime

NEW TERM   The *Common Language Runtime (CLR)* is a software program that can run MSIL code. Because the MSIL code is identical, regardless of the programming language used to write it, languages can interact in ways not possible before. Java applications are, by definition, written in Java. CLR applications can be written in any MSIL-emitting language. Microsoft currently provides three of these languages: C++, C#, and Visual Basic. Third-party vendors have announced their intention to create .NET versions of just about every other language that you ever worked with.

The ability to use several different languages to write Web services is more important to developers who are proficient in other languages. Microsoft has attempted to attract Java developers to .NET by releasing Visual J#, a Java syntax language that is closer to Java than C# is.

The CLR is responsible for tasks such as creating objects, making method calls, opening sockets, performing I/O, and so on. An additional feature of this framework is the theoretical possibility that you could port the CLR to another hardware platform and run it there. Some parts of .NET have been submitted for standardization to ECMA, but this doesn't necessarily mean that other vendors will create versions of it for platforms.

The .NET Framework

Another core part of the .NET architecture is the base framework, or class library. The framework is a set of classes that enable your code to access functionality within the .NET CLR. In addition, many of the classes provide your program with utility functions such as the C-runtime library, the Visual Basic runtime library, or the Java optional downloads (formerly known as standard extensions) provide.

All the classes in the framework start with the namespace System. It contains classes for exception handling, garbage collection, and console I/O, as well as data type conversions, random number generation, and math functions. Many of these classes have a concrete implementation that is instantiated by the .NET CLR. These objects are always available to your code without having to instantiate them. Figure 15.2 shows a graphic representation of the framework.

FIGURE 15.2

The framework provides utility functions as well as runtime services.

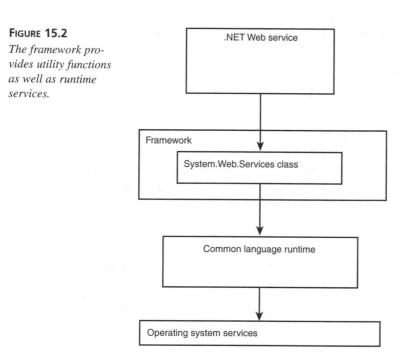

From our point of view, the most important of these classes is the `System.Web.Services` class. This class is imported and used in the creation of Web services. The power of this class is what makes Web service creation so much easier with .NET than with other technologies. This class handles all the SOAP message creation and consumption as the service is communicating with a client. In addition, the client can use this same class to perform SOAP messaging tasks. Table 15.1 shows several of the important `System` classes.

TABLE 15.1   Some Critical System Classes

Class	Purpose
System.Web.Services	Provides client and server support for SOAP-based Web service
System.Timers	Timing services
System.Collections	Collections such as lists, queues, hash tables, and so on
System.Net	Support for networking
System.Threading	Multithreaded programming
System.Drawing	2D Graphics
System.Runtime Serialization	Binary and SOAP encoding
System.Security	Security services
System.Cryptography	Encryption and decryption

Namespaces and Naming Conventions

Literally hundreds of classes are built in to the .NET framework. In addition, you have the opportunity to create new functionality by extending the framework. With this many classes hanging around, naming conflicts are all but certain to occur.

NEW TERM   .NET provides a solution to this problem by borrowing the concept of a namespace from other technologies such as Java and XML schema. A *namespace* is a unique string that is prepended to every classname. This namespace has no effect on visibility, member access, inheritance, security, or binding. The only reason that it exists is to distinguish between identical classnames.

If I create a class called `Printer` and store it in the namespace `Xyz`, the fully qualified name of the class is `Xyz.Printer`. If you create a class named `Printer` and store it in the namespace `Abc`, the real name of the class becomes `Abc.Printer`. A program could include both of these namespaces and never have a problem because the namespaces guarantee uniqueness.

The convention for user-created objects is to place your company name at the top level, followed by intermediate levels of your choice. The last name in the string will be the name that you know your object by. In this way, classes with identical names but from different companies can be distinguished.

For example, if you created a Security class, it could conflict with the `System.Security` class that is included with .NET. To avoid confusion, you could give your Security class a namespace prefix such as `Apex.Security` to make it clear which class is being referenced.

Building a Simple Web Service

ASP.NET is the recommended mechanism for implementing both Web services and Web forms in .NET. When we create a Visual Basic Web services project later in this section, you will see that you are really creating an ASP.NET application.

ASP .NET framework SDK also contains a tool to generate a proxy class that a client application can use to access the Web service.

Now that you have some understanding of the advantages of the .NET platform, let's build a simple Web service. In the best computing book tradition, the first example will be a variation of the Hello World program. The first step in building the Web service is to create a Visual Basic solution. A VB solution is simply a collection of projects. Often, the projects in this collection work together to perform a single task or accomplish a single goal. In other cases, these projects are grouped together for convenience. In our case, we will place all the Web services that we create in the same solution for convenience. You create a solution by selecting the File menu, and then New, followed by Blank Solution. We named our solution WS24Solution.

The next step is to create a Web service by choosing New from the File menu, and then selecting Project. The dialog shown in Figure 15.3 will appear.

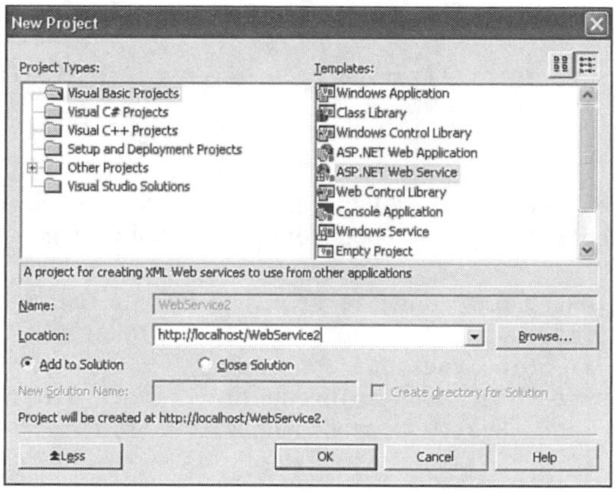

FIGURE 15.3

The New Project dialog allows you to create a Web services project.

Make sure that IIS is running on your machine. Choose ASP .NET Web Service for the project type and set the location as `http://localhost/WebService2`.

> It might seem odd to create an ASP .NET Web service when you really wanted to create a Visual Basic Web service. The reason for this is historical. Prior to .NET, Visual Basic programs had to use the ASP intrinsic objects to communicate via the Web.

Visual Studio will automatically create a dummy program such as the one in Listing 15.1.

LISTING 15.1   The Service1.asmx File

```
Imports System.Web.Services

<WebService(Namespace := "http://tempuri.org/")> _
Public Class Service1
    Inherits System.Web.Services.WebService
```

LISTING 15.1   continued

```
#Region " Web Services Designer Generated Code "

    Public Sub New()
        MyBase.New()

        'This call is required by the Web Services Designer.
        InitializeComponent()

        'Add your own initialization code after the InitializeComponent() call

    End Sub

    'Required by the Web Services Designer
    Private components As System.ComponentModel.IContainer

    'NOTE: The following procedure is required by the Web Services Designer
    'It can be modified using the Web Services Designer.
    'Do not modify it using the code editor.
    <System.Diagnostics.DebuggerStepThrough()> Private Sub InitializeComponent()
        components = New System.ComponentModel.Container()
    End Sub

    Protected Overloads Overrides Sub Dispose(ByVal disposing As Boolean)
        'CODEGEN: This procedure is required by the Web Services Designer
        'Do not modify it using the code editor.
        If disposing Then
            If Not (components Is Nothing) Then
                components.Dispose()
            End If
        End If
        MyBase.Dispose(disposing)
    End Sub

#End Region

    ' WEB SERVICE EXAMPLE
    ' The HelloWorld() example service returns the string Hello World.
    ' To build, uncomment the following lines then save and build the project.
    ' To test this web service, ensure that the .asmx file is the start page
    ' and press F5.
    '
    '<WebMethod()> Public Function HelloWorld() As String
    '   HelloWorld = "Hello World"
    ' End Function

End Class
```

The first line of code declares that we intend to use one of the classes in this framework namespace in this program.

```
Imports System.Web.Services
```

The next line declares the namespace for the project. Normally, you change the namespace name to the URL for your company. It serves to uniquely identify your Web service's name.

```
<WebService(Namespace := "http://tempuri.org/")> _
```

Next comes the declaration of the Web service class. Notice that the declaration must state that it inherits the WebService framework class.

```
Public Class Service1
    Inherits System.Web.Services.WebService
```

Visual Studio automatically generates two methods that you are instructed not to modify. By default, they are created in a region that is collapsed so that you do not see them.

```
Public Sub New()
Protected Overloads Overrides Sub Dispose(ByVal disposing As Boolean)
```

Next, a comment section is provided that contains some sample code, along with instructions on how to run it. You must uncomment this code for the rest of the example to run. The uncommented code looks like this:

```
<WebMethod()> Public Function HelloWorld() As String
    HelloWorld = "Hello World"
  End Function
```

This code represents a very simple Web service. Web services contain no user interface because they run on the server. In order to access their functions, Visual Studio automatically generates a simple Web page for you.

You can run this example by choosing Build Solution from the Build menu, and then pressing F5.

The first thing that you will see is a screen that gives you the opportunity to run the example as shown in Figure 15.4.

If you click on the name of the operation, you will be shown another page that will let you invoke the service by clicking on a button as shown in Figure 15.5.

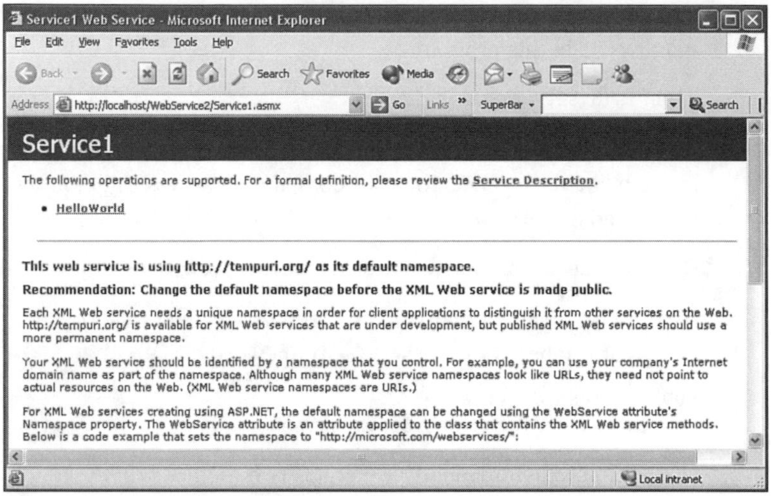

FIGURE 15.4

*Visual Studio gener-
ates a service sum-
mary for you.*

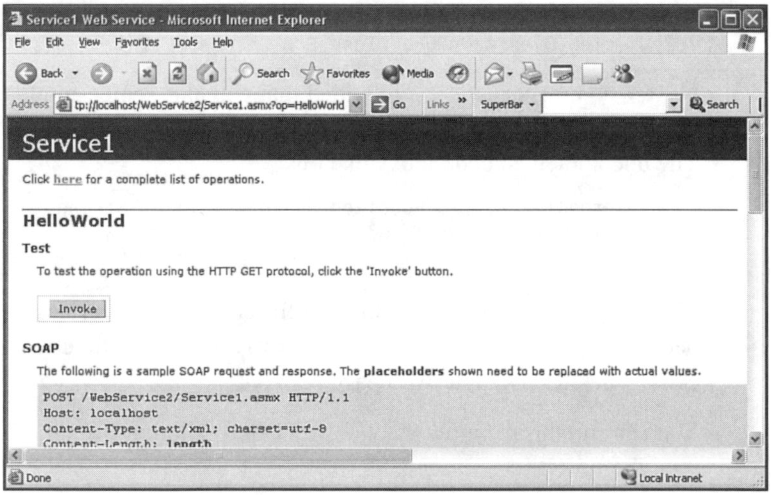

FIGURE 15.5

*By clicking on the
Invoke button, you can
run a client that tests
the operation of the
Web service.*

The result that you get back from doing this may be a little disappointing. It is shown here:

```
<?xml version="1.0" encoding="utf-8" ?>
  <string xmlns="http://tempuri.org/">Hello World</string>
```

Essentially, this is the Hello World string surrounded by enough metadata to allow it to be displayed. You can copy this result into a file called HelloWorld.xml as shown in Listing 15.2.

15

LISTING 15.2 The HelloWorld.xml File

```xml
<?xml version="1.0" encoding="utf-8" ?>
  <string xmlns="http://tempuri.org/">Hello World</string>
```

If you run this example in a Netscape browser, you will see the result shown in Figure 15.6.

FIGURE 15.6

You can display the result of running the Web service in a browser.

The generated client is not particularly useful for anything other than verifying that the service works. Hour 16 provides several examples of more interesting clients.

Creating Your Own Web Service

Creating your own Web service is only slightly more complicated than writing any other Visual Basic subroutines or functions. The next Web service that we will create takes advantage of a special feature of Visual Basic .NET—the capability to pass values to a Web service by reference.

As you recall, when a parameter is passed by value, a copy of the parameter value is passed. When it is passed by reference, the actual location of the value is passed, allowing the called method to modify code in the original program. Because Web services are called via a wire protocol and not by passing addresses, it is clear that values cannot really be passed by reference. However, the trickery available in the .NET CLR enables Visual Basic Web services to simulate a call by reference.

We will work an example to see how this works. Create a new Web services project under the WS24 solution and call it RefService1. When the default `Service1` class is created, rename it to `ByRefService1` by changing the classname in the code and in the Solution Explorer window on the right, as shown in Figure 15.7.

FIGURE 15.7

You can rename the Web service by changing both the classname and the name in the Solution Explorer.

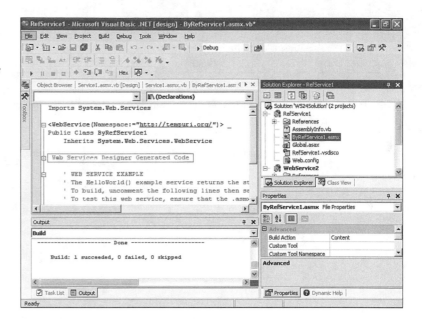

Next, delete all the Hello World code out of the class and modify the code until it looks like Listing 15.3.

LISTING 15.3   The ByRefService1.asmx File

```
Imports System.Web.Services

<WebService(Namespace:="http://tempuri.org/")> _
Public Class ByRefService1
  Inherits System.Web.Services.WebService

#Region " Web Services Designer Generated Code "
#End Region
<WebMethod()> Public Function PassByRef(ByRef int1 As Integer,
       ➡ByRef dateArg As Date) As String
       int1 = int1 + 300
       dateArg = dateArg.AddYears(1)
       Return "Finshed changing the parameters"
  End Function

End Class
```

Several things are different now. The name of the class is different, though it still inherits the `System.Web.Services.WebService` class.

```
Public Class ByRefService1
```

The Function is different also. In this example, two parameters are both marked with the ByRef qualifier, which means that they are to be passed by reference.

```
<WebMethod()> Public Function PassByRef(ByRef int1 As Integer,
   ➥ ByRef dateArg As Date) As String
```

Notice that the return value of the function is of a different type than either of the parameters. Before you can run this example from the IDE with the F5 key, you first need to alter the solution's properties to start this project. Select the solution's properties by right-clicking on the solution name and choosing Properties from the context menu that appears. The dialog shown in Figure 15.8 will appear.

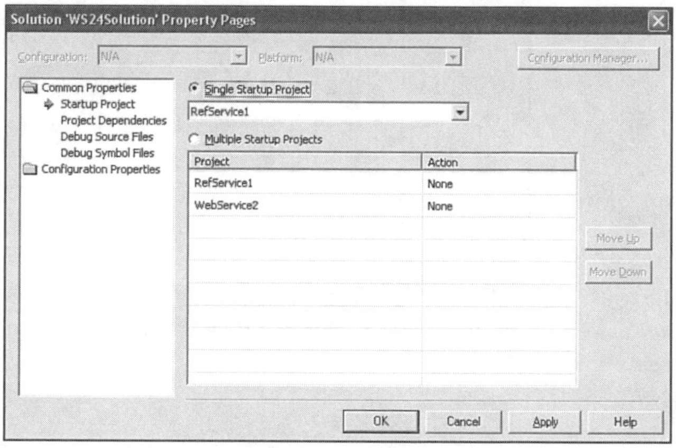

FIGURE 15.8

You change the name of the startup project in the Solution Properties dialog.

Change the properties to use RefServices1 as the Single Startup project, and then click the OK button. Next, press the F5 key to try and run the project. When the window appears, click on the PassByRef hyperlink. A window that looks like Figure 15.9 will appear.

Because of the complexity of the parameters, the HTTP Get protocol cannot be used. SOAP is the only choice of protocols for this service. An example of the SOAP message needed to communicate with this Web service is listed on the page in Figure 15.10.

The response will look something like the one in Figure 15.11.

Figures 15.10 and 15.11 appear at the bottom of the same window as shown in Figure 15.9.

FIGURE **15.9**
No automatic test page can be generated when complex parameters are passed.

FIGURE **15.10**
The Web service can be called using a SOAP message that looks like this.

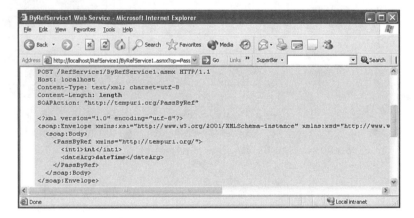

FIGURE 15.11
A SOAP message is used to make the call.

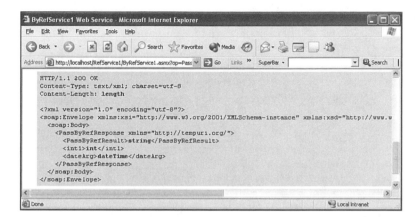

The SOAP messages are important if you are communicating with this service via a non-.NET language. Luckily for us, we can create a .NET project that can call this Web service's methods without having to dive into SOAP at all.

Create a client by creating a new Visual Basic Windows application. In that project, create a single form. Use the toolbox to add one button on the form named btnPassByRef. Modify the code to match Listing 15.4, choose the Project menu, and then Add Web Reference to make the association between this project and the Web service that we want to use. Figure 15.12 shows what this dialog looks like.

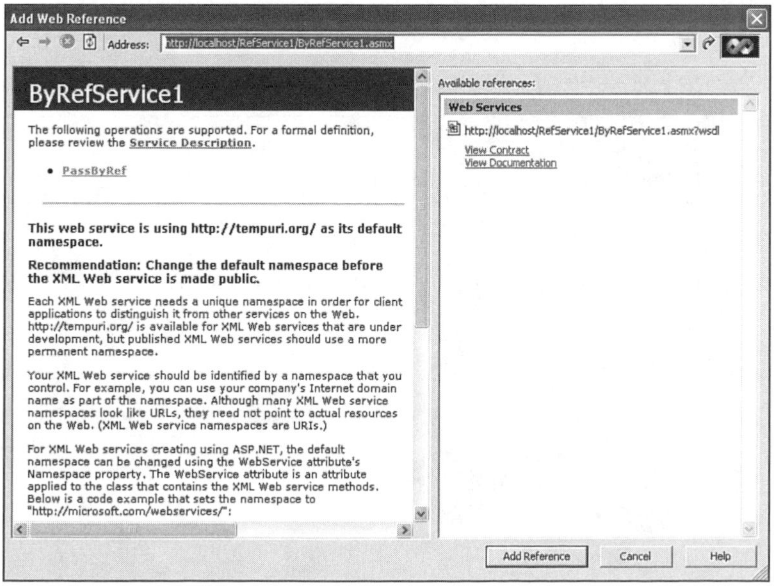

FIGURE 15.12
We must add a Web reference to the project before we can call its methods.

You might have to manually enter the URL of the Web service when the dialog appears.

Now we are ready to add some code. Enter the code from Listing 15.4 into our project.

LISTING 15.4   The Form1.vb File

```
Public Class Form1
    Inherits System.Windows.Forms.Form

#Region " Windows Form Designer generated code "
#End Region

Private Sub btnPassByRef_Click(ByVal sender As System.Object,
        ➥ByVal e As System.EventArgs) Handles btnPassByRef.Click
        Dim WS As New localhost.ByRefService1()

        MsgBox("Button Clicked")

        Dim D As Date = Now()
        Dim Int As Integer = 100
        Dim Str As String
        Str = WS.PassByRef(Int, D)
        Console.WriteLine("Return value = " & Str)
        Console.WriteLine("Integer arg = " & Int)
        Console.WriteLine("Date arg = " & D)

    End Sub
End Class
```

In the event handler for the button, we first declare an instance of the Web service.

```
Dim WS As New localhost.ByRefService1()
```

Following that, we display a message box just to provide assurance that the procedure ran.

```
MsgBox("Button Clicked")
```

We declare three local variables—a Date, an Integer, and a String.

```
Dim D As Date = Now()
Dim Int As Integer = 100
Dim Str As String
```

Next, we use the handle to the Web service to make a call, passing in the Date and the Integer and getting a String return value.

```
Str = WS.PassByRef(Int, D)
```

We then write the return value to the console.

```
Console.WriteLine("Return value = " & Str)
```

We also write the local variables to the console.

```
Console.WriteLine("Integer arg = " & Int)
Console.WriteLine("Date arg = " & D)
```

The results that we get back might surprise you.

```
Return value = Finshed changing the parameters
Integer arg = 400
Date arg = 1/14/2004 10:18:35 PM
```

The return value is what you would expect. The Integer and Date parameters have been changed locally, which is what you want if you pass by reference. This is accomplished by cleverness in the .NET framework, however.

Summary

In this hour, you saw how Microsoft has positioned the .NET platform to be a Web services creation tool. You first learned about the pros and cons of using Microsoft tools. Following that, you were introduced to the features of .NET and Visual Studio that are the most important to Web services developers.

You also learned how to use the framework to create a simple application to demonstrate how Web services are created. Finally, you were shown a demonstration of how .NET can emulate the passing of parameters by reference to and from a Web service.

Q&A

Q Is a .NET version of an application slower than an unmanaged version of the same application?

A Yes, the runtime will always introduce some overhead. This overhead might not keep your application from performing, however, because of the speed of the hardware running it.

Q Can .NET be used for all programs?

A No, games and certain types of communication programs will always need to be written in compiled code.

Q Is .NET a better platform for creating Web services or Web services clients?

A It can be used for either. Although many products are oriented toward creating Web services, Visual Studio .NET is stronger than most in creating clients.

Workshop

The Workshop is designed to help you review what you've learned and begin learning how to put your knowledge into practice.

Quiz

1. What is the purpose of the CLR?
2. Do Visual C++ Web services perform better than Visual Basic Web services?
3. What .NET class is the Web services workhorse?

Quiz Answers

1. The common language runtime (CLR) is the .NET equivalent of the Java Virtual Machine. It runs interpreted code and exposed operating system objects to the program.
2. No. All .NET Web services run the exact same bytecode. The choice of language is just for human convenience.
3. The System.Web.Services.WebService class that is part of the .NET framework does all the heavy lifting associated with creating a Web service.

Activities

1. Create a Web service that accepts a date parameter and tells you how old you will be on that date.
2. Create a Web service that doubles any integer value passed in.
3. Create a Web service that converts your name to all lowercase letters when you pass it in by reference.

HOUR 16

Creating .NET Web Service Clients

Many of the early Web services products are heavily oriented to the server side of the transaction. Microsoft .NET is different in this regard in that it provides considerable support to the client, or consuming side, of the task at hand.

Web services are created in such a way that any SOAP-compliant client can access them. There are some mechanical considerations to deal with, however, when you start creating a client. This hour shows you how .NET languages can use the framework as a foundation for creating clients that consume the Web services that we write. In addition, you will create several more sophisticated Web services and the clients that communicate with them. You will learn specifically how to

- Create a client that requests data.
- Return a structure from a Web service.
- Create a Web services client.
- Create a client to access a Web service from another company.

Exchanging Complex Data

You could write a program that generates SOAP messages by concatenating characters together one at the time. Although this would be possible to achieve, it would be tedious and unnecessary for most applications. It is far easier to use a combination of a tool and the WSDL document for service to generate the code for that client. Even better than that is the .NET approach in which the framework can dynamically read the WSDL in order to create the correct SOAP messages. In this section, we will step through the process of creating a simple Web service and a client that can access it.

Creating a Web Service to Connect with

NEW TERM The first example that we will work will demonstrate how user-defined data types, sometimes called *structures* or objects, can be passed from a Web service to a client. We can define a simple structure within a Web service as shown in Listing 16.1.

LISTING 16.1   The StructService1.asmx File

```
Imports System.Web.Services

<WebService(Namespace:="http://www.samspublishing.com")> _
Public Class StructService1
    Inherits System.Web.Services.WebService

#Region " Web Services Designer Generated Code "

    Public Structure Employee
        Dim Name As String
        Dim Age As Integer
        Dim SSN As String
        Dim HDate As Date
    End Structure

    <WebMethod()> Public Function GetEmployee() As Employee
        Dim emp As Employee

        emp.Name = "John Libby"
        emp.Age = 48
        emp.SSN = "234-56-7890"
        emp.HDate = #1/6/1955#

        Return (emp)
    End Function

End Class
```

You will recognize much of this code from the examples that we worked in the last hour. The unique part of this example is the definition of a structure inside the Web service file.

```
Public Structure Employee
    Dim Name As String
    Dim Age As Integer
    Dim SSN As String
    Dim HDate As Date
End Structure
```

We will create a Web method to send this structure to a client. Notice that we don't send it as individual data items, but as a unit.

```
<WebMethod()> Public Function GetEmployee() As Employee
    Dim emp As Employee

    emp.Name = "Steve Potts"
    emp.Age = 48
    emp.SSN = "234-56-7890"
    emp.HDate = #1/6/1955#

    Return (emp)
End Function
```

You can find the WSDL for a Web service in the Web References section of the Solution Explorer pane of the IDE. The WSDL declaration that .NET has generated for this Web service contains some interesting features, as shown here:

```
<types>
<s:schema elementFormDefault="qualified"
                      targetNamespace="http://www.samspublishing.com">
<s:element name="GetEmployee">
  <s:complexType />
  </s:element>
<s:element name="GetEmployeeResponse">
<s:complexType>
<s:sequence>
  <s:element minOccurs="1" maxOccurs="1"
                        name="GetEmployeeResult" type="s0:Employee" />
  </s:sequence>
  </s:complexType>
  </s:element>
<s:complexType name="Employee">
<s:sequence>
  <s:element minOccurs="0" maxOccurs="1" name="Name" type="s:string" />
  <s:element minOccurs="1" maxOccurs="1" name="Age" type="s:int" />
  <s:element minOccurs="0" maxOccurs="1" name="SSN" type="s:string" />
  <s:element minOccurs="1" maxOccurs="1" name="HDate" type="s:dateTime" />
  </s:sequence>
```

16

```
</s:complexType>
<s:element name="Employee" type="s0:Employee" />
</s:schema>
</types>
```

Notice that the GetEmployeeResponse element contains a complexType.

```
<s:element name="GetEmployeeResponse">
<s:complexType>
<s:sequence>
  <s:element minOccurs="1" maxOccurs="1"
                       name="GetEmployeeResult" type="s0:Employee" />
```

The complexType is composed of simple types.

```
<s:complexType name="Employee">
<s:sequence>
  <s:element minOccurs="0"
           maxOccurs="1" name="Name" type="s:string" />
  <s:element minOccurs="1"
           maxOccurs="1" name="Age" type="s:int" />
  <s:element minOccurs="0"
           maxOccurs="1" name="SSN" type="s:string" />
  <s:element minOccurs="1"
           maxOccurs="1" name="HDate" type="s:dateTime" />
  </s:sequence>
  </s:complexType>
```

Notice that each element in the complexType represents a field in the structure that we want to convey.

The messages are defined here:

```
<message name="GetEmployeeSoapIn">
  <part name="parameters" element="s0:GetEmployee" />
  </message>
<message name="GetEmployeeSoapOut">
  <part name="parameters" element="s0:GetEmployeeResponse" />
  </message>
```

The bindings for SOAP are shown here:

```
<binding name="StructService1Soap" type="s0:StructService1Soap">
  <soap:binding transport=
    "http://schemas.xmlsoap.org/soap/http" style="document" />
<operation name="GetEmployee">
  <soap:operation soapAction=
    "http://www.samspublishing.com/GetEmployee" style="document" />
<input>
  <soap:body use="literal" />
  </input>
<output>
```

```
    <soap:body use="literal" />
    </output>
    </operation>
    </binding>
```

The WSDL service element is defined, which contains the URL of the Web service.

```
<service name="StructService1">
<port name="StructService1Soap" binding="s0:StructService1Soap">
  <soap:address location=
      "http://localhost/StructService/StructService1.asmx" />
  </port>
```

Creating the Web Services Client

Creating the client for the StructService1 Web service is easy to do using Visual Basic .NET. The first step is to create a new Windows Application project that contains a form. Using the toolbox, add four text boxes called txtName, txtAge, txtSSN, and txtHireDate to the form. The code for this form is shown in Listing 16.2.

LISTING 16.2   The Form1.vb File

```
Public Class Form1
    Inherits System.Windows.Forms.Form

#Region " Windows Form Designer generated code "
#End Region

Private Sub Form1_Load(ByVal sender As System.Object,
        ➡ByVal e As System.EventArgs) Handles MyBase.Load
        Dim WS As New localhost.StructService1()

        Dim employee1 As localhost.Employee

        employee1 = WS.GetEmployee()

        txtName.Text = employee1.Name
        txtAge.Text = employee1.Age
        txtSSN.Text = employee1.SSN
        txtHireDate.Text = employee1.HDate

    End Sub
End Class
```

We chose the Form1_Load event procedure to populate the form with information retrieved from the StructService1 Web service. The first thing that we must do is make the connection with the service. The WSDL file becomes part of the client project when you add the Web reference to the project. Until then, the name `StructService1()` will be meaningless.

```
Dim WS As New localhost.StructService1()
```

The `Employee` type is known because it exists in the WSDL.

```
Dim employee1 As localhost.Employee
```

The call to retrieve the employee is made using the handle to the Web service class.

```
employee1 = WS.GetEmployee()
```

We display the values on our form by referencing the employee's information using the Visual Basic dot notation. The text box's `Text` property controls what is displayed. By assigning a value to it, you cause it to be displayed on the screen.

```
txtName.Text = employee1.Name
txtAge.Text = employee1.Age
txtSSN.Text = employee1.SSN
TxtHireDate.Text = employee1.HDate
```

Adding the Web reference is the only complicated part of this example. The easiest way to do this is to choose Add Web Reference from the Project Menu. The Add Web Reference dialog box will appear as shown in Figure 16.1.

FIGURE 16.1

The Add Web Reference dialog box gives you an opportunity to specify a connection to a Web service.

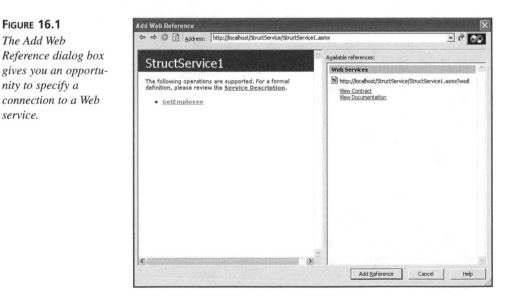

Now, all that is left is to run the StructClient application by pressing the F5 key or by choosing Start from the Debug menu. The result is shown in Figure 16.2.

FIGURE 16.2

*You can display infor-
mation gathered from
a Web service on a
Visual Basic form.*

16

Compared to the complicated process required by some tools, the Visual Basic .NET approach is very simple to learn and use.

Discovering a Web Service

Up to this point, we have limited our examples to Web services that we have created. Much of the development that you will do in your career will consume Web services written by others. You can call the methods that those services expose almost as easily as you can call methods on the services running on your own machine.

The Visual Studio IDE provides a built-in way to find Web services to communicate with: the Add Web Reference dialog box. A Web reference is a reference to an object that is located somewhere on the Web. When we add a Web reference to a project, we are asking .NET to add the "plumbing" needed for your application to make requests of this remote reference and to get responses from them. To do this, create a new Windows Application project. When the skeleton project appears in the Solution Explorer, right-click on the project name and choose Add Web Reference from the context menu. When the dialog box appears, click on the UDDI Directory hyperlink.

This will bring up the dialog box shown in Figure 16.3.

Type **"IBM"** in the Provider Name text box, and then click the Search button. This will retrieve a number of possible selections as shown in Figure 16.4.

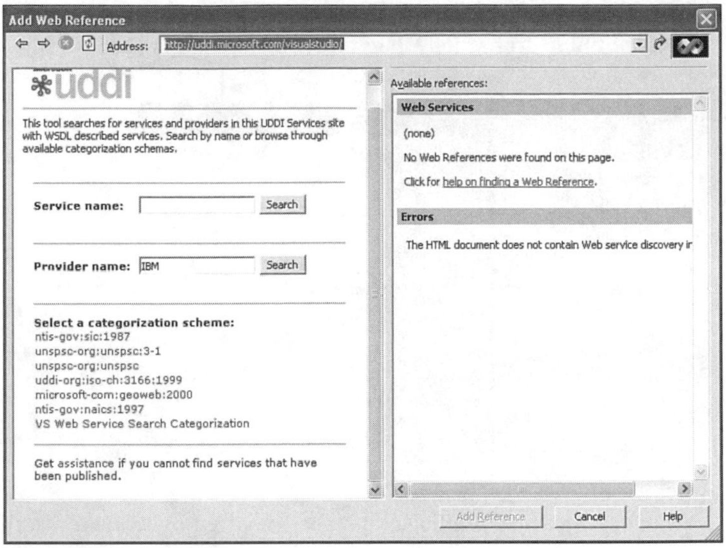

FIGURE **16.3**
A UDDI directory can help you find a Web service that you need for your project.

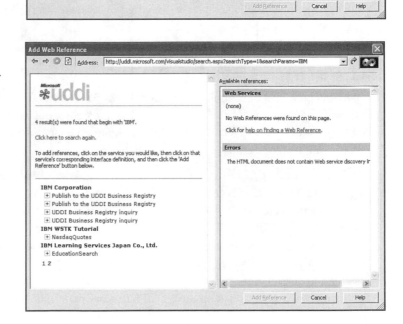

FIGURE **16.4**
A single provider might make dozens of different Web services available for you to use.

After some frustration with the fact that we couldn't find any Web services that provided decent references, we decided to copy the URL from one of these entries as shown here:

```
http://dwdemos.alphaworks.ibm.com/IBM_WSI_Sample/
```

We copied and pasted this link into the address bar of our dialog and pressed Enter. The following page appeared in the Add Web Reference dialog box as shown in Figure 16.5.

FIGURE 16.5

The Apache Axis Web services engine is employed by IBM to serve its demo Web services.

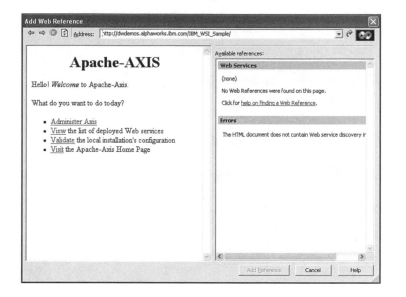

Next, we chose the View the List of the Deployed Web Services hyperlink, which caused the screen shown in Figure 16.6 to appear.

FIGURE 16.6

The IBM site offered a variety of demonstration-quality Web services to connect to.

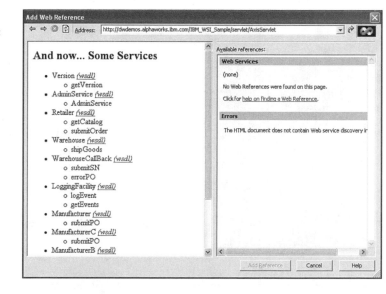

Because we wanted a simple Web service for this example, we chose the first one, the Version Web service. This caused the dialog box to display the WSDL for that service to appear in the left panel, as shown in Figure 16.7.

FIGURE 16.7
Finding the WSDL for the service that we want to connect to is the goal of the search.

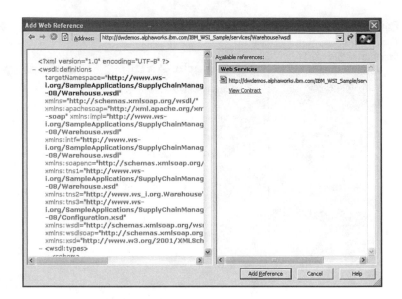

We clicked on the Add Reference button at the bottom of this dialog box to add this WSDL to our project. Figure 16.8 shows the Solution Explorer window with the Version.wsdl file listed under the Web References tree.

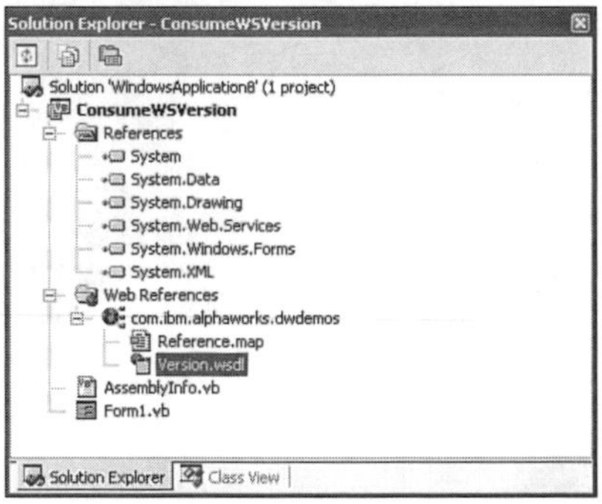

FIGURE 16.8
Once the WSDL is added to a project, all the information needed to communicate with the service is present.

The WSDL document itself is fairly easy to understand. Listing 16.3 shows what it looks like.

LISTING 16.3   The Version.wsdl File

```xml
<?xml version="1.0" encoding="utf-8"?>
<definitions xmlns:soap="http://schemas.xmlsoap.org/wsdl/soap/"
xmlns:tns="http://dwdemos.alphaworks.ibm.com/IBM_WSI_Sample/services/Version"
```

LISTING 16.3   continued

```
xmlns:s=http://www.w3.org/2001/XMLSchema
                xmlns:http="http://schemas.xmlsoap.org/wsdl/http/"
xmlns:tm="http://microsoft.com/wsdl/mime/textMatching/"
xmlns:mime="http://schemas.xmlsoap.org/wsdl/mime/"
xmlns:soapenc="http://schemas.xmlsoap.org/soap/encoding/" targetNamespace=
    "http://dwdemos.alphaworks.ibm.com/IBM_WSI_Sample/services/Version"
xmlns="http://schemas.xmlsoap.org/wsdl/">
  <types />
  <message name="getVersionResponse">
    <part name="getVersionReturn" type="s:string" />
  </message>
  <message name="getVersionRequest" />
  <portType name="Version">
    <operation name="getVersion">
      <input name="getVersionRequest" message="tns:getVersionRequest" />
      <output name="getVersionResponse"
                                    message="tns:getVersionResponse" />
    </operation>
  </portType>
  <binding name="VersionSoapBinding" type="tns:Version">
    <soap:binding transport=http://schemas.xmlsoap.org/soap/http
                                          style="rpc" />
    <operation name="getVersion">
      <soap:operation soapAction="" />
      <input name="getVersionRequest">
        <soap:body use="encoded"
namespace=
   "http://dwdemos.alphaworks.ibm.com/IBM_WSI_Sample/services/Version"
encodingStyle="http://schemas.xmlsoap.org/soap/encoding/" />
      </input>
      <output name="getVersionResponse">
        <soap:body use="encoded"
namespace=
    "http://dwdemos.alphaworks.ibm.com/IBM_WSI_Sample/services/Version"
encodingStyle="http://schemas.xmlsoap.org/soap/encoding/" />
      </output>
    </operation>
  </binding>
  <service name="VersionService">
    <port name="Version" binding="tns:VersionSoapBinding">
      <soap:address location=
   "http://dwdemos.alphaworks.ibm.com/IBM_WSI_Sample/services/Version" />
    </port>
  </service>
</definitions>
```

NEW TERM   The binding tells us how to communicate with this service. We are going to use
SOAP and the *rpc* style on an operation (method) called getVersion.

16

```
<binding name="VersionSoapBinding" type="tns:Version">
  <soap:binding transport=http://schemas.xmlsoap.org/soap/http
                                          style="rpc" />
  <operation name="getVersion">
    <soap:operation soapAction="" />
    <input name="getVersionRequest">
      <soap:body use="encoded"
```

The address that we will use to access the SOAP version of this Web service is shown here:

```
<port name="Version" binding="tns:VersionSoapBinding">
  <soap:address location=
"http://dwdemos.alphaworks.ibm.com/IBM_WSI_Sample/services/Version" />
  </port>
```

The information in this document is sufficient for .NET to communicate with this Web service directly using SOAP.

Writing a Client for the Discovered Service

Now that we have a Web reference to a service on the IBM site, we can try and make calls to it. The code in Listing 16.4 gives us a client to test it with.

LISTING 16.4   The Version's Form1 Class

```
Public Class Form1
    Inherits System.Windows.Forms.Form

#Region " Windows Form Designer generated code "

    Private Sub Form1_Load(ByVal sender As System.Object,
              ByVal e As System.EventArgs) Handles MyBase.Load

    End Sub

    Private Sub Button1_Click(ByVal sender As System.Object,
              ByVal e As System.EventArgs) Handles Button1.Click
        Dim WS As New com.ibm.alphaworks.dwdemos.VersionService()

        Dim s1 As String

        s1 = WS.getVersion()
        txtVersionInfo.Text = s1

    End Sub

End Class
```

Add a button, Button1, and a text box, txtVersionInfo, to the form and place this code in the Form1 class. Access to the Web service is provided by the fact that the Web reference for this service has been added to the project and the following line of code has been included:

```
Dim WS As New com.ibm.alphaworks.dwdemos.VersionService()
```

Here, we are creating a handle to an object located on another computer somewhere on the Internet. We use that handle to make a call to the method of that service.

```
s1 = WS.getVersion()
```

The return value from this is a String, so we will assign it directly to the Text property of a text box.

```
txtVersionInfo.Text = s1
```

You can run this example by choosing Start from the Debug menu or pressing the F5 key. After the window appears, click on the Get Version button. Figure 16.9 shows what the result looks like.

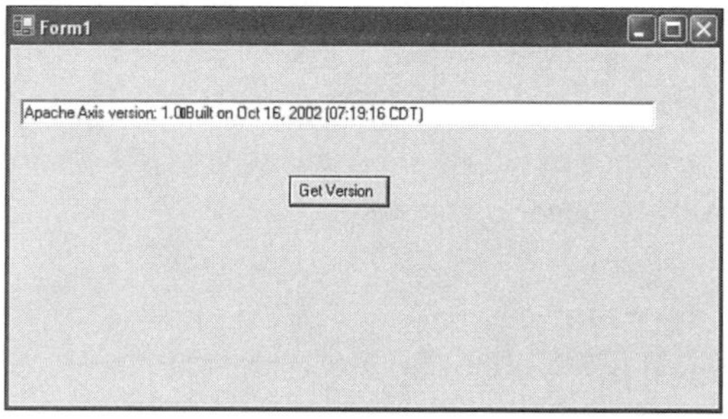

FIGURE 16.9
The Version Web service communicates information about the SOAP engine to the client.

Notice that we are using a .NET client to talk to an Apache Axis Web service, without any special effort on our part. The WSDL provides all the information that we need to communicate. Notice also that we have no information about the language that the Version Web service was written in, nor do we need to know it. The SOAP engine on the server translates the SOAP messages into the programming language of the server in the same way that the CLR translates the SOAP messages into Visual Basic for us.

Summary

In this hour, you learned how to create Web service clients using Visual Basic and the .NET platform. You first learned how to create a client that could make a request and receive a complex data type.

After that, you learned how to use Visual Studio to create a client to connect to a Web service that we found by searching directory services.

The .NET approach to creating clients is by far the most advanced of any on the market. It will be interesting to see whether the current Web service development community will be open to a Microsoft solution, given that so many of them sided with Sun Microsystems in the "Java Wars" of the past decade.

Q&A

Q Why is Visual Studio .NET considered to be a good client-creation platform?

A Microsoft is known for its client-side technology, and it isn't surprising that its client Web services tools are among the best and easiest to use.

Q How can a client be generated from just the WSDL? Where does the rest of the information come from?

A There is no need for any other information. A properly created WSDL document contains all the information needed for successful connection.

Workshop

The Workshop is designed to help you review what you've learned and begin learning how to put your knowledge into practice.

Quiz

1. What is the goal of the discovery process?

2. What is the .NET approach to creating a client?

3. What type of data can be sent to a client?

Quiz Answers

1. To locate a WSDL document for the remote service.

2. The .NET framework exposes a class called `System.Web.Services.WebServices` that handles most of the communication details for you.

3. Web services can return data of arbitrary complexity. The WSDL describes the data so that your client program can be written to receive it.

Activities

1. Create a calculator Web service and a client on your computer. Make the Web service support `add()` and `subtract()` methods. Create a client that can gather this information from the user and display the answer.

2. Create a client that accesses a Web service that you find over the Internet or using the discovery features of Visual Studio.

16

Creating Web Services with BEA WebLogic Workshop

NEW TERM WebLogic Workshop is a product of BEA Systems. BEA is a major player in the *J2EE* server arena with its product WebLogic Server. In fact, Workshop runs on top of WebLogic Server.

In this hour, we are going to take a look at the BEA offering in the Web services development arena, WebLogic Workshop. You will learn the following:

- The WebLogic Workshop architecture
- The Visual Development environment
- How to build a WebLogic Workshop Web service
- How to build a WebLogic Workshop Web service client
- How to create a Workshop conversation service
- How to test a Web service using WebLogic Workshop

The Architecture of the WebLogic Workshop Product

The WebLogic Workshop, or simply Workshop, is an ease-of-use oriented product. The emphasis of this product is on making the creation and deployment of Web services as painless as possible.

NEW TERM Workshop features a design-time visual development environment that is reminiscent of a Java IDE such as Visual Café. Developers create Web services by adding controls and methods, setting properties, and writing Java code to add business logic. The basic unit of work in Workshop is the *.jws* file, which stands for Java Web service. JWS files are standard Java files containing special annotations that add the Web service functionality to the application.

The second part of the Workshop product is a runtime framework that does the heavy lifting associated with the deployment of the Web service classes. In addition, the framework provides debugging and testing services. The framework generates J2EE components that are then installed and run on the WebLogic server product. Figure 17.1 shows this architecture.

FIGURE 17.1

The WebLogic Workshop product is built on top of the WebLogic J2EE server.

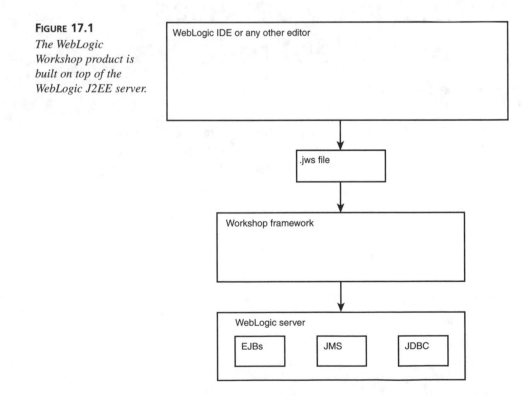

The basic advantage of the framework is that it can perform most of the complex plumbing work for you and free up your efforts to concentrate on creating the business logic that makes your applications valuable. Figure 17.2 shows the Workshop IDE.

FIGURE 17.2

The WebLogic Workshop IDE is used to specify the details of your Web services.

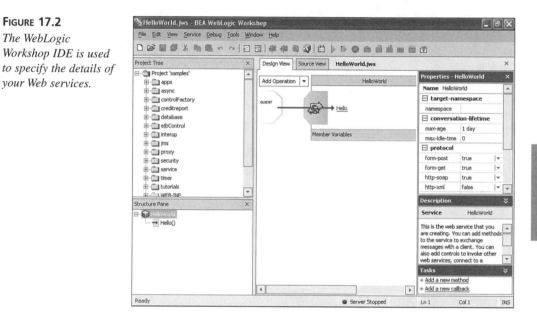

The basic parts of the IDE are

- **The Project Pane**—Displays all the projects under development and the files that compose it.

- **The Structure Pane**—Displays the details of the Web service project that you are currently working on. The client interface, private methods, and controls are all listed here.

- **The Design View**—Provides you with a graphical representation of the public portions of the Web service.

- **The Source View**—Displays the source code for the service.

- **The Properties Pane**—Allows you to set the properties of the objects in your project.

- **The Description Pane**—Shows you a text description of the project.

- **The Tasks Pane**—Suggests tasks that are commonly performed on an object.

All of these user interface elements will be used to create Web services and clients later in this hour.

17

Creating a Web Service with WebLogic Workshop

The creation of a WebLogic Workshop Web service is straightforward. The first step is to choose File, New Project. This will bring up the dialog box shown in Figure 17.3.

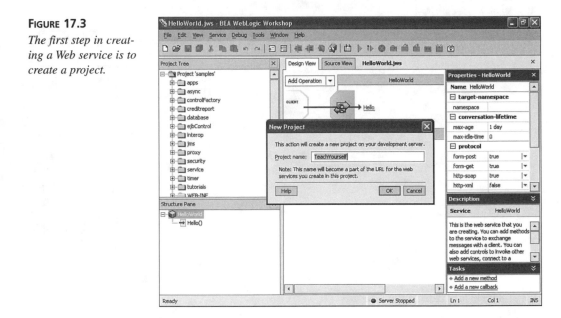

Enter a project name and click on the OK button. We named this project TeachYourself. The next step is to create a Web service by choosing File, New, New Web Service. This will bring up the dialog box shown in Figure 17.4.

We will name our service Watson. Click OK. Notice that the Project Pane, the Structure Pane ,the Design View, and the Source View are all populated with the skeleton of a Web service. Listing 17.1 shows this skeleton from the Source View.

LISTING 17.1   The Watson.jws File

```
import weblogic.jws.control.JwsContext;

public class Watson
{
    /** @jws:context */
    JwsContext context;
}
```

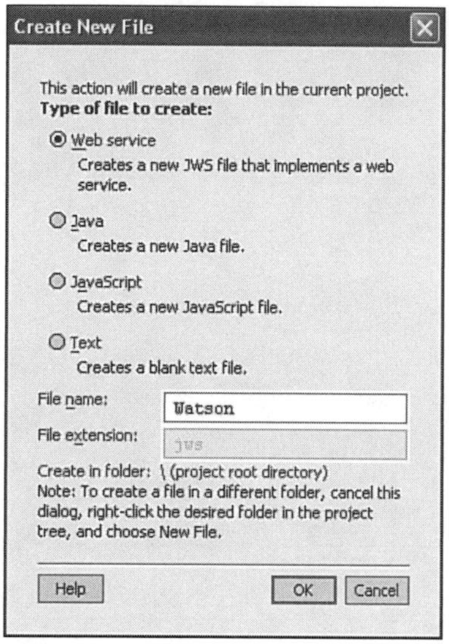

FIGURE 17.4

The next step is to create a Web service by using a dialog box.

This class is simply instantiating the `JwsContext` object. This tag that appears in the Javadoc comment in Listing 17.1 is really a directive to the framework. It is telling Workshop to connect the object following the tag to the runtime objects of the framework.

```
/** @jws:context */
```

The actual declaration of the class is shown next:

```
JwsContext context;
```

The `JwsContext` instance is normally present in a JWS file. This object can be used to access aspects of the Web service context at runtime. Some of the methods defined by the `JwsContext` interface are `getService()`, `getLogger()`, and `isFinished()`.

Adding a Method to the Web Service

We will need a method that is callable by a client in our service. To do this, bring up the Edit Maps and Interface dialog box. This is done by clicking on the Add Operation control located in the Design View. When the operation graphic appears, name it **callWatson**. Right-click on this name and select Edit Maps and Interface. The dialog box shown in Figure 17.5 appears.

17

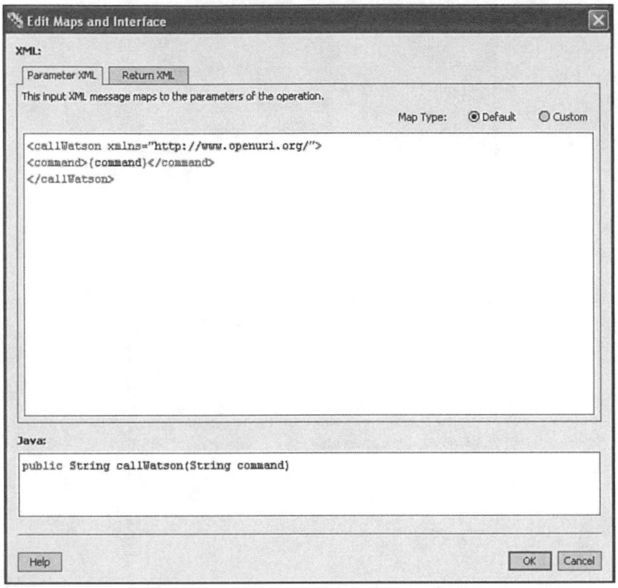

FIGURE 17.5

*You add a method
using the Edit Maps
and Interface
dialog box.*

In the lower pane, add the following line of Java code:

```
public String callWatson(String command)
```

Next, click on the OK button. Change the code for the Web service now to look like
Listing 17.2.

LISTING 17.2   The Changed Watson.jws File

```
import weblogic.jws.control.JwsContext;

public class Watson
{
    /** @jws:context */
    JwsContext context;


    /**
     * @jws:operation
     */
    public String callWatson(String command)
    {
        return "Watson is coming";
    }

}
```

Notice the @jws:operation tag in this listing. This notifies Workshop that this operation is part of the public interface of this Web service.

Building the Web Service in WebLogic Workshop

To build the Web service, select Build from the Debug menu. The output message at the bottom of the screen should read as follows:

```
"Build complete - 0 error(s), 0 warning(s)"
```

Next, you can run the service by choosing Start from the Debug menu. A browser will open and show you a screen that looks like the one in Figure 17.6.

FIGURE 17.6

A special page appears that allows you to test your service.

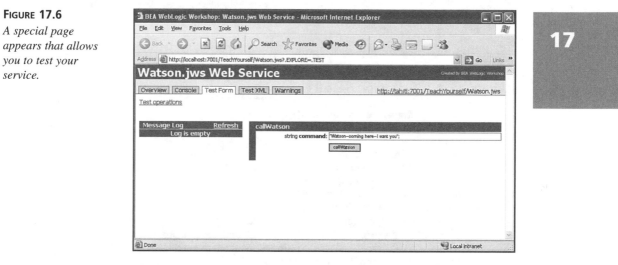

This HTML page is created by Workshop as an aid for testing. Type in a message for Watson and click the callWatson button. You will see a new page appear in the browser that should look a lot like Figure 17.7.

A WSDL file is generated for this by Workshop. It is shown here in Listing 17.3. To view it, select the Overview tab and then select Complete WSDL.

17

FIGURE 17.7

A results page is generated that shows you both the request and the response.

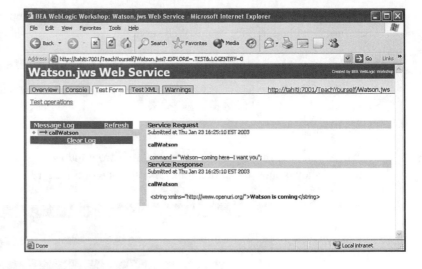

LISTING 17.3   The Watson.wsdl File

```
<?xml version="1.0" encoding="utf-8" ?>
<definitions xmlns="http://schemas.xmlsoap.org/wsdl/"
xmlns:conv="http://www.openuri.org/2002/04/soap/conversation/"
xmlns:cw="http://www.openuri.org/2002/04/wsdl/conversation/"
xmlns:http="http://schemas.xmlsoap.org/wsdl/http/"
xmlns:jms="http://www.openuri.org/2002/04/wsdl/jms/"
xmlns:mime="http://schemas.xmlsoap.org/wsdl/mime/"
       xmlns:s="http://www.w3.org/2001/XMLSchema"
xmlns:s0="http://www.openuri.org/"
     xmlns:soap="http://schemas.xmlsoap.org/wsdl/soap/"
xmlns:soapenc="http://schemas.xmlsoap.org/soap/encoding/"
xmlns:xm="http://www.bea.com/2002/04/xmlmap/"
                    targetNamespace="http://www.openuri.org/">
<types>
 <s:schema attributeFormDefault="qualified"
                    elementFormDefault="qualified"
                    targetNamespace="http://www.openuri.org/">
  <s:element name="callWatson">
  <s:complexType>
  <s:sequence>
   <s:element minOccurs="0" maxOccurs="1"
                         name="command" type="s:string" />
   </s:sequence>
   </s:complexType>
   </s:element>
   <s:element name="callWatsonResponse">
  <s:complexType>
  <s:sequence>
   <s:element minOccurs="0" maxOccurs="1"
```

LISTING 17.3 continued

```
                                    name="callWatsonResult" type="s:string" />
    </s:sequence>
    </s:complexType>
    </s:element>
    <s:element nillable="true" name="string" type="s:string" />
    </s:schema>
    </types>
<message name="callWatsonSoapIn">
  <part name="parameters" element="s0:callWatson" />
  </message>
<message name="callWatsonSoapOut">
  <part name="parameters" element="s0:callWatsonResponse" />
  </message>
<message name="callWatsonHttpGetIn">
  <part name="command" type="s:string" />
  </message>
<message name="callWatsonHttpGetOut">
  <part name="Body" element="s0:string" />
  </message>
<message name="callWatsonHttpPostIn">
  <part name="command" type="s:string" />
  </message>
<message name="callWatsonHttpPostOut">
  <part name="Body" element="s0:string" />
  </message>
  <portType name="WatsonSoap">
  <operation name="callWatson">
  <input message="s0:callWatsonSoapIn" />
  <output message="s0:callWatsonSoapOut" />
  </operation>
  </portType>
  <portType name="WatsonHttpGet">
  <operation name="callWatson">
  <input message="s0:callWatsonHttpGetIn" />
  <output message="s0:callWatsonHttpGetOut" />
  </operation>
</portType>
<portType name="WatsonHttpPost">
<operation name="callWatson">
 <input message="s0:callWatsonHttpPostIn" />
 <output message="s0:callWatsonHttpPostOut" />
 </operation>
 </portType>
<binding name="WatsonSoap" type="s0:WatsonSoap">
 <soap:binding transport="http://schemas.xmlsoap.org/soap/http"
                                    style="document" />
<operation name="callWatson">
```

17

LISTING 17.3   continued

```
<soap:operation soapAction="http://www.openuri.org/callWatson"
                                   style="document" />
<input>
 <soap:body use="literal" />
 </input>
<output>
 <soap:body use="literal" />
 </output>
 </operation>
 </binding>
<binding name="WatsonHttpGet" type="s0:WatsonHttpGet">
 <http:binding verb="GET" />
<operation name="callWatson">
 <http:operation location="/callWatson" />
<input>
 <http:urlEncoded />
 </input>
<output>
 <mime:mimeXml part="Body" />
 </output>
 </operation>
 </binding>
<binding name="WatsonHttpPost" type="s0:WatsonHttpPost">
 <http:binding verb="POST" />
<operation name="callWatson">
 <http:operation location="/callWatson" />
<input>
 <mime:content type="application/xwwwformurlencoded" />
 </input>
<output>
 <mime:mimeXml part="Body" />
 </output>
 </operation>
 </binding>
<service name="Watson">
<port name="WatsonSoap" binding="s0:WatsonSoap">
 <soap:address location="http://tahiti:7001/TeachYourself/Watson.jws" />
 </port>
<port name="WatsonHttpGet" binding="s0:WatsonHttpGet">
 <http:address location="http://tahiti:7001/TeachYourself/Watson.jws" />
 </port>
<port name="WatsonHttpPost" binding="s0:WatsonHttpPost">
 <http:address location="http://tahiti:7001/TeachYourself/Watson.jws" />
 </port>
 </service>
</definitions>
```

Notice that Workshop generates bindings for SOAP, HTTP Get, and HTTP Post.

```
<port name="WatsonSoap" binding="s0:WatsonSoap">
 <soap:address location="http://tahiti:7001/TeachYourself/Watson.jws" />
 </port>
<port name="WatsonHttpGet" binding="s0:WatsonHttpGet">
 <http:address location="http://tahiti:7001/TeachYourself/Watson.jws" />
 </port>
<port name="WatsonHttpPost" binding="s0:WatsonHttpPost">
 <http:address location="http://tahiti:7001/TeachYourself/Watson.jws" />
```

Notice also that the URL for all three bindings is the same.

Creating Web Services Clients with WebLogic Workshop

17

The process for creating client applications that consume Web services is also made easier by using WebLogic Workshop. The first step is to obtain the proxy jar files from the Test application for the service that you want to communicate with. To do this, go to the Overview tab in the Test View as shown in Figure 17.8.

FIGURE 17.8

The results page contains links that allow you to get client proxy files.

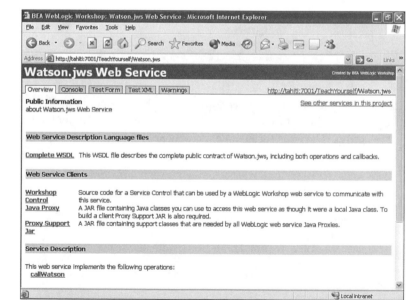

Click on the Java Proxy link and specify the directory that you are going to build your application in as the save destination. Next, click on the Proxy Support Jar link and save it to the same directory.

The next step is to add both of these jar files, Watson.jar and webservicesclient.jar, to the classpath of the client machine. This will enable the client that you write to access them. The jar files are located in the directory that you specified for the Java Proxy.

The Watson.jar file contains classes that are specific to the Watson Web service as shown in Figure 17.9.

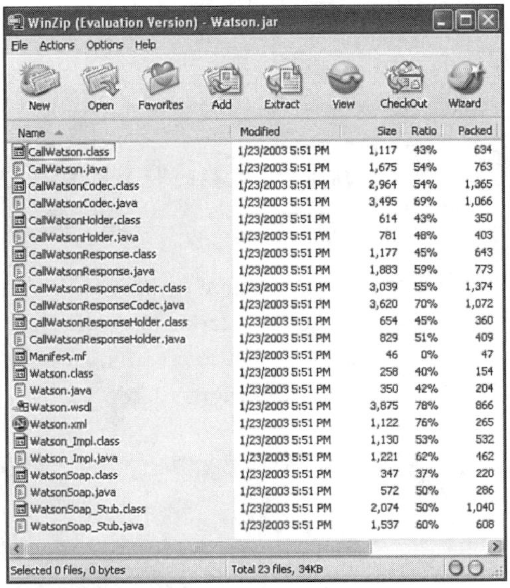

FIGURE 17.9
The Watson.jar file is created for one specific Web service.

The webservicesclient.jar contains classes that pertain to all Web services clients. These classes are not called directly by your code, but rather by the generated code in the proxy. The code for the client is shown in Listing 17.4. Type this code in to a new java file called TestWWClient.java.

LISTING 17.4   The TestWWClient.java File

```java
import weblogic.jws.proxies.*;

public class TestWWClient
{
   public static void main(String[] args)
  {
     try
     {
        Watson_Impl proxy = new Watson_Impl();
        WatsonSoap soapProxy = proxy.getWatsonSoap();
        System.out.println(soapProxy.callWatson("Watson--come here"));
```

LISTING 17.4 continued

```
    }
    catch (Exception e)
    {
        e.printStackTrace();
    }
  }
}
```

This package contains the generated proxy classes.

```
import weblogic.jws.proxies.*;
```

First, we obtain a handle to the proxy class for this Web service:

```
Watson_Impl proxy = new Watson_Impl();
```

Next, we get a handle to the Soap-specific proxy through the generic proxy handle:

```
WatsonSoap soapProxy = proxy.getWatsonSoap();
```

Next, we use the Soap-specific proxy handle to make a call to the public method in that Web service:

```
System.out.println(soapProxy.callWatson("Watson--come here"));
```

You compile and run this just as you would any other Java program. The result is shown here:

```
G:\Books\ws24\chapters\ch17>javac TestWWClient.java
G:\Books\ws24\chapters\ch17>java TestWWClient
Watson is coming
```

Creating a Conversation That Maintains State

WebLogic Workshop is able to maintain state in a Web service in an almost automatic fashion using the Enterprise Java Bean (EJB) capabilities of WebLogic server.

NEW TERM State is important because many Web services need to behave like a session instead of a like a stateless, single-hit Web page. In fact, Workshop calls its session facility a *conversation*. A conversation is simply a set of method calls that are able to find out about activities that occurred earlier by the same user. The classic example of a stateful session is the online retail store. The user selects items and places them in a virtual shopping cart. When she is ready to check out, the items in the shopping cart are "removed" and shipped to her. Her credit card is charged the agreed amount plus any taxes or fees.

17

HTTP provides a session object that can be used for this purpose. Instead of using the session object, Workshop takes advantage of the session facility of EJBs that are available in J2EE-compliant servers.

Three special tags are used by Workshop to communicate: the start, continue, and finish of a session.

- * @jws:conversation phase="start"—Tells the runtime to begin maintaining state for this user.

- * @jws:conversation phase="continue"—Tells the runtime to use the current state for this user in this method call.

- * @jws:conversation phase="finish"—Tells the runtime to discard the state for this user.

Working an Example

In order to show how a conversation can be conducted, we can work the following example. Create the following Web service by following the same procedure that you did in the first example in this hour. Name it Conversation. Listing 17.5 shows the service's code.

LISTING 17.5   The Conversation.jws File

```
import weblogic.jws.control.JwsContext;

/**
 * @jws:protocol soap-style="rpc"
 */
public class Conversation
{

    public String userName;
    /** @jws:context */
    JwsContext context;

    /**
     * @jws:operation
     * @jws:conversation phase="start"
     */
    public void setUserName(String userName)
    {
        this.userName = userName;
    }

    /**
     * @jws:operation
```

LISTING 17.5   continued

```
  * @jws:conversation phase="continue"
  */
 public String getUserName()
 {
     return "The current user is " + this.userName;
 }

 /**
  * @jws:operation
  * @jws:message-buffer enable="false"
  * @jws:conversation phase="continue"
  */
 public String orderAProduct()
 {
     return this.userName + " ordered a product";
 }

 /**
  * @jws:operation
  * @jws:conversation phase="continue"
  */
 public String cancelAnOrder()
 {
     return this.userName + " cancelled an Order";
 }

 /**
  * @jws:operation
  * @jws:conversation phase="finish"
  */
 public String checkOut()
 {
     return this.userName + " checked out";
 }
}
```

17

Once again, we use the `JwsContext` object to provide us with access to the facilities inside Workshop.

```
import weblogic.jws.control.JwsContext;
```

We will use the remote procedure call style of communication for this service.

```
/**
 * @jws:protocol soap-style="rpc"
 */
```

All of the methods are created in a class that has the same name as the service.

```
public class Conversation
{
```

The userName is the state variable that we want to keep track of between method calls.

```
    public String userName;
    /** @jws:context */
    JwsContext context;
```

The starting operation is called setUserName().

```
    /**
     * @jws:operation
     * @jws:conversation phase="start"
     */
    public void setUserName(String userName)
    {
        this.userName = userName;
    }
```

The getUserName() is a continue-type method call, meaning that it neither starts nor ends a conversation.

```
    /**
     * @jws:operation
     * @jws:conversation phase="continue"
     */
    public String getUserName()
    {
        return "The current user is " + this.userName;
    }
```

The orderAProduct() method is also of type continue.

```
    /**
     * @jws:operation
     * @jws:conversation phase="continue"
     */
    public String orderAProduct()
    {
        return this.userName + " ordered a product";
    }
```

The cancelAnOrder is also of type continue.

```
    /**
     * @jws:operation
     * @jws:conversation phase="continue"
     */
    public String cancelAnOrder()
    {
```

```
        return this.userName + " cancelled an Order";
    }
```

The `checkout()` method is of type `finish`. It tells the runtime that the state for this user can be discarded after this method completes.

```
    /**
     * @jws:operation
     * @jws:conversation phase="finish"
     */
    public String checkOut()
    {
        return this.userName + " checked out";
    }
}
```

Workshop provides a handy graphical representation of this service in the Design View, as shown in Figure 17.10.

FIGURE 17.10

The Design View shows a graphical representation of the Web service.

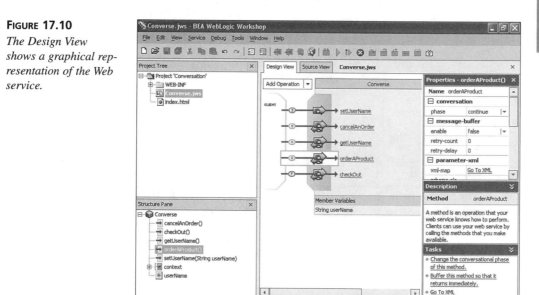

The little circled letters *S*, *C*, and *F* indicate whether a method is of the `start`, `continue`, or `finish` type.

Testing the Example

Even though many methods are associated with this Web service, the Test application
that is generated automatically can still be used to test it. You start the Test application
by choosing Start from the Debug menu. This will bring up the Web page shown in
Figure 17.11.

FIGURE 17.11

*The Test Web page will
display only the* start
method at first.

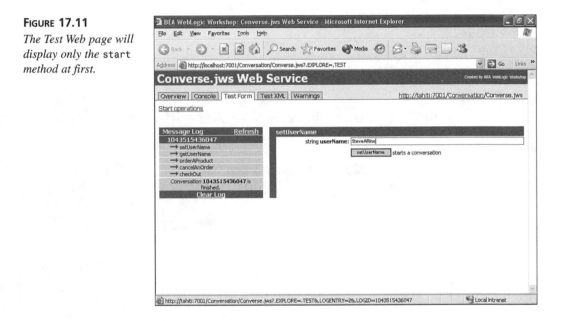

After you type in the name of your user and click on the setUserName button, a second
dialog box will appear. Clicking on the Continue This Conversation hyperlink will bring
up the Web page shown in Figure 17.12.

This page will give you an opportunity to run the other methods and see what they
return. For instance, clicking on the orderAProduct button will return the following:

```
<string xmlns="http://www.openuri.org/">SteveARino ordered a product</string>
```

The next step, which we won't show here, is to create a real client for this service using
the generated jar files. The process for doing this is exactly the same as you saw in the
Watson Web services that we created earlier in this hour.

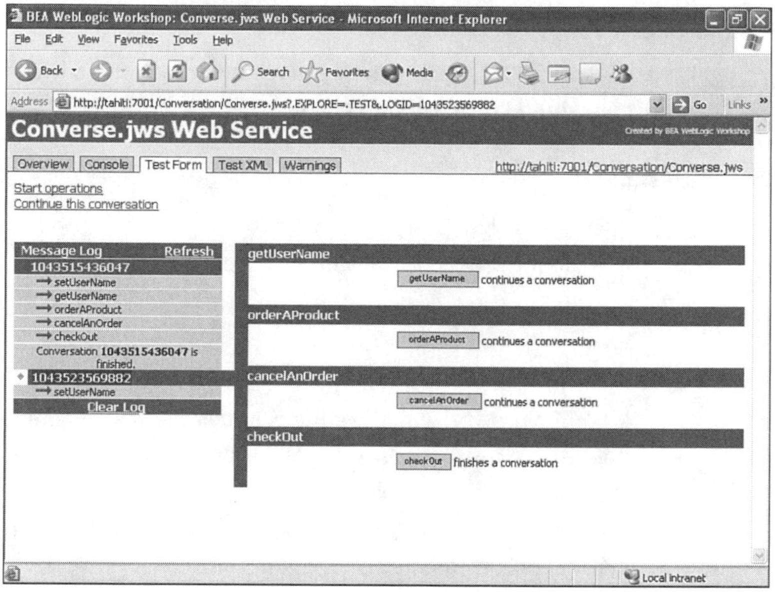

FIGURE 17.12

*A browser will display
the second Web page.*

Summary

In this hour, you learned how to create a Web service using BEA's Weblogic Workshop. You first learned how to create a simple Web service using the Workshop IDE. Next, you learned how to use the jar files that the IDE generates to create a client.

Following that, you learned how to create a conversation-oriented Web service. Finally, you learned how to use the Test application that the IDE generates automatically to test the conversation Web service.

Q&A

Q What specific group of developers will WebLogic Workshop appeal to?

A Developers who are already familiar with BEA WebLogic Server will be a natural fit for WebLogic Workshop. A second group will be developers who like a graphical interface that guides them through the creation process.

Q How does the generation of the proxy jar files compare with other products' client-development procedures?

A Proxy files are a common way to provide client support. As you saw, they were easy to use and reliable.

Workshop

The Workshop is designed to help you review what you've learned and begin learning how to put your knowledge into practice.

Quiz

1. What is a .jws file?
2. Why do the tags appear inside Javadoc comments?
3. Why do we need conversational Web services?

Quiz Answers

1. A WebLogic Workshop .jws file is a Java file that contains special Javadoc tags that provide instructions to the Workshop framework about how to create the Web service.
2. Keeping these tags inside comments makes it easy to use the javac compiler to create bytecode to run on the virtual machine.
3. We need conversational Web services because some Web services need to be able to treat a series of calls as one logical operation. The conversation preserves state between calls, enabling the user to perform a more complex operation.

Activities

1. Create a calculator Web service and a client on your computer by following the same basic procedure that we used to create the HelloWatson Web service.
2. Create a client for the Conversation Web service by generating the proxy jar files and using them in a Java program.

HOUR 18

Creating Web Services with IBM WebSphere

IBM has been an active participant in the formation of Web services standards from the beginning. In fact, most of the current proposed standards that we discuss in the latter hours of the book were created with heavy IBM involvement.

In this hour, you will learn about IBM's WebSphere Studio Application Developer (WSAD). We will pay particular attention to the features of this product that pertain to the creation of Web services. In particular, you will learn

- How to use WSAD to create a Web service
- How to generate a trial client application
- How to run the trial application to verify that your Web service works

IBM and Web Services

IBM became involved with Web services in its early stages. It has provided strong support for the activities of all the major standards bodies for several years. IBM is also closely allied with Sun Microsystems in the area of Java and J2EE. IBM joined with Microsoft in submitting SOAP 1.1 to the *World Wide Web Consortium (W3C)*.

IBM's product offerings are less well known than those of Microsoft and BEA. This is primarily because IBM doesn't actively market its development tools to independent consultants. IBM's major marketing efforts are aimed at Fortune 500 companies. Most of its marketing efforts seem to be focused on getting these clients to use its flagship development product, WebSphere Application Developer.

WebSphere Studio Application Developer

NEW TERM   IBM's *WebSphere Studio Application Developer (WSAD)* is a full-service Java development environment that is based on the *Eclipse* code base. The value that it adds to the Eclipse code is found in the wizards that it includes for creating projects of a specific type. Later in this hour, you will use these wizards to create a simple Web service and other wizards to generate a sample application.

> You can download a trial version of WSAD 5.0 from `http://www14.`
> `software.ibm.com/webapp/download/product.jsp?cat=ad&fam=SPAT-`
> `535HNG&s=s&id=SPAT-524G3S&pf=&k=ALL&q=websphere+application+`
> `developer&dt=&v=&rs=&sr=1&S_TACT=&S_CMP=&sb=n.` If this link is not current,
> go to `www.ibm.com` and follow the links to find it.

WSAD's primary advantage is in a large development team. Each installation contains its own test version of WebSphere Application Server that allows an individual programmer to test his code before deploying it to the team's server. This means that two different developers can test their changes to the same part of the application without fear of interfering with each other.

WebSphere Application Server is built upon the foundation of the Apache products. This provides WebSphere with both a Web server and a SOAP engine. These products are so heavily wrapped in the user interface that you might not even realize you are running them if no one told you about it.

Developing a Web Service with WSAD

The WSAD approach to creating a Web service is very Java-centric. It is based on the creation of a Java class that fits into the basic bean pattern with private variables that come with a full set of get() and set() methods, along with any other logic that is required. One or more public methods is defined as the interface into the Web service. WSAD generates all the code needed to turn this class into a Web service.

The scenario that we will use is a new customer scenario. We will create two classes—a new customer class that contains the data and a CustomerManager class that keeps track of all the customers. No database will be used in order to keep the complexity of the example to a minimum.

Creating the Project

The first step is to create the project. You do this by starting up WSAD and then choosing New, Project from the File menu. This will bring up the New Project dialog box. Choose Web, Web Project, Next. A dialog box similar to the one shown in Figure 18.1 will appear.

FIGURE 18.1
WebSphere Studio Application Developer requires that a project be created.

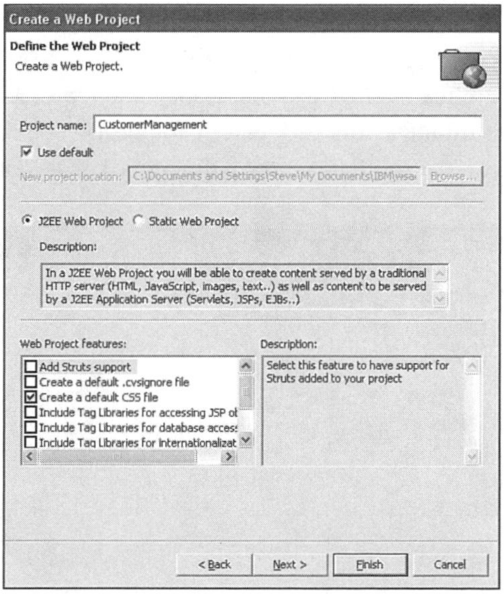

18

Name the project CustomerManagement, accept all the defaults on this page, and click Next. Name the Enterprise Application project CustomerManagementEAR as shown in Figure 18.2.

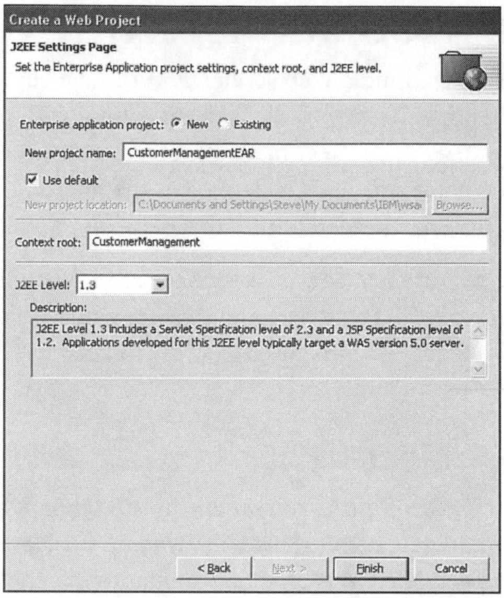

FIGURE 18.2
*WebSphere Studio
Application Developer
also requires that an
Enterprise project be
created.*

The Enterprise project will manage the server instances that are created to run your
application. Make sure that the New radio button is selected and accept the defaults for
everything else. Click Finish. Two projects, the Web and EAR projects, will appear in the
Navigator pane. Right-click on the CustomerManagement project in the Navigator pane
and choose Properties from the context menu that appears. Selecting Java Build Path on
the left and Libraries on the right will show a dialog box that looks like Figure 18.3.

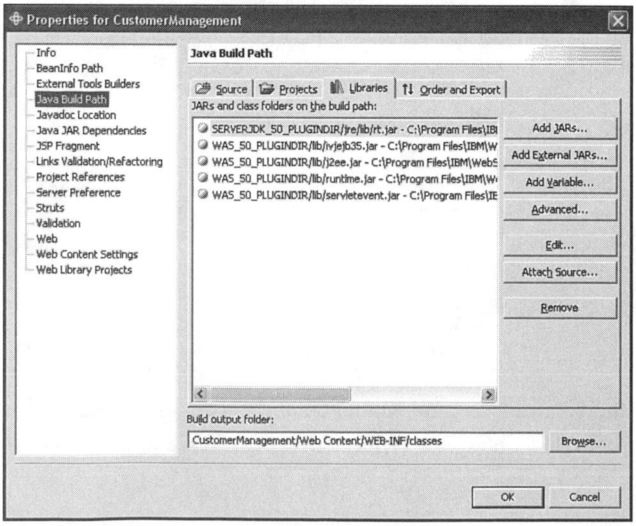

FIGURE 18.3
*The Libraries tab
allows you to add jar
files to the Build Path
for your project.*

The Build Path is a set of all directories and jar files that will be used to locate the classes needed by your project. The default Web project doesn't need either Xerces or SOAP, so these jar files are not included by default. You add them by clicking on the Add External JARs button and then using the File dialog box to locate soap.jar and xerces.jar. The version of WSAD that we ran had them stored in

```
C:\Program Files\IBM\WebSphere Studio\runtimes\base_v5\lib
```

Locate both of them and click on the OK button.

Adding the Code

As we stated earlier in the hour, WSAD builds Web services by using Java classes as input. We now need to create the Java classes that will be used in this process. The first class that we will create will be called Customer. In WSAD, the appearance of the IDE changes depending on your choice of "perspective." You choose a perspective to suit the role that you are filling at any given moment. Until now, you were creating a Web project, so you were in the Web perspective. Now you want to be a Java developer for a while, so you change your perspective by selecting Open Perspective, Java from the Window menu. This will transform the IDE to look like Figure 18.4.

FIGURE 18.4

The Java perspective provides you with a set of tools that are designed for Java development.

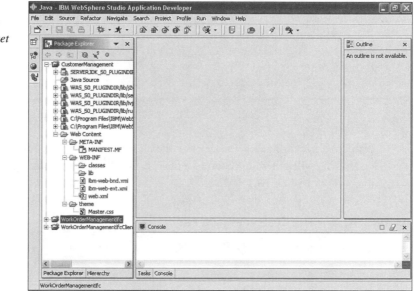

18

The primary areas of the Java perspective are the Package Explorer on the left, the Editor pane in the middle, and the Task pane on the bottom. The Task pane shows you errors and warnings.

> WSAD perspectives can be thought of as different but complimentary products in the same IDE. The Server perspective is for running the application, the Debug perspective is for debugging, the Java perspective is for editing and compiling code, and so on.

We need a couple of classes for this example. First, we need a class to represent the customer. You create a new Java class by right-clicking on the Java Source folder in the Navigator Pane. This will bring up the dialog shown in Figure 18.5.

FIGURE 18.5

The Java perspective provides you with tools to create Java classes.

Name the package com.mycompany and the class Customer. Click Finish to generate the code. This will generate a Stub of a class called Customer. Complete the class by adding the code in Listing 18.1.

LISTING 18.1   The Customer.java File

```
package com.mycompany;

import java.util.Date;
import java.lang.String;


/**
 * @author Steve Potts
```

LISTING 18.1   continued

```
    */

public class Customer
{
    private int customerNumber;
    private String customerName;
    private String street;
    private String city;
    private String state;
    private String zip;

    static int nextCustomerNumber = 1000;

    //constructor
    public Customer()
    {
        this.customerNumber = nextCustomerNumber;
        nextCustomerNumber++;
    }

    //getters

    public String getCustomerName()
    {
        return this.customerName;
    }

    public String getStreet()
    {
        return this.street;
    }

    public String getCity()
    {
        return this.city;
    }

    public String getState()
    {
        return this.state;
    }

    public String getZip()
    {
        return this.zip;
    }
```

18

LISTING **18.1**   continued

```
        public int getCustomerNumber()
        {
            return this.customerNumber;
        }

//Setters

        public void setCustomerName(String customerName)
        {
            this.customerName = customerName;
        }

        public void setStreet(String street)
        {
            this.street = street;
        }

        public void setCity(String city)
        {
            this.city = city;
        }

        public void setState(String state)
        {
            this.state = state;
        }

        public void setZip(String zip)
        {
            this.zip = zip;
        }

}
```

This class is a garden-variety Java class. The static variable allows us to keep up with the customer numbers that have already been given out.

```
//constructor
public Customer()
{
    this.customerNumber = nextCustomerNumber;
    nextCustomerNumber++;
}
```

The constructor allocates the next number.

We also need another class to provide method calls for the Web service. This class, the CustomerManager class, is shown in Listing 18.2.

LISTING 18.2   The CustomerManager.java File

```java
package com.mycompany;

import java.util.Date;
import java.util.Vector;
import java.lang.String;

/**
 * @author Steve Potts
 *
 */
public class CustomerManager
{

    static Vector customers = new Vector();

    public int createNewCustomer(
    String customerName,
    String street,
    String city,
    String state,
    String zip)
    {
        Customer newOne = new Customer();

        newOne.setCustomerName(customerName);
        newOne.setStreet(street);
        newOne.setCity(city);
        newOne.setState(state);
        newOne.setZip(zip);

        customers.addElement(newOne);

        return newOne.getCustomerNumber();
    }
}
```

18

Cut and paste Listings 18.1 and 18.2 into WebSphere, and continue with the exercise. This class is very ordinary, by design, so that your attention will be on the creation of the Web service itself.

```java
customers.addElement(newOne);
```

After the customer is created, you add it to the customers vector.

Generating the Web Service

Your next task is to generate the Web service from these classes. Choose New, Other from the File menu. When the dialog box shown in Figure 18.6 appears, choose Web Services in the left pane and Web Service in the right pane and click Next.

FIGURE 18.6

*Web services are cre-
ated by the IDE.*

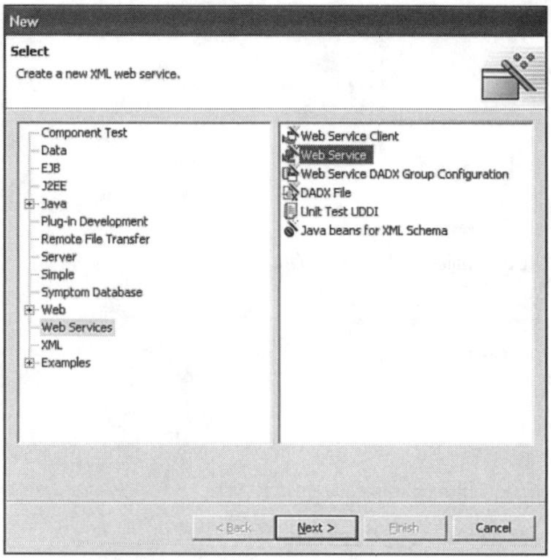

This will bring up the dialog box shown in Figure 18.7.

FIGURE 18.7

*The Web service that
we are creating is of
type Java Bean.*

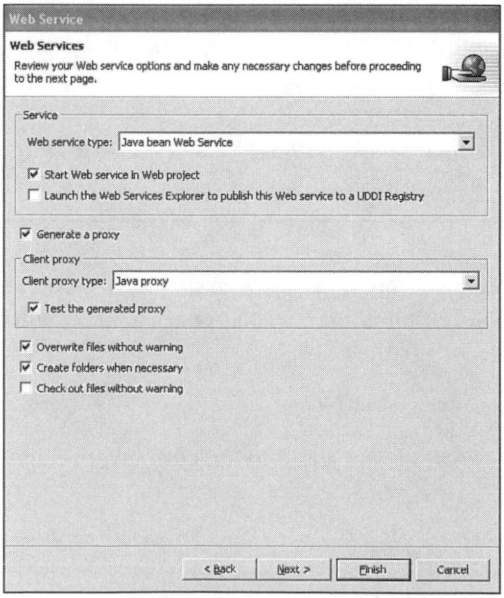

Choose Java Bean Web Service as the Web service type, check the boxes as shown in the figure, and click on Next.

> The term "Java Bean Web Service" is one that is generated from a class that follows the Java Bean pattern. You can also use WSAD to generate a Web service from an EJB.

One of the boxes, Test the Generated Proxy, will cause the test application to be generated. This will bring up the dialog box shown in Figure 18.8.

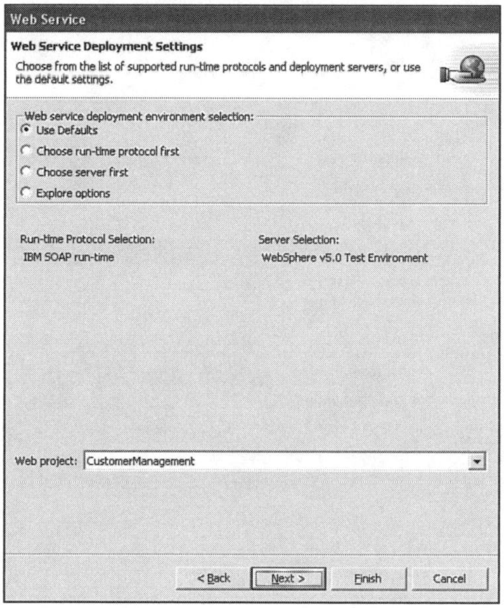

FIGURE 18.8

We specify the name of the project containing the bean.

18

The CustomerManagement class is chosen because it contains the Java code for the Web service. Clicking on Next brings up the dialog box shown in Figure 18.9, which allows us to specify the class containing the methods that we want to expose.

Click on Next to see the names of all the files that will be generated. This is shown in Figure 18.10.

Accept the defaults and click Next. This will bring up the dialog box shown in Figure 18.11.

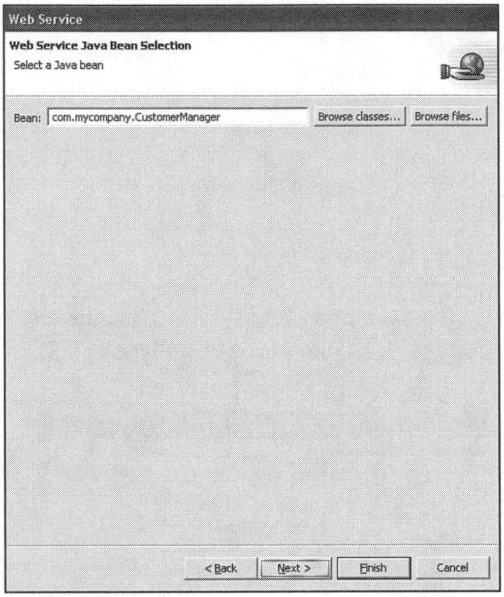

FIGURE 18.9

You specify the Java bean to be used to cre ate the Web service.

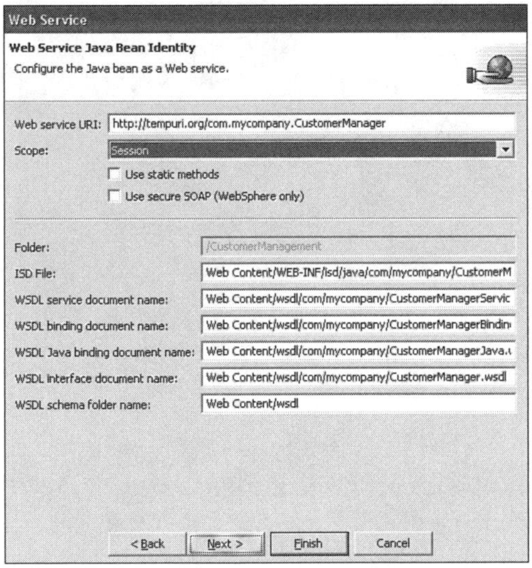

FIGURE 18.10

You can modify the default locations of the files generated for the Web service.

Accept the defaults and click Next again. This will bring up the Binding Proxy Generation screen shown in Figure 18.12. The proxy is created so that we can test the Web service.

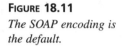

FIGURE 18.11
The SOAP encoding is the default.

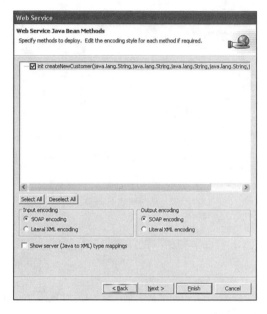

FIGURE 18.12
The proxy allows clients to communicate with the service.

18

Click Next. The screen that comes up is shown in Figure 18.13. It asks whether you want to run the test application. Check the Test the Generated Proxy box, and click Next.

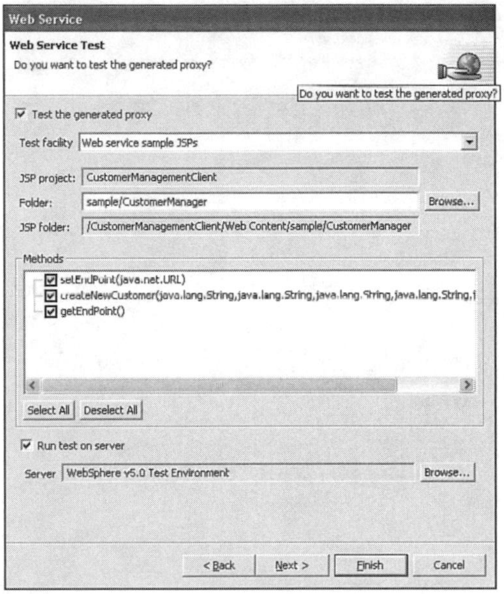

FIGURE 18.13

Testing the proxy is done by creating test JSPs that use the Web service.

The dialog box in Figure 18.14 asks whether you want to publish the Web service to a UDDI registry. For this example, we will not publish it.

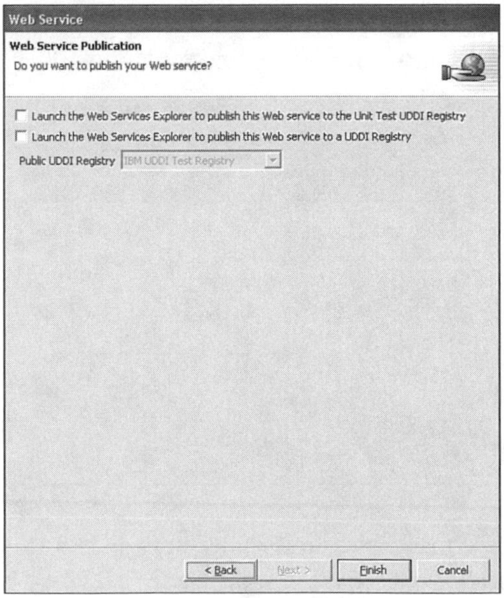

FIGURE 18.14

Publishing the Web service to a UDDI registry can be done at the same time.

Clicking Finish will cause WSAD to go off and generate code, start up servers, and so on for several minutes.

Testing the Web Service

When WSAD finishes, it will display a browser in the center pane. Clicking on the `createNewCustomer()` method will display a generated form in the right panel. Entering data and pressing the Invoke key will produce a result like the one displayed in Figure 18.15.

FIGURE 18.15

The test program runs in the browser.

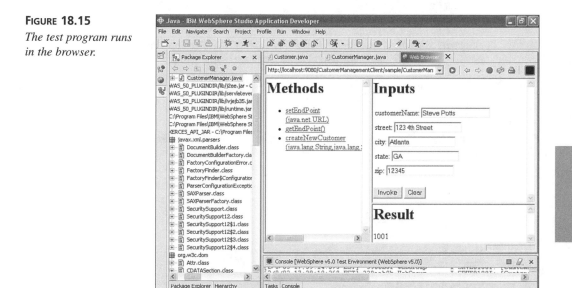

You will see a different customer number in the bottom pane based on how many times you have executed the service. This magic effect was created by WSAD in a new project called CustomerManagementClient. The proxy file that was generated by WSAD is shown in Listing 18.3.

LISTING 18.3   The CustomerManagerProxy.java File

```
package proxy.soap;

import java.net.*;
import java.util.*;
import org.w3c.dom.*;
import org.apache.soap.*;
```

LISTING 18.3   continued

```java
import org.apache.soap.encoding.*;
import org.apache.soap.encoding.soapenc.*;
import org.apache.soap.rpc.*;
import org.apache.soap.util.xml.*;
import org.apache.soap.messaging.*;
import org.apache.soap.transport.http.*;

public class CustomerManagerProxy
{
  private Call call;
  private URL url = null;
  private String stringURL =
    "http://localhost:9080/CustomerManagement/servlet/rpcrouter";
  private java.lang.reflect.Method setTcpNoDelayMethod;

  public CustomerManagerProxy()
  {
   try
   {
     setTcpNoDelayMethod = SOAPHTTPConnection.class.getMethod(
                      "setTcpNoDelay", new Class[]{Boolean.class});
   }
   catch (Exception e)
   {
   }
   call = createCall();
  }

  public synchronized void setEndPoint(URL url)
  {
    this.url = url;
  }

  public synchronized URL getEndPoint() throws MalformedURLException
  {
    return getURL();
  }

  private URL getURL() throws MalformedURLException
  {
    if (url == null && stringURL != null && stringURL.length() > 0)
    {
      url = new URL(stringURL);
    }
    return url;
  }
```

Listing 18.3 continued

```
public synchronized int createNewCustomer(
    java.lang.String customerName,java.lang.String street,
    java.lang.String city,java.lang.String state,java.lang.
                                String zip) throws Exception
{
String targetObjectURI =
            "http://tempuri.org/com.mycompany.CustomerManager";
String SOAPActionURI = "";

if(getURL() == null)
{
  throw new SOAPException(Constants.FAULT_CODE_CLIENT,
  "A URL must be specified via CustomerManagerProxy.setEndPoint(URL).");
}

call.setMethodName("createNewCustomer");
call.setEncodingStyleURI(Constants.NS_URI_SOAP_ENC);
call.setTargetObjectURI(targetObjectURI);
Vector params = new Vector();
Parameter customerNameParam = new Parameter(
        "customerName", java.lang.String.class, customerName,
                                        Constants.NS_URI_SOAP_ENC);
params.addElement(customerNameParam);
Parameter streetParam = new Parameter("street",
                    java.lang.String.class, street, Constants.NS_URI_SOAP_ENC);
params.addElement(streetParam);
Parameter cityParam = new Parameter("city",
                java.lang.String.class, city, Constants.NS_URI_SOAP_ENC);
params.addElement(cityParam);
Parameter stateParam = new Parameter("state",
                java.lang.String.class, state, Constants.NS_URI_SOAP_ENC);
params.addElement(stateParam);
Parameter zipParam = new Parameter("zip",
                java.lang.String.class, zip, Constants.NS_URI_SOAP_ENC);
params.addElement(zipParam);
call.setParams(params);
Response resp = call.invoke(getURL(), SOAPActionURI);

//Check the response.
if (resp.generatedFault())
{
  Fault fault = resp.getFault();
  call.setFullTargetObjectURI(targetObjectURI);
  throw new SOAPException(fault.getFaultCode(),
                                fault.getFaultString());
}
else
{
```

18

LISTING 18.3   continued

```
   Parameter refValue = resp.getReturnValue();
   return ((java.lang.Integer)refValue.getValue()).intValue();
 }
}

 protected Call createCall()
 {
   SOAPHTTPConnection soapHTTPConnection = new SOAPHTTPConnection();
   if ( setTcpNoDelayMethod != null)
   {
     try
     {
       setTcpNoDelayMethod.invoke(soapHTTPConnection,
                                           new Object[]{Boolean.TRUE});
     }
     catch (Exception ex)
     {
     }
   }
   Call call = new Call();
   call.setSOAPTransport(soapHTTPConnection);
   SOAPMappingRegistry smr = call.getSOAPMappingRegistry();
   return call;
 }
}
```

If you want to look at the generated code, choose the Web perspective. The code is located under the CustomerManagementClient project. Open the Java source folder, and then look in the proxy.soap package for the file.

You should not expect to understand everything that is included in this generated file, but you might notice some interesting parts.

```
private Call call;
private URL url = null;
private String stringURL =
  "http://localhost:9080/CustomerManagement/servlet/rpcrouter";
```

The Call object is commonly used to represent the SOAP call. The URL is the actual servlet that routes the call to the call handler.

This Java file is called by a JSP that was also generated for you by WSAD. Listing 18.4 shows this JSP.

LISTING 18.4   The Result.jsp File

```
<HTML>
<HEAD>
<TITLE>Result</TITLE>
</HEAD>
<BODY>
<H1>Result</H1>

<jsp:useBean id="CustomerManagerid" scope="session"
                        class="proxy.soap.CustomerManagerProxy" />

<%!
public static String markup(String text) {
    if (text == null) {
        return null;
    }

    StringBuffer buffer = new StringBuffer();
    for (int i = 0; i < text.length(); i++) {
        char c = text.charAt(i);
        switch (c) {
            case '<':
                buffer.append("&lt;");
                break;
            case '&':
                buffer.append("&amp;");
                break;
            case '>':
                buffer.append("&gt;");
                break;
            case '"':
                buffer.append("&quot;");
                break;
            default:
                buffer.append(c);
                break;
        }
    }
    return buffer.toString();
}
%>


<%
String method = request.getParameter("method");
if (method == null) method = "";

boolean gotMethod = false;
```

18

LISTING 18.4   continued

```
try {
if (method.equals("setEndPoint(java.net.URL)")) {

        gotMethod = true;
        String url0id= markup(request.getParameter("url5"));
        java.net.URL url0idTemp = new java.net.URL(url0id);
        CustomerManagerid.setEndPoint(url0idTemp);
}else if (method.equals("getEndPoint()")) {

        gotMethod = true;
        java.net.URL mtemp = CustomerManagerid.getEndPoint();
if(mtemp == null){
%>
<%=mtemp %>
<%
}else{
        String tempResultresult8 = markup(mtemp.toString());
        %>
        <%= tempResultresult8 %>
        <%
}
}else if (method.equals("createNewCustomer(java.lang.String,java.lang.String,
                   java.lang.String,java.lang.String,java.lang.String)")) {

        gotMethod = true;
        String customerName1id= markup(request.getParameter("customerName13"));
        java.lang.String customerName1idTemp = customerName1id;
        String street2id= markup(request.getParameter("street15"));
        java.lang.String street2idTemp = street2id;
        String city3id= markup(request.getParameter("city17"));
        java.lang.String city3idTemp = city3id;
        String state4id= markup(request.getParameter("state19"));
        java.lang.String state4idTemp = state4id;
        String zip5id= markup(request.getParameter("zip21"));
        java.lang.String zip5idTemp = zip5id;
        int mtemp = CustomerManagerid.createNewCustomer(customerName1idTemp
                   ,street2idTemp,city3idTemp,state4idTemp,zip5idTemp);
        String tempResultresult11 = markup(String.valueOf(mtemp));
        %>
        <%= tempResultresult11 %>
        <%
}} catch (Exception e) {
%>
exception: <%= e %>
<%
return;
}
if(!gotMethod){
```

LISTING 18.4 continued

```
%>
result: N/A
<%
}
%>
</BODY>
</HTML>
```

You can locate this code in WSAD by going to the Web perspective and looking in the Navigator under the CustomerManagerClient project. The folder chain is Web content, sample, and then CustomerManager.

The actual call is shown here:

```
}else if (method.equals("createNewCustomer(java.lang.String,java.lang.String,
                         java.lang.String,java.lang.String,java.lang.String)")) {

    gotMethod = true;
    String customerName1id= markup(request.getParameter("customerName13"));
    java.lang.String customerName1idTemp = customerName1id;
    String street2id= markup(request.getParameter("street15"));
    java.lang.String street2idTemp = street2id;
    String city3id= markup(request.getParameter("city17"));
    java.lang.String city3idTemp = city3id;
    String state4id= markup(request.getParameter("state19"));
    java.lang.String state4idTemp = state4id;
    String zip5id= markup(request.getParameter("zip21"));
    java.lang.String zip5idTemp = zip5id;
    int mtemp = CustomerManagerid.createNewCustomer(customerName1idTemp
             ,street2idTemp,city3idTemp,state4idTemp,zip5idTemp);
    String tempResultresult11 = markup(String.valueOf(mtemp));
    %>
    <%= tempResultresult11 %>
    <%
```

Notice that each of the values in the object is obtained from the request object.

The connection between this JSP file and the Web service is found in the useBean tag of the JSP.

```
<jsp:useBean id="CustomerManagerid" scope="session"
                            class="proxy.soap.CustomerManagerProxy" />
```

This JSP is declaring that it intends to use the proxy code to communicate with the Web service. You can cut and paste from this JSP to create an application that fits your requirements. Alternatively, you could write a Java application that uses this proxy to access the Web service also.

18

Another alternative would be to take the WSDL file generated for this project and use it to create a client using any number of tools such as WebLogic Workshop or Visual Studio .NET. The WSDL for this project is stored in

```
...\IBM\wsad\workspace\CustomerManagement\Web Content\wsdl\com\mycompany
```

The root of this is where you installed WSAD. Normally it is c:\Program Files. The files in this directory can be combined to create a WSDL that can be used by any tool to communicate with this Web service.

Summary

In this hour, you learned about IBM's entry into the Web services tools market. You first learned about IBM's role in Web services. Next, you learned about its flagship Java Development tool, WebSphere Studio Application Developer. You then developed a business application in Java and transformed it into a Web service using WSAD. Finally, you used WSAD to create a JSP that can be used to test your Web service.

Q&A

Q What isn't WSAD more popular with independent consultants?

A IBM's marketing of WSAD tends to be aimed at large companies. It tends to be expensive compared to .NET and other comparable products.

Q What type of resources are available for learning WSAD?

A Unfortunately, they are limited. IBM offers some courses in WSAD. You can find articles on WSAD at www.ibm.com, but there are no "WSAD Unleashed" books on the market.

Workshop

The Workshop is designed to help you review what you've learned and to test your understanding of WebSphere.

Quiz

1. What type of program is used to provide functionality for WSAD Web services?
2. What type of Web services test program is generated by WSAD?
3. What other types of programs besides Web services can be generated using WSAD?

Quiz Answers

1. A Java Bean is used to hold data and an ordinary Java class is used to provide methods.

2. A Java Server Page (JSP) is created for testing the Web service.

3. WSAD is a full-service J2EE development environment that can be used to create servlets, EJBs, JSPs, and Java applications.

Activities

1. Create a calculator Web service and a client on your computer using WSAD. Follow the same methodology that we used previously.

2. Move the generated client to another computer and access the Web service from it. The same URL that you are using on your own computer will be used on that computer also.

18

Hour **19**

Creating Web Services with Other Toolkits

In Hours 13–18, we examined some of the well-known Web services toolkits. Although they are the more popular toolkits from the larger vendors, it does not always mean that they are better. Because Web services are still a fairly young technology, there are still many smaller companies and groups offering competing solutions. In some cases, these offerings fill needs the larger companies have ignored. In this hour, we'll examine the following toolkits:

- The Mind Electric GLUE
- PocketSOAP
- SOAP::Lite

For each toolkit, we'll also demonstrate how to build a client using the toolkit, and in the case of GLUE and SOAP::Lite, how to build a service as well. Finally, we'll discuss some of the advantages of each tool.

The Mind Electric GLUE

One of the smaller, yet very popular, Java-oriented Web services toolkits is GLUE by The Mind Electric. The company's slogan for GLUE is "The Power of Java, the Simplicity of .NET." In many cases, GLUE delivers on this promise and as such has built up quite a following in the Java-based Web services community since its introduction in August 2001.

One of the great features of GLUE is its capability to work either as a complete server or as the Web services module for another application server product (such as Websphere). When running as a standalone server, it supports JSP, servlets, JMS, and many other features typically found in full-fledged application servers.

The package itself is also quite small (around 500K). It comes in two versions: Standard and Professional. The Professional version adds a number of features, but the Standard version is quite capable in its own right for performing Web services development.

GLUE can be used to build both clients and services. For the service side, the user builds her code, and a simple Java servlet is wrapped around it, providing the SOAP interface. The system comes with a series of tools to create WSDL from java classes and vice versa.

Finally, the best part about GLUE is the price. In most noncommercial and even in many commercial situations, the package is free for 30 days.

See the terms and conditions for the GLUE product license at
http://www.themindelectric.com/glue/license-STD.html for the Standard
version and http://www.themindelectric.com/glue/license-PRO.html for
the Professional version.

GLUE provides full support of all the current standards including SOAP 1.1 and 1.2, UDDI 1 and 2, SOAP headers, SOAP with attachments, and so on. As such, GLUE is one of the most fully featured toolsets available at this time. Several benchmarks have also shown it to be quite fast compared to many of the other popular solutions. Also of interest is GLUE's excellent integration with Enterprise Java Beans (EJB). This capability allows for easy exposure of your EJB services via Web services.

Building a Service with GLUE

Let's build a simple service with GLUE to show you how it's done. Later, we'll build a client that can access this service also with GLUE. For our example, we'll make a service that has two methods. The first will take a temperature sent to it in degrees F and return the equivalent temperature in degrees C. The second method will perform the opposite conversion. The code for our simple service can be seen in Listing 19.1.

LISTING 19.1   A Class to Perform Temperature Conversions

```
public class TempConverter
{
    public double CtoF(double degreesC)
    {
      System.out.println("finding the F equivalent for "
          +degreesC+" degrees C");
      return (9.0/5.0)*degreesC+32.0;
    }

    public double FtoC(double degreesF)
    {
        System.out.println("finding the C equivalent for "
            +degreesF+" degrees F");
        return (degreesF-32.0)*(5.0/9.0);
    }
}
```

As you can see from the code, there is nothing specific to GLUE or Web services added to the code. It looks like any other Java class you might write to perform this function.

In order for GLUE to turn the TempConverter class into a Web service, it is necessary to write a small wrapper program. This wrapper program will register the class with the server and assign it a specific service name. The code for the wrapper can be found in Listing 19.2.

19

LISTING 19.2   The GLUE Wrapper That Makes TempConverter Act As a Service

```
import electric.registry.Registry;
import electric.server.http.HTTP;

public class TempConverterService
{
   public static void main(String[] args) throws Exception
   {
     HTTP.startup("http://localhost:8888/glue");
     Registry.publish("urn:TempConverter"
         , new TempConverter());
   }
}
```

In this file, we first import a pair of support classes provided by GLUE: Registry and HTTP. We then create a Java class that contains a `main()` method, so we can run it as a program. That main method establishes an HTTP connection to the GLUE server, and then instructs the GLUE service registry to create a new entry for `TempConverter` and instantiates a copy of `TempConverter` for use.

If you downloaded the code from the Web site, you will find these two java files in the \webservice24hours\ch19\glue\service directory. You can compile both of these files by typing the following command:

```
javac *.java
```

Provided everything is installed and configured correctly, you should receive no compile errors. Start the service up by typing:

```
java TempConverterService
```

You should see the following output:

```
[STARTUP] GLUE standard 4.0b2 © 2001-2003 The Mind Electric
[STARTUP] soap/http server started on http://thismachinesIPaddress>:8888/glue
```

That's all there is to it. You now have a service running on GLUE ready to handle requests.

Building a Client Application with GLUE

Now that you have a service running on GLUE, let's access it with a client written using GLUE. As normal, the first part of writing a client is to access the service's WSDL to determine the call structure. GLUE provides an excellent tool called `wsdl2java` that will take a WSDL and build the needed interface and helper classes for you.

If you downloaded the code from Sams' Web site, you should find a directory named webservice24hours\ch19\glue\client. Open a new command-line window and CD to that directory. Then type the following command to generate the interface classes using `wsdl2java`:

```
wsdl2java http://localhost:8888/glue/urn:TempConverter.wsdl
```

You should get back the following output:

```
[STARTUP] GLUE standard 4.0b2 © 2001-2003 The Mind Electric
write file ITempConverter.java
write file TempConverterHelper.java
```

If you perform a DIR command, you will see that two new java files were created corresponding to the ones named in the output from the `wsdl2java` command you ran. Let's briefly examine those files. ITempConverter.java can be seen in Listing 19.3 and TempConverterHelper.java is shown in Listing 19.4.

LISTING 19.3 The ITempConverter.java File Created by the `wsdl2java` Tool

```
// generated by GLUE standard 4.0b2 (wsdl2java) on
// Sun Feb 02 15:35:44 EST 2003
public interface ITempConverter
  {
  double CtoF( double arg0 );
  double FtoC( double arg0 );
  }
```

LISTING 19.4 The TempConverterHelper.java File Created by the `wsdl2java` Tool

```
// generated by GLUE standard 4.0b2 (wsdl2java)
//on Sun Feb 02 15:35:44 EST 2003
import electric.registry.Registry;
import electric.registry.RegistryException;

public class TempConverterHelper
{
  public static ITempConverter bind()
      throws RegistryException
  {
    return bind("http://localhost:8888/glue/urn:TempConverter.wsdl");
  }

  public static ITempConverter bind(String url)
      throws RegistryException
  {
    return (ITempConverter) Registry.bind(url,ITempConverter.class);
  }
}
```

19

As you can see from Listing 19.3, ITempConverter is a simple interface that lists the two methods found in our service. That's all it does!

In Listing 19.4, you see the code for TempConverterHelper. This class is responsible for performing the actual binding of the method calls from our client to the service. You'll notice that two versions of the bind method are given. The first takes no parameters and will create a binding to the exact service location that we provided during the wsdl2java tool invocation. The other is a more generic version that allows us to specify a different service URL. This can be helpful when you build both your client and service on one machine, and then deploy them on different machines because you can then specify their new addresses.

Now that we have the support classes created, let's go ahead and build a client to call them. We have provided a simple client in the webservice24hours\ch19\glue\client directory called TempClient.java. The code for this file can be found in Listing 19.5.

LISTING 19.5   The TempClient.java File Is Our Client Program

```java
import electric.registry.Registry;

public class TempClient
{
    public static void main(String[] args) throws Exception
    {
        if(args.length<2)
        {
            System.out.println("You must give temp and scale.");
            System.out.println("For instance: 21 F");
            System.exit(-1);
        }

        if(!(args[1].equals("C") || args[1].equals("F")))
        {
            System.out.println("Incorrect Temperature Scale.");
            System.out.println(" You must specify either 'F' or 'C'");
            System.exit(-1);
        }
        ITempConverter tempconverter = TempConverterHelper.bind();
        String temp_as_string = args[0];
        double starttemp = (new Double(temp_as_string)).doubleValue();
        double endtemp;
        if(args[1].equals("F"))
        {
            endtemp = tempconverter.FtoC(starttemp);
            System.out.println("The equivalent temperature is: "+endtemp
                +" degrees C");
        }
        else if(args[1].equals("C"))
        {
            endtemp = tempconverter.CtoF(starttemp);
            System.out.println("The equivalent temperature is: "+endtemp
                +" degrees F");
        }
    }
}
```

Only part of this program is any different than it would be if the `TempConverter` class was local—the line where we instantiate the class. Instead of creating an instance of the `TempConverter`, we create an `ITempConverter` reference and link it to an object that the `TempConverterHelper` class gives us after binding to the remote service. Then we call and use this reference as though it were a normal local object.

To run our client, first double-check that you have the service up and running in another window. Then, in this window, type the following:

```
java TempClient 100 C
```

You should get the following output:

```
The equivalent temperature is: 212.0 degrees F
```

In the service window, you should see output such as this:

```
Finding the F equivalent for 100.0 degrees C
```

That's all there is to it. GLUE takes care of all the heavy lifting. This is one of the reasons that it has become so popular in the Java developer community. There is a lot more to GLUE than what we've shown here though. The Mind Electric provides excellent documentation on its product, and a number of good references are on the Web that can show you how to build more complex systems using GLUE. If you're planning to do a Java-based Web services project, GLUE is an excellent choice and is highly recommended.

PocketSOAP

19

In late 2000, Simon Fell released the first version of PocketSOAP. His goal was to implement a mechanism to enable Web services to be easily built for Microsoft PocketPC-based PDAs (hence the "Pocket" in "PocketSOAP"). Because PocketPC machines are small and low powered, his goal was only to create a system to enable these machines to act as clients, not to provide a framework for building services.

Over the course of time, PocketSOAP has expanded its reach and capabilities. It now supports all versions of Windows from Windows 95 (OSR2) up to the current Windows XP releases, as well as PocketPC 2000 and 2002.

How is this any different from the Microsoft .NET platform? First of all, .NET will not run on Windows 95 or 98; PocketSOAP will. Second, the .NET tools for PocketPC are in beta at the time of this writing (although they should be released by the time you read this). PocketSOAP supports SwA (MIME-based attachments), which Microsoft seems to have no plans to do in .NET. As a result, PocketSOAP is a good alternative to .NET in some situations.

PocketSOAP really should be considered as one of a group of tools. They are

- **PocketSOAP**—Provides both message and RPC-style (section 5) SOAP communications.
- **PocketXML-RPC**—Provides RPC-XML style Web services (as opposed to SOAP-based communications).
- **WSDL Wizard**—Helps create proxies based on a WSDL definition. The proxies are generated as Visual Basic 6 classes. The proxy classes can then be used by PocketSOAP or PocketXML-RPC.
- **PocketSOAP TransportPak**—Provides additional transports other than HTTP for PocketSOAP.
- **4s4c**—A package for creating SOAP-based services. It exposes COM objects as Web services that can be called.
- **TcpTrace**—An excellent tool for monitoring SOAP communications.
- **PcapTrace**—Another monitoring tool similar to TcpTrace, but one that monitors through the Windows Packet Capture library.
- **ProxyTrace**—Another tool for monitoring HTTP SOAP traffic. Works better with WSDL than TcpTrace.

The current version of PocketSOAP is 1.4.1. This version supports DIME, SOAP with attachments, Section 5 (RPC style) encoding, complex objects, multidimensional arrays, and HTTP 1.1. The current version is SOAP 1.1–compliant only, however. Upcoming versions are expected to include SOAP 1.2 support.

PocketSOAP has been tested to work cleanly against many of the other Web services toolkits such as Axis, GLUE, .NET, SOAP::Lite, XMLBus, and many others. As such, there is no reason to think it wouldn't work when communicating with any other standards-compliant services.

An excellent Yahoo! group is set up at `http://groups.yahoo.com/group/pocketsoap/`. The developers of PocketSOAP and many of the supporting tools frequent the message board here and provide excellent assistance. If you run into problems with PocketSOAP, post to the message board here for help.

Now that you've gotten the background on PocketSOAP, let's build a simple example client with it.

 Appendix C, "Installing and Configuring Other Toolkits," contains instructions on how to download and set up PocketSOAP and the various supporting tools.

Building a Client Application with PocketSOAP

Because PocketSOAP is meant for client-side development only, we'll build our example client to communicate with a service found on the www.xmethods.com Web services directory site. In this case, we'll write a client to interface with the Weather-Temperature service found on the site. Weather-Temperature takes a U.S. ZIP Code and returns the current temperature to the client.

PocketSOAP allows the developer to write client code in a number of languages. In this case, we'll use VBScript because it is built in and readily available on all Windows-based machines.

In order to write our client, we'll need to first examine the methods that the Weather-Temperature service understands. To do this, open your browser and point it to http://www.xmethods.net. Scroll to the bottom of the page. Near the bottom is the link for Weather-Temperature. Clicking on the link opens up some initial details about the service. The first point of interest on this page is the endpoint value. We'll need this for our code, so remember where you see it.

In the yellow block near the top of the screen is a link named Analyze WSDL. Click that link to get the WSDL analysis page provided by xmethods. This new page tells us the name of the service, the number of methods it supports, the call style, the transport protocol it uses, and the endpoint information again.

Click on the link that says 1 Operation. At this point, a new screen will appear listing the methods this service supports, the SOAP Action (in this case, none), the call style (in this case, RPC), and the input and output messages. If you click on the links for Input or Output message, you'll see the list of parameters that this method expects, their types, and so on.

From the information in the screens we just viewed, we can conclude that a service with an endpoint at http://services.xmethods.net:80/soap/servlet/rpcrouter responds to a single method call named getTemp, which takes a single String parameter for the ZIP Code and returns a float for the temperature. You'll note that we could also have gotten all this

19

information by examining the WSDL file. (There's a link for it on the main page for this service.) This method is just a bit easier for us humans.

Now that we have the specifics we need to call the service, let's write our client. We'll make it take a single parameter at the command line that contains the ZIP Code of the area in the United States that we want to get the temperature of. It will then build up the SOAP call, make the communication with the service, and get back the results. The results will be displayed in a small pop-up dialog box on our screen. Listing 19.6 shows the code for our example client.

LISTING 19.6   The Example Temperatureclient.vbs File Retrieves the Current Temperature for a U.S. ZIP Code Through the Weather-Temperature Service Found on xmethods.net.

```
' get the command line parameter
dim objArgs
set objArgs = WScript.Arguments

' Create a new envelope object,
'this is the core part of any pocketSOAP usage.
dim env
set env = CreateObject("pocketSOAP.Envelope.2")

' set the methodName and methodname Namespace values
env.SetMethod "getTemp", "urn:xmethods-Temperature"

' create the parameter, pass along the zip code the user types
' at the command line.
env.Parameters.Create "zipcode", objArgs(0)

' now, we need to send the SOAP request to the
' endpoint, so we create a transport object
dim http
set http = CreateObject("pocketSOAP.HTTPTransport.2")

' we need to set the SOAPAction header
http.SOAPAction = ""
' now we send the request, the call to env.serialize,
' takes the envelope object we've been working with
' and serializes it out to the SOAP/XML format for sending.
strLoc = "http://services.xmethods.net:80/soap/servlet/rpcrouter"
http.Send strLoc, env.serialize

' now, we need to parse the SOAP message we get as a response
env.parse http

' and now, extract the return value
wscript.echo "Temp for "&objArgs(0)&"="&env.Parameters.Item(0).Value
```

Let's examine the code of our client and see how the PocketSOAP system comes into play. In the first three lines, we do some setup to retrieve the ZIP Code as a command-line parameter to be passed in at runtime.

Next, we'll set up the SOAP envelope object:

```
dim env
set env = CreateObject("pocketSOAP.Envelope.2")
```

Then, we'll tell it what method we're calling and from which service:

```
env.SetMethod "getTemp", "urn:xmethods-Temperature"
```

In this next step, we'll pass in the parameters for the getTemp method. In this case, we're going to pass in the "zipcode", which is stored in objArgs(0):

```
env.Parameters.Create "zipcode", objArgs(0)
```

Okay, now that the envelope for our request is all built, we'll need to set up the transport object. We'll do that with the next two lines of code:

```
Dim http
Set http = CreateObject("pocketSOAP.HTTPTransport.2")
```

No SOAP action is required for this method, so we'll tell the transport not to use anything for it:

```
http.SOAPACtion = ""
```

At this point, all the setup work is finished. Now, we can make the actual call out to the service. We do that with these lines:

```
StrLoc = "http://services.xmethods.net:80/soap/servlet/rpcrouter"
http.Send strLoc, env.serialize
```

Next, we need to parse out the response. We can reuse the envelope object by using it to store the data returned by the http.Send command that we just executed. We'll need to tell the envelope to parse the data that http returns to it. We do that here:

```
env.parse http
```

Now that we have the results, we report them back to the user:

```
Wscript.echo "Temp for "&objArgs(0)&"="&env.Parameters.Item(0).Value
```

19

As you can see, we requested the results of the service call by getting the first item's value out of the envelope.

To run our new client, open a command prompt, navigate to the directory that you have the code in, and then type the following:

TemperatureClient.vbs 30096

You can replace the 30096 with any valid U.S. ZIP Code. The remote service will be called, and you should get back a prompt similar the one in Figure 19.1, but with a different temperature depending on current weather conditions.

FIGURE 19.1

Results of the
TemperatureClient
VBScript program, utilizing the Weather-Temperature service on xmethods.net.

As you can see, the process of using PocketSOAP is quite simple and easy to understand. Although we have demonstrated using only the PocketSOAP package to build your client and having to get the needed information manually, it is possible to automate some of this by making use of the WSDL Wizard and other tools found on the PocketSoap Web site. Regardless, the limited work involved in building Web service clients using PocketSOAP and its wide range of language support and features should make it quite useful to anyone looking to quickly prototype a Web service client.

SOAP::Lite

SOAP::Lite is a Perl-based toolkit built to provide Web service capability through the Perl language. It has proven to be very popular with many users, particularly the UNIX crowd because Perl is usually found on most UNIX machines. SOAP::Lite is actually part of a suite of tools that provide the various pieces of the Web services puzzle. These tools include UDDI::Lite, XMLRPC::Lite, and XML::Parser::Lite.

Currently, SOAP::Lite supports SOAP 1.1, 1.2, the SOAP with attachments specifications, WSDL schemas, multiple transports such as MQSeries and Jabber, and COM interface capabilities. SOAP::Lite can be used to build both the client and service sides of the equation.

Building a Service with SOAP::Lite

In order to demonstrate the SOAP::Lite system, we'll once again use our Temperature Conversion example. We'll write a service using SOAP::Lite that will convert temperatures in degrees Celsius to degrees Fahrenheit and vice versa.

In Listing 19.7, you can see how easy it is to write the Perl SOAP::Lite-based service.

LISTING 19.7   The TempConverter.pl Web Service Program

```perl
#!perl -w
use SOAP::Transport::HTTP;
SOAP::Transport::HTTP::CGI
  -> dispatch_to('TemperatureConverters')
  -> handle;
package TemperatureConverters;
sub c2f
{
    my ($class, $degreesc) = @_;
    return 32+($degreesc*9/5);
}
sub f2c
{
    my ($class, $degreesf) = @_;
    return (5/9)*($degreesf-32);
}
```

This Perl code looks very similar to virtually any other Perl model except for the first couple of lines. Just to be sure that we understand what's happening, let's walk through the code line by line.

```perl
#!perl -w
```

This line tells the computer what to do with this code. Here, we're indicating that this is Perl code and to use the Perl runtime interpreter to execute it.

```perl
use SOAP::Transport::HTTP;
```

Here, we're indicating what transport mechanism to use for the SOAP communications. In this case, we're indicating HTTP. We could have chosen Jabber or any number of others supported by SOAP::Lite.

```
SOAP::Transport::HTTP::CGI
    ->dispatch_to('TemperatureConverters')
    ->handle;
```

Here is where we set up the linkage between the Web server's CGI engine and the SOAP::Lite engine. We're telling SOAP::Lite to accept calls to the CGI via HTTP and route them to the `TemperatureConverters` package. It will be the one responsible for returning the results.

```
package TemperatureConverters;
```

Here we're declaring the package that our functions will be referenced by.

The rest of the code simply builds the two conversion functions—one for converting Celsius to Fahrenheit and the other to go in the opposite direction.

To deploy this service, simply place the file into the IIS default Web server's cgi-bin subdirectory with the name TempConverterService.pl.

Building a Client Application with SOAP::Lite

Much as you saw that building services using SOAP::Lite was easy, so to is it relatively simple to write clients using the SOAP::Lite tools. Here we'll examine how to write a client to use our new SOAP::Lite service. The code for our client can be seen in Listing 19.8.

LISTING 19.8   The SOAP::Lite Temperature Conversion Client

```perl
#!perl -w
use SOAP::Lite;

my $soap = SOAP::Lite
   -> uri('http://127.0.0.1/TemperatureConverters')
   -> proxy('http://127.0.0.1/cgi-bin/TempConverterService.pl');
print "Enter the temperature you wish to convert";
print "\n";
print "for example: 100.0";
print "\n";
$temp = <STDIN>;
print "\nEnter the scale to convert FROM (either C or F)\n";
$scale = <STDIN>;

if($scale =~"C")
{
   print $soap
     -> c2f($temp)
```

LISTING 19.8 continued

```
      -> result;
   print " degrees F";
}
elsif($scale =~ "F")
{
   print $soap
     -> f2c($temp)
     -> result;
   print" degrees C";
}
else
{
   print "You must enter a valid scale. Either C or F";
}
```

Let's examine this code as we did with the service. First, we start out with the usual declaration telling the system what to do with the file:

```
#!perl -w
```

We then tell the Perl runtime engine that we want to make use of the SOAP::Lite service module and that we want to link this code to the TemperatureConvertors module found in the TempConvertorService.pl file. This sets up the call binding for us to make use of the functions found in the service:

```
use SOAP::Lite;
```

```
my $soap = SOAP::Lite
   -> uri('http://127.0.0.1/TemperatureConverters')
   -> proxy('http://127.0.0.1/cgi-bin/TempConverterService.pl');
```

In the remaining code, we request some input from the user, both the temperature and then the scale that the users are converting from. Depending on which scale the user tells us he is converting from, we pick the correct function of the service and call it. We take the results and display them back out to the user.

Now that we have the code for our client, let's try it out. Type the following command:

perl TempConverterClient.pl

You should see the following prompt:

```
Enter the temperature you wish to convert
for example: 100.0
```

19

Enter a value, say 212 (the boiling point of water in degrees F) and press the Enter key. You'll next be prompted to enter the scale you're converting from as seen here:

```
Enter the scale to convert FROM (either C or F)
```

In this case, type in the letter F and press Enter. You should get back the following results:

```
100 degrees C
```

That's all there is to it. Try the program a few more times, entering different values for the temperature and the scale, and see what happens.

As you can see, there isn't much involved in terms of creating the binding to the remote service. This really is the only difference between calling the remote functions and what would be needed for calling local ones. That's why SOAP::Lite has the word lite in its name!

 Although the view of SOAP::Lite that we have shown is very basic, it should be enough to get you started. Much like the other tools we've examined in this hour, a good support group can be found on the Yahoo! Groups system at http://groups.yahoo.com/group/soaplite/.

Summary

In this hour, we briefly covered several additional Web services toolkits. Each of these products, although not quite as big as the others we've looked at in this book, are quite capable and have strong followings among the developer communities that they service. We've seen how to build services for deployment on GLUE and SOAP::Lite. In addition, we've seen how to write clients on each of the toolsets that can talk to and use those services. We also have examined where each toolset's strength in the market lies and what makes it unique in relation to other offerings.

Although we've only shown the basics for how to use each of these toolsets, they all have a lot more to offer. We encourage the reader to look into each of these tools further because each contains a wealth of capabilities.

Q&A

Q **You've only covered the basics for creating and deploying a service. Is there more involved with these packages?**

A Although it is true that we have only demonstrated the very basics in order to give you an idea how to get up and running, each of these toolsets has a lot more to it. If you are interested in using any of them, we encourage you to explore the online documentation and ask questions of the various discussion boards found online for each of these tools.

Q **What is different or lacking in these tools compared to the others covered in this book?**

A Frankly, nothing is missing from any of these toolsets. Each is quite capable of providing complete Web services capabilities (albeit some with add-on packages in the case of PocketSOAP and SOAP::Lite). We simply chose not to cover these toolsets as extensively because they are less likely to be found in a commercial development setting.

Workshop

This section is designed to help you anticipate possible questions, review what you've learned, and begin learning how to put your knowledge into practice.

Quiz

1. What are the advantages of using PocketSOAP instead of .NET if both work on MS platforms?

2. Can you write services in PocketSOAP?

3. What is the name of the tool in GLUE that builds the helper classes from a WSDL schema?

4. What transport protocols are supported by SOAP::Lite?

19

Quiz Answers

1. PocketSOAP was available first. At the time of this writing, no .NET system is available for PocketPC, and PocketSOAP supports some of the older versions of languages such as VB6.

2. No, PocketSOAP is for client-side development only. However, an excellent package called 4s4c provides service creation capabilities from COM objects.

3. `wsdl2java`.

4. A good number—HTTP, Jabber, MQSeries, and so on.

Activities

1. Take a look at the documentation for each of these packages. Each has a lot more to it than what we've covered in this hour. If you're planning to use one of these for a project, you'll need to be aware of the additional information and capabilities.

2. Pick the toolset of your choice and attempt to make a client to interface with some service available on the xmethods.net site.

3. Pick the toolset of your choice and attempt to write your own version of one of the services found on the xmethods.net site. See if you can make yours do the same sort of work as one of theirs.

Hour **20**

Comparing the Different Web Services Tools

The goal of Hours 13 through 19 was to provide you with a summary of what each of these vendor's products could do and provide you with a glimpse of what development with this tool is like.

By this point, you are probably wondering how to choose the right tool for you with so many options available. In this hour, you will learn

- What factors need to be considered when making a choice
- How the tools stack up in each area
- The advantages and disadvantages of each tool

The Importance of Choosing the Best Web Services Tool

With many of the technologies that were created to enable software to interoperate across hardware boundaries, the choices that you make early on commit you for years to come. Fortunately, Web services are different in this area. Because all the Web services tools that you can download or purchase comply to the same set of core standards, you have the option of changing development environments. In addition, you have the option of allowing different groups in the same organization to use different tools to create and consume Web services.

As a further complication/advantage, some tools that we have covered in this book—such as Axis—excel in creating Web service providers, whereas others—such as Visual Studio .NET—excel in creating Web service consumers. It might make sense to choose one tool for the server side and another for the client side. There are still reasons to use the same tool where possible, such as maintenance and training costs.

Some of the tools that we covered are free for downloading, whereas others are quite pricey. It might make sense for you to begin with one of the free tools, but migrate to a more expensive one after you have gained experience and proven to your organization that this technology is practical. Some of the tools do much more than just Web services—both IBM WebSphere Studio Application Developer and Microsoft .NET are full blown software versions of the Swiss Army knife.

You will need to see the load that will be placed on the system in production. If the load is light, you might be able to get away with using the free tools. If the application needs to scale to handle a large user base, you might have to purchase a more scalable tool.

The Products Chosen for Evaluation

The products selected for evaluation in this book were chosen based on our experience, with a real effort made to cover as broad a spectrum as possible. We made an effort to include products by small independent vendors as well as those by the big players such as Microsoft and IBM. We tried to include the freeware products as well as the commercial products. We could not evaluate every product on the market. As a result, our choices should be seen as a representative sampling of the products available. Many products that we failed to include in the evaluation might be as good or even better than those that were evaluated.

The list of evaluated products along with the abbreviation that we will use in this hour is shown in Table 20.1.

TABLE 20.1 The Evaluated Products

Tool	Abbreviation
Apache Axis	Axis
Java Web Services Developer Pack	Java WSDP
Microsoft Visual Studio .NET	.NET
BEA WebLogic Workshop	BEA Workshop
IBM WebSphere Studio Application Developer	WSAD
The Mind Electric GLUE	Glue
PocketSOAP	PocketSOAP
SOAP::Lite	SOAP::Lite

Details about each product are available in the individual hours where these products are introduced:

- Apache Axis—Hour 13
- Java Web Services Developer Pack—Hour 14
- Microsoft Visual Studio .NET—Hours 15 and 16
- BEA WebLogic Workshop—Hour 17
- IBM WebSphere Studio Application Developer—Hour 18
- The Mind Electric GLUE—Hour 19
- PocketSOAP—Hour 19
- SOAP::Lite—Hour 19

Establishing the Evaluation Criteria

In order to assist you in your evaluation of the different options, we have created a set of issues in which these products differ from one another. In each section, we will point out products that stand out in that area. Keep in mind that these impressions are opinions based on our experience with the product in varying periods of time. You might disagree with our conclusions, but we believe that it is more valuable to you for us authors to take a stand and not just lead you through pages of "happy talk" designed to please everyone.

20

Cost

Cost is a factor in nearly every decision made by an organization. It would be a mistake, however, to focus solely on the cost of acquisition while ignoring other, often-larger issues such as development cost, support costs, outside resource expenses, the cost of hardware, and the long-term maintenance of the systems created with these tools.

Because full life-cycle costs are impossible to estimate without knowing the specifics of your organization, we will have to limit our specific discussion to acquisition costs. Table 20.2 shows the approximate acquisition cost of each product.

TABLE 20.2 The Evaluated Products' Estimated Cost of Acquisition

Tool	Cost
Axis	Free
Java WSDP	Free
.NET	$1,000 to $2,000
BEA Workshop	$2,495
WSAD	$3,500
GLUE	Free
PocketSOAP	Free
SOAP::Lite	Free

Notice the wide variation in prices among the different products. Nearly all the products listed in the table have a free evaluation version available at their vendor's Web site. The cost of training and hardware would have to be considered separately.

Legacy Experience

Both the learning curve and the speed of development are a function of the language background of the developer. Naturally, a Java developer will be productive sooner in a Java-oriented tool than in one that is focused on the C++ developer. Table 20.3 shows the language background that is most natural for each tool.

TABLE 20.3 The Evaluated Products' Natural Programming Language

Tool	Language
Axis	Java
Java WSDP	Java
.NET	Visual Basic, C++, C#
BEA Workshop	Java
WSAD	Java
GLUE	Java
PocketSOAP	Visual Basic, C++, C#
SOAP::Lite	Perl

You will notice that Java is the language for most of the products listed here. The reason for this is that much of the server development taking place outside of Web services is done in Java. This makes Java a natural, but not the only, language suited to Web service development.

Steepness of Learning Curve

All the previously listed products require some level of expertise to use. With some products, it takes very little time to get a simple Web service up and running. Others are less automatic and require quite a bit more education before you can be productive. Speaking generally, the more costly tools provide more GUI support for the development of the Web service. In some cases, the product itself is complex, but when you understand how to use the interface, creating Web services is not hard. Table 20.4 rates the learning curve steepness for each evaluated product.

TABLE 20.4 The Evaluated Products' Learning Curve Steepness

Tool	Steepness
Axis	Medium for Java programmers
Java WSDP	Medium for Java programmers
.NET	Easy for VB, C++, C# programmers
BEA Workshop	Easy for Java programmers
WSAD	Steep
GLUE	Easy for Java programmers
PocketSOAP	Easy for VB, C++, C# programmers
SOAP::Lite	Easy for PERL programmers

Most of the complexity of the WSAD and .NET products comes from the fact that the product is a full-scale development environment that can be used for creating any type of Web service or J2EE type of application. After the tool is mastered, learning how to create Web services with it is not too difficult.

Axis and Java WSDP are free downloads that are intended for the Java programmer audience. This group of developers is not that fond of graphical tools, or perhaps they are just not fond of the Java-based graphical tools that they have been given to use. As a result, none are provided.

Many open source projects don't have graphical tools because they're hard to do, and it's seen as overhead code that doesn't actually contribute to solving the problem defined by the project.

20

Development Speed

The development speed can be measured by how long it takes a developer to complete a task after he is familiar with the tool and the development process imposed by the tool. Table 20.5 gives our opinions on how productive you will be when proficient.

TABLE 20.5   The Evaluated Products' Development Speed

Tool	Speed
Axis	Medium for Java programmers
Java WSDP	Medium for Java programmers
.NET	Fast for VB, C++, C# programmers
BEA Workshop	Fast for Java programmers
WSAD	Fast for Java programmers
GLUE	Medium for Java programmers
PocketSOAP	Medium for VB programmers
SOAP::Lite	Medium for PERL programmers

The tools that provide greater automation enable higher productivity in exchange for an increase in cost. For all these tools, after you develop a solution with their framework, it can be very difficult to migrate your business logic to another framework.

Compatibility with Legacy Systems

In the real world, every organization has a history. That history is studded and strewn with the decisions made in years gone by. Many of these systems were state-of-the-art in the day that they were created and, more importantly, they contain data that is the basis for your organization.

NEW TERM   Many of the products such as PocketSOAP or GLUE provide no special leverage when working with legacy data. MS .NET contains special tools that make the conversion of *legacy code* (DCOM) to .NET code easier. For IBM mainframe developers, WSAD provides a good environment for writing Web services that retrieve data from DB2 databases running on the big computer.

BEA Workshop makes it easy to expose existing EJB session beans as Web services, and Axis fits seamlessly into a Tomcat installation. Table 20.6 shows these relationships.

TABLE 20.6 The Evaluated Products' Synergy to Legacy Systems

Tool	Legacy System
Axis	Tomcat servers
Java WSDP	Existing Java code
.NET	DCOM and COM objects
BEA Workshop	WebLogic EJBs
WSAD	Mainframe DB2 and CICS

If you have experience and a base of code in the Legacy System section, you will find that the tool in the left column of Table 20.6 provides some advantages when transforming these objects into Web services.

Keep in mind though, that all these products can be used to access any of the data. It is a question of convenience, not a question of capability.

Vendor Track Record and Commitment

It is not yet clear whether there will be a consolidation of Web service vendors. Because of the open-minded nature of Web services, a vendor doesn't have to command a huge market share to be viable. He does, however, have to make more money than he spends in order to survive.

In other situations, a vendor will change directions without a visible reason and start preaching a different lesson than he was preaching the year before, which was different than the one preached the year before that. Bearing that in mind, we evaluated who, in our opinions, was the most likely to continue investing in the vendor's toolkits and who was likely to remain faithful to the Web services approach. Table 20.7 contains our predictions on whether a vendor will be active in Web services in five years.

TABLE 20.7 The Evaluated Products' Commitment

Tool	Future Prospects
Axis	Certain
Java WSDP	Certain
.NET	Less Certain
BEA Workshop	Less Certain
WSAD	Less Certain
GLUE	Uncertain
PocketSOAP	Uncertain
SOAP::Lite	Uncertain

20

This is all very unscientific, but based on the following reasoning: Axis is an open-source project. Volunteers do all the software development on open-source projects. It's a grass-roots effort with people using their own resources and investing their own time to build free software for the community. This allows them to survive without a profit margin. Java WSDP is similar to an open-source project: It doesn't have to be profitable to survive as long as Sun Microsystems survives.

Microsoft will be in business in five years, but it has a history of changing direction every few years. Microsoft brought us the VBX, followed by OCX, followed by ActiveX, COM, DCOM, and now .NET and Web services. Management swears that they have bet the company's future on Web services, and we believe them. The company's track record does not instill confidence, however.

IBM will also be in business in five years, but it has a similar history of changing directions. Like Microsoft, the company has contributed much time and energy to the establishment of Web services standards, so we tend to believe that it will maintain its commitment.

BEA is well respected as a technology company, but it is still in the formative years of its history. WebLogic is most popular as a J2EE server, but that hasn't translated into huge profits yet. It lacks the cash-cow business lines that rivals, Microsoft and IBM, live off of. WebLogic is, however, the sentimental favorite because it is good at what it does. We believe that the company will still be a force in five years.

The small vendors of SOAP::Lite, GLUE, and PocketSOAP face an uncertain future. Their products are free, so their revenue stream is nonexistent, at least for Web services. They are not open-source projects, so they don't get donated labor. We are not sure that they will still be improving their products in five years, though it is likely that today's versions will still be around in the future.

Vendor Niche

Many of the vendors offer their product into a niche market. PocketSOAP was originally written for handheld computers such as the Palm and Pocket PCs. It runs on Windows 95 and 98, unlike .NET.

Microsoft has carved out a big niche in the desktop computer area with Visual Basic and Visual C++. The Web services client support in .NET is outstanding. It is easy to foresee Microsoft as a dominant player in the Web services client area.

Apache Axis is a companion product to Apache Tomcat. Given that more than half of all Web servers run Tomcat, it seems logical that a large number of those shops will choose

Axis as their SOAP engine. The fact that Axis is a well-crafted but spartan tool is appealing to those Java programmers who never really liked graphical development environments very much anyway.

IBM will leverage its mainframe business and contacts in Fortune 500 companies to use WebSphere AD. This is a good fit for large companies that can afford $3,500/seat for a development tool and the training budget needed to become productive. WebSphere is a powerful tool in the hands of those who understand how to use it.

Quality of Documentation

As writers, documentation is near and dear to us. Unfortunately, the documentation that surrounds Web services tools is not very good overall, except with .NET. Microsoft does an average job of documenting its products, but the book writers do a bang-up job on all Microsoft tools. As a result, .NET developers can always find answers. Table 20.8 shows the quality of documentation available from all sources.

TABLE 20.8   The Evaluated Products' Documentation

Tool	Documentation Quality
Axis	Fair
Java WSDP	Good
.NET	Great
BEA Workshop	Good
WSAD	Poor
GLUE	Fair
PocketSOAP	Fair
SOAP::Lite	Fair

The Java programming language is well documented both at Sun and in third-party books. Java Web services books are not rare either, though they often concentrate on the Java WSDP, which is not really a production environment.

Apache Axis suffers from the typical lack of documentation that surrounds open-source projects. It seems that volunteers write better software than they do manuals. Few Axis books are on the shelves at your local book store. They will likely appear over time.

WebLogic Workshop has some following in the book world, but BEA does a better-than-average job in its online docs. IBM writes much better software than it does documentation. There doesn't seem to be much organization in what the company publishes. For

20

example, it is not unusual to find four articles on how to do an obscure task in Web services, but not one "Hello,World" style example can be found on the whole Web site. IBM product books don't sell well either, so there is no hope of getting much help there. Unless this situation changes, WSAD might be the software world's best-kept secret. Other well-engineered IBM products like OS/2 and PowerPC have failed to capture market share.

PocketSOAP, GLUE, and SOAP::Lite have no following to speak of in the book world. There is quite a bit of informal online documentation, and Pocket::SOAP has a fine following in the Yahoo! groups.

Other Benefits of the Products

Before concluding, we need to mention that several of the products evaluated here are far more than just Web services development tools. Both WSAD and Microsoft .NET are full-blown software versions of the Swiss Army knife. Both products allow you to develop dozens of different products in addition to Web services providers and clients. If you have a need for a full-service IDE, they might be an affordable choice, but only if you are going to use them a lot.

Summary

In this hour, you were led through a series of sections that dealt with one characteristic of Web services tools. The goal of this was to help you decide which Web services development toolkit is right for you at this time.

We looked at each toolkit from many angles such as cost, quality of documentation, availability of support, and professional services. Finally, we looked at issues such as vendor niche, track record, and commitment to the technology.

Q&A

Q What category of toolkits tend to be the most expensive to acquire?

A Toolkits that generate the Web service for you tend to be more expensive. In addition, full-service IDEs tend to cost more than single-purpose Web service tools.

Q What computer languages can be used to develop Web services?

A Java is very popular, but C++, Perl, C#, and Visual Basic are also used.

Q Why is the total life-cycle cost of a tool important?

A All tools provide some services to the programmer, and the programmer writes the rest of the functionality. Organizations have to pay for both the tool and the labor of the programmer. A more expensive tool might have a lower life-cycle cost if a programmer can accomplish the same tasks in fewer hours.

Workshop

The Workshop is designed to help you review what you've learned, and begin learning how to put your knowledge into practice.

Quiz

1. What is the most popular programming language for Web services?
2. What toolkit has the best third-party documentation?
3. What type of developers gravitate to IBM WSAD?

Quiz Answers

1. Overall, Java is the most popular. In the Microsoft Windows realm, Visual Basic is the most popular.
2. The .NET framework is very popular with independent writers because there are so many developers.
3. WSAD is popular with companies that have a lot of IBM mainframe software.

Activities

1. Create a list of the evaluation criteria that are most important to your organization.
2. Create a chart that shows products on one axis and features on another.
3. Rank the products by the criteria that you value most and select a toolset for your organization.

20

PART IV
Advanced Topics

Hour

Hour 21

Web Services Interoperability

The primary reason that Web services have gathered so much attention from the vendors of software products and professional software developers is the promise of interoperability across platforms and programming languages. But, before you jump into the fray, you might be wise to stop and consider how true this promise of interoperability is.

In this hour, we will cover the issues surrounding interoperability. We will begin by stating the goals of Web services, and then move on to the limitations that have been discovered in the real world. Following that, we will discuss the industry's efforts to work through these issues.

In this hour you will learn about

- Interoperability goals
- Interoperability limitations
- How interoperability is attained
- The Web Services Interoperability (WS-I) Proposal

Making Web Services Interoperate

NEW TERM   If you take interoperability out of Web services, you have yet another single-vendor solution for making remote procedure calls. At the core of Web services is the dream of *universal interoperability*.

At present, Web services transactions will be successfully exchanged only if the following are true:

- They use the same version of the same transport. The most common communication now in use is TCP/IP running Hypertext Transfer Protocol (HTTP 1.1).
- They are created with the same version of XML schema.
- They both use the same version of the WSDL specification.
- They interpreted the ambiguous areas of the WSDL specification in the same way.
- They are using the same version of SOAP.
- They interpreted the ambiguous areas of the SOAP specification in the same way.
- No additional headers were used in the SOAP message without prior agreement.
- No additional features like WS-Signature, WS-Transaction, and so on were used.

The preceding list seems intimidating, and it should. In reality, there are many opportunities for failure mentioned on this list.

The Limitations of Interoperability

To suggest that there are limitations to the interoperability of Web services sometimes causes gasps in the first row of pews. Many exclaim that because the entire premise of Web services is interoperability, there shouldn't be any interoperability problems. Here in the real world, however, there are limitations that you must be aware of before you ruin your technical reputation by recommending that your organization head down an immature path.

Ambiguous Standards

Some readers will scoff at the idea that the basic Web services specifications can have interpretation problems. In the ideal world, all specification would be written by people with great foresight and unlimited time to get everything exactly right. The user community is far too impatient to wait too long for the standards bodies to act. If a standard is slow in coming, software vendors will implement their own solutions, thereby making it harder later to get them to adopt the new standard.

All standards bodies operate on a feedback loop in which interested parties make comments on what has been proposed. The feedback loop provides the perfecting mechanism whereby the oversights and omissions that appear in an initial version of a specification are worked out. In the mean time, misunderstandings are a problem whenever a clause is vague enough for two different interpretations to exist.

In SOAP 1.1, consider the case in which a message is received where the namespace name of the Envelope is not `http://schemas.xmlsoap.org/soap/envelope/`. The SOAP 1.1 specification states that this message might be discarded. If one vendor discards, but another chooses to generate a fault instead, a difference in behavior occurs. Later in this hour, you will see how the WS-I proposal handles this type of situation.

Versions of Standards

The perfecting process requires that standards bodies respond to the feedback that they get from the user community. The customary way to respond to feedback is to issue a modified version of the standard complete with a new version number; HTTP 1.0 was superceded by HTTP 1.1.

At present, five core standards form the foundation of Web services:

- XML
- XML schema
- SOAP
- WSDL
- UDDI

If there were two versions of each of these in common use, there would be 32 (two raised to the fifth power) different combinations of these standards that a product could be programmed to. If you add in all the proposed standards, and the underlying standards like HTTP and UTF-16, the number of combinations becomes very large.

Distributed Support Model

In the good old days, you purchased a computer, operating system, and much of the layered software from one vendor. If you had a problem, you called 1-800-MyFavoriteVendor and they handled it (sometimes). This model began to break down when the personal computer came on the scene because the computer, operating system, and each application were purchased from different vendors.

With the advent of Web services, this model is completely destroyed. In the PC world, a transaction was normally handled by one application. In the new Web services world, a

21

single transaction might invoke 5, 10, or who knows how many different Web services. In addition, each of them might have been built with a different tool, and they might be running a different SOAP processor. This is the hurdle for a lot of companies that want to use open-source software, but are afraid of the lack of support. If you are using a vendor's implementation, you can call them.

Who are you going to call when something goes wrong? Your customers know who to call: YOU! What vendor is going to accept responsibility for a problem if it is only one of a dozen different programming staffs that have contributed code to this transaction's processors?

Look for the third-party support model now in its infancy to become the standard way of tackling these kinds of problems. They will accept the problem and work it because you pay them to, either on a retainer or on a per-case basis.

In addition, look for a new generation of tools to emerge that are able to analyze long transactions throughout their life cycles in order to isolate the Web service that is misbehaving.

New Standards on the Horizon

In the ideal world, customers would wait to ask for new features until clear, well-tested standards existed for all the technology needed to support it. In the real world, customers ask for the moon and want delivery tomorrow. They pressure us to make modifications to our systems that push them beyond the approved standards and into areas where either no standard exists yet or where only immature standards exist.

The following is a only a partial list of the proposed standards that were in some workgroup at the time of this writing:

- **BPELWS**—Business Process Execution Language for Web Services provides an XML-based programming language for defining business processes.
- **SAML**—The Security Assertion Markup Language allows clients to identify themselves to Web services.
- **WS-Coordination**—Defines an XML grammar to coordinate complicated Web services requests.
- **WS-Security**—Provides a framework for Web services security solutions.
- **WS-Transaction**—Defines an XML way of creating both atomic transactions that can be rolled back as well as long transactions that cannot.
- **XML-Encryption**—Allows a confidential message or part of a message to be sent.

- **XML-Signature**—Provides a way for clients and Web services to verify their identity.

It is safe to say that the suite of standards that define Web services will grow without an end in the foreseeable future. This creates several opportunities and problems:

- You will be able to use a standard instead of a homegrown approach to provide the functionality mentioned previously. On the flip side, you can get out of synch with the providers and consumers that you interact with if they don't upgrade to the same standard at the same time you do.

- The number of possible combinations of standards that will be in use at the same time will grow exponentially. Because nothing happens in an instant, there will be a transition period with each standard in which the old standard version of proprietary approach is replaced by the new one.

- Some overlap exists between these standards. You might implement one standard to handle an issue, but the consumers of your service might choose another.

Those developers who have created public sites that don't know in advance who the consumers of their services will be are going to have a never-ending task of deciding which of the standards to support, and when to support them.

Meeting the Challenge

It would be great if this section could describe the silver-bullet solution to the challenges previously described. As you have probably suspected, there is no silver bullet, nor is there likely to be one in the future.

> Human nature tells us that as soon as we solve one interoperability problem, the user community will demand even more ambitious systems from us, which will lead us into another set of interoperability challenges. This could discourage us, or we could see it as an almost endless demand for analysts, programmers, and managers who are up to the challenge.
>
> Keep in mind, however, that although the challenges never cease, the Web services that we design, program, implement, and deploy will be improving steadily and moving closer to the strategic center of your organization.

21

The solution, or rather solutions, to the problem of interoperability all require a strategy instead of a technique.

Leading Without Bleeding

We all try to stay off the "bleeding" edge of technology but we are all enticed to enter it from time to time. Sometimes our customers pressure us to become involved before the time is really right, but many times we treat new technology similar to birthday presents—we get so excited that we open the present before the guests arrive.

Your first job is to understand both the technology and what stage it is at in the collective mind of the computing business. Reading about the progress of a standard or technology will give you a sense of when "critical mass" has been reached.

Testing for Interoperability

Testing for interoperability is not something that you want to tackle on your own. The amount of resources required to perform a thorough test of one vendor's product that implements one suite of standards would be forbidding. A thorough test would have to create a Web service. Then it would have to create clients using every other popular product. Finally, it would have to test every client against the server.

A faster and less-expensive approach is to become acquainted with the testing already going on in the industry. One of the most promising of these efforts is called SOAPBuilders.org (`www.SOAPBuilders.org`). This organization states that

> The purpose of SOAPBuilders is so the techie types from the various SOAP implementations can ensure interop isn't just a buzzword. Part of that involves having a low barrier to entry.

From this informal mission statement flows a series of tests. These tests are organized into rounds—with later rounds providing a more rigorous set of tests than the earlier ones. In addition to the tests, each round provides some general guidelines to vendors who are planning on testing their applications. These guidelines are refinements to the specifications that instruct the participants such as "SOAPAction should be present, and quoted." or "Method namespace should be a well-formed, legal URI." As you can see, they don't raise the bar too high.

The first three rounds tested to see if the various vendor products could perform the following:

- **Round One**—Echoed the most common different data types back when sent to them.
- **Round Two**—Echoed some more data types (Hex binary, Base64, and so on) back when sent to them.

- **Round Three**—A more thorough test that involved generating a WSDL and using the generated WSDL to communicate with Web sites, and so on.

NEW TERM Periodically, *SOAPBuilders* hosts what they call face-to-face events, normally in conjunction with a Web services conference. During these events, different vendors demonstrate their compliance with the test suite that has been developed for them. By keeping up with the proceedings from these conferences, you can learn about the different vendors and what sort of effort they are willing to expend to make their products interoperable. If your requirements are less ambitious than the tests that have been run, you will be able to have confidence that your efforts will not be wasted.

The Web Services Interoperability Organization

On October 24, 2002, Sun Microsystems announced that it was planning to join the Web services Interoperability Organization (WS-I, `www.ws-i.org`), the consortium of companies that is working to make Web services interoperate. IBM and Microsoft, Oracle, BEA, HP, and Intel had already joined along with a huge number of other companies such as Ariba, Iona, and VeriSign.

The addition of Sun to this group is critical because of the following that Sun has among the Java development community. Because of Web services' position on the leading edge of technology, many of the early technical converts are Java heavyweights in companies around the world. Now that Sun has joined, these technical leaders will feel comfortable bringing their development efforts in line with decisions made by the consortium and its budding proposed standard WS-I.

As specifications go, WS-I is a newborn. Because of the central role that interoperability will play in the future of Web services, however, it is hard to imagine a standard that is more critical to its long-term success.

The stated goal of WS-I is

> To accelerate the adoption of Web services by assisting in the selection and interpretation of Web services specifications, and in the development of common best practices for their usage in the development, deployment, and integration of business applications.

The WS-I organization is producing three primary sets of deliverables: profiles, testing tools, and sample applications.

Profiles

NEW TERM A *profile* is a named set of versioned specifications. Included in the profile is a set of guidelines that provide interpretations of these specifications. In addition, the profile includes a set of recommendations on how to use these specifications.

21

As you recall, earlier in this hour, we discussed the difficulty caused by the multiplicity of specification versions that are available at any one time. The profile narrows this list to exactly one version of each specification. If either the versions or the number of specifications changes, the profile would be given a new name and would therefore be a different profile.

The effect of constraining a profile in this way is far reaching. If a Web service provider claims that it is compliant with profile X, a potential consumer of that service can have a high degree of confidence that it will succeed in communicating with the other service.

The addition of the guidelines will tighten up the specifications so that the number of potential conflicts because of incompatibilities can approach zero over time. The vision is to provide a logo that states what profile a particular service is compliant with. This would provide one name for a potential customer to look for, instead of *n* different specification names and version numbers.

At this writing, the only profile that has been published is the Basic Profile Version 1.0. This profile names the following standards:

- HTTP/1.1
- RFC2965:HTTP State Management Mechanism (cookies)
- SOAP 1.1
- UDDI Version 2.0 XML Schema
- UDDI Version 2.03 Data Structure Reference
- UDDI Version 2.03 Replication Specification
- UDDI Version 2.03 Replication XML Schema 2001
- UDDI Version 2.03 XML Custody Schema
- UDDI Version 2.01 Operator Specification
- UDDI Version 2.04 API
- WSDL 1.1
- XML 1.0 (Second Edition)
- XML Schema Part 1: Structures
- XML Schema Part 2: Datatypes

In addition, dozens of pages of guidelines serve to tighten up these specifications to the point at which misunderstandings are unlikely to occur if both parties in a transaction comply with them.

Testing Tools

In order to determine conformance to a certain profile, WS-I will also provide a set of testing tools that can be used to observe the messages being exchanged by different services and their consumers. Monitors would capture messages and hand them to analyzers that determine the conformance, or lack thereof, to a particular profile.

Sample Applications

Sample applications allow vendors to gain a better understanding of the specifications and guidelines as they pertain to the system that they are trying to create. If a picture is worth a thousand words, a piece of code that is known to be correct is worth ten thousand. If there is a question on how to use a certain message feature, the programmer can look at the sample application to find an example to mimic.

In addition, the sample applications will provide a test bed to prove that the profile is correctly written. If the sample application isn't capable of conforming, the profile will need to be modified.

Another area in which the profiles are wonderful is in the area of new standards. We stated earlier that when new standards are proposed, the timing of when to incorporate them into your Web services can be tricky. As a result, everyone tends to wait on everyone else just like cars at a four-way stop. The publication of a profile that includes a new specification might serve as the "coming-out party" for a new standard. Once the WS-I agrees that a profile is needed that includes the new specification, it will signal that everyone agrees that it has value and that it is ready for prime time.

Summary

In this hour, we covered the problems associated with writing Web services that interoperate well. We first looked at some of the issues that keep our services from communicating. Next, we looked at some basic strategies for handling this problem. Finally, we looked at the WS-I and its attempts to remove the risk from committing to an implementation.

Q&A

Q Aren't Web services built on the promise of interoperability?

A In the ideal world, they are. In the real world, standards are loose enough for misunderstandings.

21

Q Why would companies spend money testing interoperability? Wouldn't it be easier for their customers to purchase software from other vendors?

A Yes, but it would also be possible to sell to new customers. In fact, the ethics of locking in a customer is questionable. We should be able to choose the best products based on quality not compatibility.

Workshop

The Workshop is designed to help you review what you've learned, and begin learning how to put your knowledge into practice.

Quiz

1. Why is interoperability an issue?
2. What is the purpose of SOAPBuilders.org?
3. What was WS-I created for?
4. What is a WS-I profile?

Quiz Answers

1. The variety of specifications and interpretations in common usage can cause compatibility problems. If a standard is interpreted differently by different vendors, the two systems won't interoperate.
2. This organization publishes tests and holds events to allow vendors to test and brag about their compatibility prowess.
3. WS-I was created to promote Web services by lowering the risk of incompatibility.
4. A profile is a document that lists a set of standards and versions that have been tested together and found to work. In addition, it contains a series of guidelines on how to interpret the ambiguous portions of the various specifications that it uses.

Activities

1. List the reasons that interoperability problems can occur.
2. Go to SOAPBuilders.org and examine the details of the upcoming round of testing. If a face-to-face event is held in your area, attend it.
3. Go to the WS-I Web site (www.ws-i.org) and read the Basic Profile 1.0. Pay particular attention to the guidelines.

Hour **22**

Web Service Security

One of the weaknesses of Web services that we talked about in Hour 3, "Disadvantages and Pitfalls of Web Services," was security. The problem is not the lack of a Web services security mechanism, but the lack of agreement on what that mechanism (or mechanisms) should be. As of this writing, security is one of the topics normally relegated to the undefined part of the SOAP header.

In this hour, we will discuss some of the proposals that have a good chance of one day making up part of the standards that get adopted. We start with an overall discussion of computer program security. Following that, we will look at applying a traditional approach, the Secure Socket Layer, to Web services. Next, we will look at two established recommendations (quasi-standards)—XML Signature and XML Encryption. Finally, we look at the proposed SAML and WS-Security standards.

In this hour you will learn about

- The need to secure a Web service
- Using SSL to send messages
- The XML Signature specification

- The XML Encryption specification
- The SAML specification
- The WS-Security specification

Defining Web Services Security

The openness of the Internet is one of its greatest assets. From the standpoint of security, however, this openness is its greatest liability. It is great to be able to connect and order an authentic South Korean Soccer Team home jersey from a Web site in Hong Kong. If you think about the number of wires that your request (that includes your credit card number) has to travel over and the number of different hubs that it must pass through to get there, you will be nervous. It you add to that fear the fact that these transactions are very attractive to criminals, you would have a justifiable panic.

Securing Web services is a conceptually simple topic. Although the details of how to program different techniques and implement different technologies can seem complex, the issues are easy to understand. For an XML transaction between your computer and mine to complete securely, you have to be able to say the following:

- **Authenticity**—We are certain that the Web services transaction took place between my client and your server. Another client could impersonate me, or another server could pose as you.
- **Privacy**—We are sure that our messages and responses were not "overheard" by any unauthorized person.
- **Integrity**—We are both sure that every message that the client sent to the server and that the server sent to the client arrived unaltered.
- **Nonrepudiation**—Both the client and the server can prove to everyone's satisfaction (including each other) that the transaction actually took place (if a question were to arise) and that the parties involved were indeed who they said they were.

We often hear that there is no such thing as a completely secure computer transaction. This is true in the sense that someone with enough motivation, money, knowledge, and time can find a way to break into any system, regardless of the security measures taken in advance. The vast majority of all transactions, however, take place in a completely secure fashion—if only by virtue of the fact that no one is listening to or trying to hack it. If a banking system that has been running for five years is attacked successfully and a thousand transactions are observed, it is considered a serious breach.

When speaking of the seriousness of a threat, we have to consider two different measurements. The first is how likely an attack is to occur and succeed. As annoying as a stolen credit card number is, it is not really that hard to remedy, given the laws governing them. For example, most credit card companies limit the liability of the cardholder to $50 or less. This means that most of the cost of any fraudulent transactions charged to your card is born by the credit card company. If you use the Internet for a lot of transactions, there is a small chance that one day a credit card number of yours will be hijacked.

The second consideration is the amount of damage that could be caused if an attack succeeds. If you were sending a message that listed the names and addresses of all the spies in a hostile country, an interception could cause the death of many people or even the loss of a war. For this reason, threats that are unlikely, but catastrophic, are treated with great seriousness.

Targets and Target Hardening

NEW TERM In this hour, we will refer to any message that you want to protect as a *target*. Doing work to make a target more secure will be referred to as hardening the target.

Your job, as a Web services software engineer, is to harden a target so that it is more expensive to break into than it is worth. The level of security you need to provide will vary according to the value of the target. Attractive targets, such as international money transfer messages, demand a very high level of hardening. A wire transfer withdrawal of $200.00 from a mom to her son at the bus station requires less hardening, but it still requires some. An XML draft of the presentation that you are going to make at the next Kennel Club national convention probably does not need any hardening at all.

Your job is to impose costs on any would-be snooper or electronic vandal. If the costs that you impose exceed the rewards of intercepting your message, you can reasonably expect that the criminal will simply move on to other, softer targets.

Attacks

NEW TERM Any attempt by an unauthorized person to access a target is called an *attack*. Every attack has unique characteristics, but in general they can be grouped in the following categories:

- **Theft of Information**—Some information is very valuable to a thief. Credit card numbers and personal identification numbers (PINs) for automated teller machines (ATMs) are very popular because they can provide quick access to your money.
- **Unauthorized Modification**—Many messages could contain information that must arrive unaltered. Intercepting, altering, and forwarding a message could cause serious problems.

22

- **Impersonation**—Many attacks occur when your system thinks that it is communicating with an authorized user when, in reality, it is communicating with a criminal.

Some Web services have characteristics that make them more likely to be attacked in one way than in another. A banking system might be more likely to suffer from a theft of information than from unauthorized modification. Your security strategy for each Web service will need to be tailored based on these characteristics.

The Web's Security Infrastructure

Fortunately for us, the Internet's security infrastructure was created long before Web services came into being. This infrastructure was created to facilitate the transfer of private information across the Internet from browsers to Web sites. The establishment of online stores such as Amazon.com and Buy.com drove much of the demand for this.

NEW TERM   A key piece of this infrastructure is the *public key certificate*. A person or organization who wants to engage in secure Internet communication can obtain a public key certificate that identifies him to actual and potential Web services trading partners. Certificate authorities such as VeriSign issue these certificates.

Certificate authorities are trusted companies who create certificates in accordance with the ITU-T X.509 Certificate Standard. They normally gather quite a bit of information about an applicant before granting him a certificate. Much of this information is placed inside the certificate before it is encoded with the authorities' private key. Two companies who provide these certificates are VeriSign, www.verisign.com, and Thawte, www.thawte.com.

The process of creating a certificate begins with the creation of a public/private key pair. The public key is made available by the owner to anyone who wants to see it, but the owner keeps the private key secret. These two keys are related mathematically, but it is computationally infeasible to try and calculate the private key given the public key.

For example, a person armed with your public key can encrypt messages that only you can decrypt because you are the only one who possesses the private key. Public keys have two features to make them useful. It is very difficult to use only a public key to decrypt a document that was encoded with that key. Next, it must be extremely difficult to figure out the private key by examining the public key. Otherwise, you might as well send clear text. Figure 22.1 shows how public and private keys work to encrypt a message.

FIGURE 22.1
*The public key can
encrypt messages that
only the private key
can decrypt.*

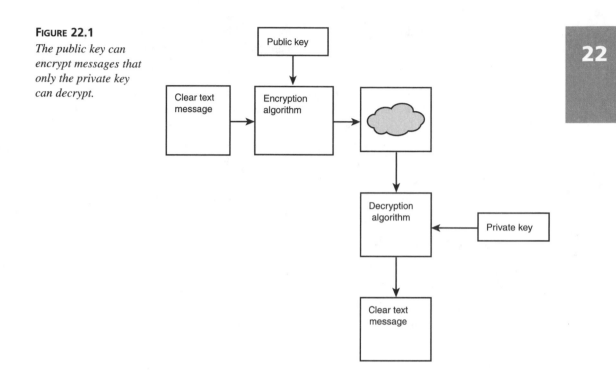

If I send you a message that is encrypted with your public key, you can decrypt it with your private key. This keeps the contents private. On the other hand, if I send you a message that is encrypted using my private key, you can use the public key to verify that it is from me—even though the message can be decrypted by anyone who takes the time to find my public key. This answers the nonrepudiation requirement.

The Secure Sockets Layer

NEW TERM The simplest, but least useful way to secure your Web services message is to use the *Secure Sockets Layer (SSL)*.

Web services that conduct electronic commerce cannot use clear text. Anyone with a laptop and some packet-sniffing software could fish out credit card numbers all day long. Netscape communications realized this and developed a protocol called the SSL to address this issue.

SSL contains two different, but related, protocols—the Secure Sockets Layer and the Transport Layer Security. These protocols are concerned with securing a socket and all of the data that passes over it rather than encrypting just a SOAP message.

You have used SSL before if you have ever typed in `https:` in a URL. HTTPS is a higher-level protocol built using SSL. SSL allows encrypted traffic to flow through the socket that it creates. A client sends a request to a server. The server sends an X.509 certificate back to the client, which contains the public key of the server. If the server's key is valid, some handshaking takes place and the session begins. SSL-based software classes such as the Java Secure Socket Extension (JSSE) hide most of this detail from the user and even the programmer. Using it is very much like using a normal socket except that the secure socket is created using a special class.

How SSL Works

All implementations of SSL use a handshaking procedure in which the client and the server exchange certain information that enables them to determine what form of communication they will use in the actual transactions. In addition, this procedure ensures that both parties in this communication are behaving in a way that the other would expect.

No unencrypted key is ever exchanged. The real beauty of this approach is in the amount of work a programmer has to do to get this to work. Aside from obtaining the proper certificate from a certificate authority, the only code that is written is similar to that used to create simple sockets.

Adding SSL to Web services doesn't change either the business or Web services code that you write. This is all handled by the HTTP container and is transparent to the application.

Using SSL to Send SOAP Messages

Using SSL to send SOAP messages is fairly easy. All that you really need is a Web server that is capable of communicating with clients that use HTTPS as well as HTTP. After your client composes the SOAP message, it specifies that it wants to send this message to the server using HTTPS. Your client needs to be written using the JSSE or some other similar library. This library will perform all the handshaking for you automatically, and then send your message to the Web server.

The Web server will decrypt the message when it arrives and hand it to your Web service. The Web service will then work its magic and formulate a response message (normally). A response will be delivered to the client securely if that was specified. Figure 22.2 shows how this works.

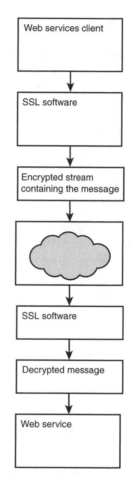

FIGURE 22.2
SSL allows a client to send a secure message to a server.

Notice that everything that goes over the Internet gets encrypted, not just the sensitive parts.

Limitations of SSL

SSL is like a tired workhorse. For all the good work that it has done over the years, it lacks the pep to go to the next level. The reasons for this are

- The fact that it provides encryption during transport ignores the fact that encryption is also needed while some documents are stored on intermediate servers.
- The whole message is encrypted and decrypted together. This keeps an intermediate end point from adding to a message without discovering its contents.
- SSL, by itself, cannot provide authentication, data integrity, and nonrepudiation for the life of the message if it is routed across more than one Web server.

The Proposed Security Specifications

When gurus talk about the Web services standards being weak on security, they do not mean that hackers are running wild and stealing information at will. What they mean is that there is no mention in the specifications for the SOAP language that specifies how a message is to be secured.

This doesn't mean that the Web services proponents are sitting on their hands and refusing to write a set of XML security standards. It means that no decision has been made, at least officially, as to what the W3C and OASIS will eventually specify. That being said, the field of Web services security is taking on a shape, and certain standards are emerging as the odds-on favorites, but it is too soon to declare a winner.

This section provides an overview of several of the proposed standards that have a direct bearing on the problems of security. Luckily, these proposal writers are aware of each other, and, thus far, they have done a good job of holding duplications to a minimum.

XML Signature

When you get an important document, you need to be certain, beyond a reasonable doubt, that the author of the document is who it says it is. A check is signed by the owner of the bank account, testifying that he does indeed have an account at that bank and that you now have rights to $47.33 of the money in it.

In the same way, your Web service needs to know that if John Q. Public orders a camera, he is a real person who wants a camera and intends to pay for it. Because of the similarities of this need and that of the person who accepts a check, the term digital signature is used to describe a solution.

A digital signature is not a signature at all, but rather a set of tags and values that serves the same purpose—identifying the originator or the transaction against unauthorized modification, impersonation, and repudiation. Your Web service needs protection against the equivalent of a check writer saying later, "That isn't my signature and I never wrote that check." Whether or not the check writer is lying, you still have a problem.

NEW TERM *Cryptography* is the basis of XML-Signature. As discussed earlier in this hour, a client needs to possess a pair of keys, one public and one private, which can be used to encrypt and decrypt messages. If you are sure of the origin of one of these keys, you can determine, via software, that the other key was used to encrypt something. This is the basis for declaring that a request is legitimate.

Secure Sockets Layer is capable of securing a message during transport. However, Web services transactions have two characteristics that SSL can't handle at all: They are often routed across many nodes while being processed, and each node can add additional information to the message as it proceeds. If you use SSL to send Web services transactions over several nodes, the encryption and decryption has to be done on each node, exposing the secrets on every node.

XML Signatures is an open standard managed by the Organization for the Advancement of Structured Information Standards (OASIS). As the name implies, XML Signature is a set of XML tags. These tags are designed to contain sufficient information to allow a client to be verified using the public/private key pair that he must possess to participate in a signed transaction.

XML signature is powerful in that it enables an endpoint to sign only one part of a document instead of the whole thing. This is important because some SOAP messages obtain additional information as they proceed through the work flow. If the XML signature were signing the whole document, adding new information would cause the message to be cryptographically invalid—even if the modifier is a legitimate part of the transaction. Because the original signer only signed part of the document, additions do not invalidate the original signature. The following XML document fragment shows a sample XML Signature:

```
<?xml version="1.0" encoding="UTF-8"?>
<Signature xmlns="http://www.w3.org/2000/09/xmldsig#">
      <SignedInfo Id="curly">
           <CanonicalizationMethod
              Algorithm="http://www.w3.org/TR/2001/REC-xml-c14n-20010315"/>
                  <SignatureMethod Algorithm=
                      "http://www.w3.org/2000/09/xmldsig#dsa-sha1"/>
              <Reference URI="http://www.mycompany.com/news/2000/sample.htm">
                  <DigestMethod Algorithm=
                       "http://www.w3.org/2000/09/xmldsig#dsa-sha1"/>
                  <DigestValue>oiuyhhlkeroiapoi987qhn</DigestValue>
              </Reference>
              <Reference URI="http://www.w3.org/TR/2000/WD-xmldsig-core-
              ➥20000228/signature-example.xml">
                  <DigestMethod Algorithm=
                       "http://www.w3.org/2000/09/xmldsig#dsa-sha1"/>
                  <DigestValue>lkhuyiydyueuu973kdk9</DigestValue>
              </Reference>
      </SignedInfo>
      <SignatureValue>MC9E-LE</SignatureValue>
      <keyInfo>
           <X509Data>
                <X509SubjectName>CN=Steve Potts,O=Potts Company,
                            ST=GA,C=US</X509SubjectName>
                <X509Certificate>
                            lkjhiouyrwelkjahdsf…8i7
                </X509Certificate>
```

```
            </X509Data>
        </KeyInfo>
</Signature>
```

This document contains a complete signature and references to two signed documents. The public key is contained in the X509Certificate, which is also included here.

When the recipient gets the message, he applies the public key to each document. If the algorithm says that it matches the one included, he can be sure that the document is unaltered. If the public and private signatures don't match, he has received a fake signature.

XML Key Management Specification

The use of the public and private keys presents a bit of a problem. On one hand, how do you write the XML that it takes to verify the information contained in the <KeyInfo> tags of the signatures? On the other hand, how can we communicate with the certificate authorities automatically? If we have to put a person on a browser every time we need to get information from a certificate authority, there would be little point in automating the rest of the service.

The XML Key Management Specification (XKMS) consists of two separate parts:

- **XML Key Information Service Specification (X-KISS)**—A protocol that enables an application to delegate the validation of the key that has been sent to another Web service. This makes programming the signature-verification part simpler.

- **XML Key Registration Service Specification (X-KRSS)**—A protocol that allows clients and Web services to communicate with a certificate authority to bind name or extended-attribute information to a public key.

Using these two protocols, your client or Web service can communicate to other Web services in a way that is more transparent than traditional approaches to key management.

XML Encryption

Encryption is the art of secret writing. For as long as there have been people, there has been a need for private communication. Sometimes the motivation for this privacy is national security, and sometimes it is financial. At other times, the primary motivator is just to keep private things away from nosey people.

The tried-and-true technique for maintaining privacy is to apply some sort of encoding scheme on a message before sending it. The recipient, who must know the decoding scheme, can then turn the garbled data back into clear text for processing.

22

The details of how encryption works is beyond the scope of this book, but it is sufficient to say that there are two basic types of encryption—symmetric, and asymmetric. Symmetric encryption uses the same key and an algorithm to convert the document from clear text into encrypted text and back again. Asymmetric encryption uses one key to encrypt and another, mathematically related, key to decrypt. Asymmetric encryption is more secure because your key doesn't ever have to be transferred. Symmetric encryption is much faster, though.

XML Encryption is a proposed standard that is being evaluated at the World Wide Web Consortium (W3C). XML Encryption is fairly simple; the original clear-text information is encrypted and placed in between the `<EncryptedData>` tags. The following code fragment shows a sample that is unencrypted:

```
<Payment xmlns="http://sampleCreditCard.com/payment">
      <Name>Bill Powell</Name>
      <CreditCard Currency="USD">
              <Number> 3456654323455432</Number>
              <Bank>Hometown Bank</Bank>
              <Expires>05/05</Expires>
      </CreditCard>
</Payment>
```

Now here is the encrypted version of the same document:

```
<Payment xmlns="http://sampleCreditCard.com/payment">
<Name>Bill Powell</Name>
<EncryptedData Type="http://www.w3.org/2001/04/xmlenc#Element'
   xmlns='http://www.w3.org/2001/04/xmlenc#'>
   <CipherData><CipherValue>u8ui7i8u7i7</CipherValue></CipherData>
</EncryptedData>
</Payment>
```

Notice that all the data except the name has been encrypted. This could be useful when part of the data needs to be visible to a clerk or an accountant, but he does not need to see sensitive data such as the credit card number.

SAML

Every secure Web service needs to be capable of answering the question, "Who is this person or system that is trying to engage in a conversation with me?" In addition, the service needs to be able to evaluate whether or not this client has permission to use our Web service in the way that he is attempting to use it. This topic is referred to generically as authentication and authorization.

We have all used the simplest form of authentication when we key in a username and password to access a site. While we try to use the same username and password for each system that we visit, it is normally impossible to do. Sometimes the rules of usernames and passwords disallow our favorite pair. Other times, someone else has chosen that username already, so we have to go to a second choice. The situation is so bad that many users have to record their information for each site in a document or a personal database.

This situation is annoying for personal Web usage, but it is debilitating when planning a complex Web service. One of the promises of Web services is the capability to create workflow-based transactions that span many individual Web services. You might have a transaction that estimates a kitchen remodeling. It could access one Web service to get the cost of materials, another to calculate labor costs, still another to determine the permits required, and a fourth one to calculate the sales tax.

What we need is a single sign-on (SSO) as well as role-based access control (RBAC). Because it is often necessary to span different companies to execute some workflows, these solutions need to span company boundaries—at least in the case of federated companies that work together on projects, but preserve their ownership independence.

Some companies have written one-off systems to accomplish this. What is needed, though, is a standard way of solving the authentication problem so that when your circle of trading partners expands, you will be able to include the new partners quickly and without high costs.

To respond to this need, OASIS approved the 1.0 version of the Security Assertion Markup Language (SAML). A security assertion is a claim to have permission to call a certain method on a Web service. The purpose of SAML is to provide a protocol whereby clients might make assertions and Web services can authenticate these claims. The "ML" in the name indicates that SAML is an XML-based solution.

SSL provides adequate security for simple point-to-point Web service calls. What is lacking is a way to establish a "community of interest" in a certain Web service that can use it securely. What SAML adds over and above SSL is a SOAP-based messaging protocol and XML-based data structures for communicating assertions.

At present, the SAML 1.0 standard places the assertion XML in the body of the SOAP message. The more logical place for this type of information is in the SOAP header. Discussions are now taking place at OASIS between the SAML committee and the WS-Security committee concerning the feasibility of enclosing the SAML assertions inside the `<wsse:Security>` tag.

SAML provides the capability for the enterprise to vouch for the identity, authentication, and authorization rights of both human and program users.

WS-Security

Another standard on the horizon is the WS-Security standard. It proposes a set of SOAP header extensions that can be used to contain the XML for the standards that we have discussed earlier in this hour, as well as standards that will emerge in the future. The goal of WS-Security is to provide the framework for a complete security solution, but one that is customizable to individual needs.

WS-Security serves as a container for a variety of elements, each of which provides a partial security solution. The elements defined in the specification are as follows:

- `<Security>`—The enclosing tag.
- `<UsernameToken>`—The username and password.
- `<BinarySecurityToken>`—Contains binary data such as X.509 certificates and Kerberos tickets.
- `<SecurityTokenReference>`—Provides for the external storage of claims (privileges).
- `<ds:Signature>`—Digital signatures specified by the XML Signature specification.
- `<xenc:EncryptedKey>`—Key data specified by the XML Encoding specification.

The primary value of this specification is the organization that it brings to the SOAP header. If this standard is adopted into the SOAP specification, it will be a major step forward in the transformation of Web services security from a series of one-off solutions to a more unified way to transfer information securely over the Web.

Summary

In this hour, we covered the topic of securing a Web service transaction against a variety of security problems related to privacy, authentication, nonrepudiation, and nonmodification. We first looked at the problem of securing transactions against attack, and then we looked at the uniqueness of Web services transactions.

We covered several emerging specifications—each of which contributes to an overall solution. SSL allows you to send a single point-to-point transaction securely. WS Signature provides a protocol for verifying the origin of a document. WS Encryption allows you to encode all or part of your transactions during its entire life cycle. SAML allows a complex transaction to use a single authentication and authorization across the entire transaction, and WS-Security provides a framework to contain the other solutions.

Q&A

Q Why don't the standards bodies just pick a proposal and approve it?

A Standards bodies fear that standardizing something too quickly might make the standard worthless. Then you would have a "scoffed" standard, which is widely ignored.

Q Why is it a problem to allow an encrypted transaction to be decrypted and encrypted at every node?

A Some of the nodes might be public entities like courthouse computers. Allowing everyone at every node to view every transaction in its entirety is a little like sending secrets on a postcard.

Workshop

The Workshop is designed to help you review what you've learned and begin learning how to put your knowledge into practice.

Quiz

1. What is a target?
2. What are the basic threats that you must guard against?
3. What specification deals with providing a digital signature to a transaction?
4. What specification provides a security extension to the SOAP header?
5. Why is SSL considered inadequate for complex Web service transactions?

Quiz Answers

1. Any transaction that contains information that is private or of value can be a target.
2. The basic threats are theft of information, unauthorized modification, and impersonation.
3. WS Signature allows for transaction signing.
4. WS-Security would add security to the SOAP header.
5. SSL encrypts an entire transaction as it moves from one computer to another. Web services need a security strategy that enables multiple servers to be involved and the adding of additional information at each server.

Activities

1. List the threats that could potentially affect the Web services that you have built or are contemplating building.

2. Go to www.verisign.com and investigate what it would take to obtain a certificate for your organization.

3. If your organization already has a certificate, investigate what is required by your organization to make use of it.

Hour **23**

Web Services in the Real World

In this hour, you will learn about how Web services have been used in the real world. As part of this, you will see

- Several case studies showing how Web services have been used to help companies achieve goals
- Web locations with Web services directories that you can tap into or register your own Web service at

As you've seen in previous hours, Web services can be used to help solve a number of distributed and client/server computing problems. Now that you understand how to build them, it's time to see some in action. Hopefully with this information at your disposal, you'll be able to convince your boss that people actually do use this technology to solve real-world problems. You should also get a number of ideas as to how you could use Web services in your own organization.

Case Studies of Real Web Service Solutions

As you've seen in previous hours, Web services can be useful both for exposing your organization's internal systems for use by external entities and also for linking together systems that completely lie within your organization. To illustrate how a number of companies have used Web services to serve both of these purposes, while simultaneously providing real benefits to their companies, we will examine six examples. The first three show how some of the biggest names on the Internet are using Web services to expose their systems for use by outside developers. The second batch of three examples shows where companies have used Web services internally to help build systems, link together various applications, improve their bottom line, and reduce development time.

Google

In April 2002, one of the largest and most well-known Web search engines, Google, decided to open up its directory of over three billion Web pages for access via Web services. This would allow application developers to integrate the Google search engine directly into their programs. The program didn't have to be a Web site, though. Some possible uses of this service include

- Automated systems that look for new or changed entries over time on a particular topic and report those back to the user
- Information gathering and dissemination systems that look at the Web and try to find patterns across search results
- Information games utilizing data found on the Web

Google has provided a beta version of its service for use with the only restriction being a 1,000 query per day limit on the account. Each developer must register for his own account.

How does this help Google? First, its engine is exposed to a larger number of users. Second, as part of its developer area, Google encourages the exchange of ideas on how to use its data engine. This gives Google new areas to look into adding to its service (much like Yahoo! has grown into more than just a Web Search engine).

The Google developer package can be downloaded from `http://www.google.com/apis/download.html`. You can examine the APIs that the Google Web services support by examining the WSDL file for them at `http://api.google.com/GoogleSearch.wsdl`.

Let's give a brief example on how to use the Google API. We'll work this example using the GLUE Web services toolset. Although the steps involved might be slightly different for whatever toolkit you use, the overall process is the same.

First, download the Google API toolkit and unzip it to some location on your machine. Included within that zip file is the WSDL schema file for the Google Web services. Next, open a command-line window and navigate to the webservice24hours\ch23 directory, which is where our client code will live. Then type the following command, replacing <rootdir> with the drive and parent directories of the location where you unzipped the Google toolkit to:

```
wsdl2java <rootdir>\googleapi\GoogleSearch.wsdl
```

The WSDL program will parse the WSDL schema and produce a number of .java code files that form the interface layer for our client. The files created are

```
IGoogleSearchPort.java
GoogleSearchServiceHelper.java
GoogleSearchResult.java
DirectoryCategory.java
ResultElement.java
GoogleSearchService.map
```

If we examine the IGoogleSearchPort.java file that is created, we see that the Google API can respond to three different calls. They are

- `doGetCachedPage()`—Sends back the HTML for a page currently stored in the Google cache

- `doSpellingSuggestion()`—Returns a suggested spelling for a passing in word or phrase

- `doGoogleSearch()`—Performs a Web page search against the Google index

Now that we have the supporting files, we can write a client. The client found in Listing 23.1 will perform a search on whatever search terms you pass in, fetch the results, and display the URLs. The Google search API has two limitations that you should be aware of. First, the `doGoogleSearch` method will restrict you to receiving 10 results at a time. If more than 10 matches exist, you'll have to perform the search again, requesting the next batch of 10 results, and so on. Second, there is a limit of 1,000 queries per day. As a result, if you perform a search that has 50,000 hits and let it run to completion with the 10 hits per search, you'll run out of queries before you can even finish the search.

23

LISTING 23.1   A Sample Google Search Client That Uses the Google Web Services

```java
import electric.registry.Registry;

public class ourSearch
{
  /**
   * Description of the Method
   *
   *@param args Description of the Parameter
   *@exception Exception Description of the Exception
   */
  public static void main(String args[])
    throws Exception
  {
    if (args.length != 1)
    {
      System.out.println("Include search terms enclosed in \".");
      System.out.println("For example \"Commodore Amiga 2000\"");
      System.exit(-1);
    }
    // This part will be different depending on your toolset.
    IGoogleSearchPort search = GoogleSearchServiceHelper.bind();

    // Your search key will be mailed to you when
    // you register to use the GoogleAPI.
    String key = "bV8vwfxQFHKmgaPdMwfu8jRaCkpgkBAS";

    // Set optional attributes

    // Invoke the actual search
    // Do this in a loop since the max number allowed to be
    // returned at a time is 10.
    GoogleSearchResult result  = null;
      result = search.doGoogleSearch(
          key,
          args[0],
          0,
          10,
          false,
          "",
          true,
          "",
          "",
          ""
          );
    // process the result
    // First we'll just show the result metrics
```

LISTING 23.1   continued

```
System.out.println("Estimated number of hits:");
System.out.println(result.estimatedTotalResultsCount);
System.out.println("Search time:");
System.out.println(result.searchTime);
System.out.println("RESULTS:");
System.out.println("----------------------------------");

// Now the actual results. The API restricts us to 10
// results per search, so we have to do the search over
// and over getting the next batch of 10 results...

ResultElement[]    elements = null;
int          startpos = 0;
boolean        flag   = true;
  while (flag == true)
  {
    result = search.doGoogleSearch(
        key,
        args[0],
        startpos,
        10,
        false,
        "",
        true,
        "",
        "",
        ""
        );

    elements = result.resultElements;

    for (int i = 0; i < elements.length; i++)
    {
      System.out.println(elements[i].URL);
    }
    if (elements.length < 10)
    {
      flag = false;
    }
    startpos = startpos + 10;
  }
 }
}
```

If you're using a toolset other than GLUE to build the interfaces, you might need to alter the code slightly. Also, you'll need to replace the key value in the program with the one sent to you by Google when you registered. Compile the program code by typing

```
javac *.java
```

To execute the search program, type

```
java ourSearch "Sams Publishing Java 2 Unleashed"
```

You should get back the time that the search took, the number of estimated hits, and a listing of all the search results. You'll probably want to press Ctrl+C to stop the program before you exhaust all of your query quota.

Amazon

In July 2002, Amazon—the largest online retailer and one of the most popular Web sites around—provided a Web services interface to its inventory. This allows users to create their own interfaces to the Amazon store. For instance, using the Amazon API, it would be possible to build all sorts of comparison shopping interfaces that currently might not be available on the Amazon.com Web site. Rather than waiting for Amazon to build those capabilities, you can build them yourself. Even better, you could build your own Web service that makes use of the Amazon Web service and then post it for others to use. This provides Amazon with even more sales opportunities. Developers can make use of Amazon's product descriptions, reviews, search systems, and wish lists, as well as other features such as the shopping cart.

Say, for instance, that you wanted to build a portal dedicated to motorcycles. In part of your site, you'd like to include links to the Amazon store for products related to motorcycles. With the Amazon Web services, you can now do that very easily without having to build your own commerce engine, shopping cart, and so on.

In fact, this arrangement has proven to be beneficial not only to Amazon, but also to members of its Associates Program. This program was started in order to allow other online retailers to link to Amazon for actual ordering of merchandise. The retailer receives up to a 15% kickback of the purchase price of any order originating through its site. The Web services engine has allowed such retailers to easily create enticing storefronts and at the same time drive up sales for both themselves and Amazon.

Prior to the Web services initiative, to build such a service required screen scraping and a lot of HTML rework to make the site be branded as the retailer's and not Amazon's. With the Web services, it is a much easier endeavor.

The Amazon.com Web Services Developers Kit can be found at `http://www.amazon.com/webservices`. The kit exposes two main areas of interest. The first is the Product Display area that allows users to search the product catalog and retrieve information about the products listed within. The second area is the Shopping Cart, which provides users with an API to add products from the catalog to the Amazon shopping cart, wish lists, and gift registries.

Much like the Google API, Amazon requires the developer to register for a unique product key that is passed during all Web service invocations to identify you. If you want to write a client that uses the Amazon API, you'll need to register for one of these keys. (Amazon refers to them as Tokens.) Also, similar to the Google API, the Amazon API has restrictions on the number of results returned during searches, the number of reviews returned for a product, and so on. Check the API documentation for the specific restrictions.

The API provides a number of different search methods, categorized by the main type of search (for instance AuthorSearchRequest, UpcSearchRequest, AsinSearchRequest, and so on).

To develop a client that utilizes the Amazon API, you can perform steps similar to what we did in the previous Google example, instructing the wsdl2java program to read the WSDL schema found at `http://soap.amazon.com/schemas2/AmazonWebServices.wsdl`. Aside from the different classes and API calls, the overall process involved is the same as it has been throughout the book. Use the WSDL to make your interfaces, and then write your client making use of the interface classes.

Microsoft's MapPoint.NET

Microsoft recently released a new version of its MapPoint Web site. This new version provides a Web services interface for developers to tie into. Microsoft, in a battle with other companies such as MapQuest, saw a need in providing a simple programmatic interface to its map database.

With the new Web services interface, developers can write software that, for instance, ties addresses in a sales database to the mapping system to fetch out driving directions for sales people. Another interesting capability of the service is *reverse geocoding*, whereby longitude and latitude information from a GPS can be converted to a street address. Web site developers can quickly integrate maps of areas—say a map of the surrounding area for a vacation resort or driving directions from the nearest airport.

Although competitor MapQuest does have a programming API to tie into its system, it is proprietary and not Web services based, which means that developers wanting to use it would require more time and effort to learn and use it than the MapPoint solution.

23

To reach the MapPoint.net technical documents and support, visit http://www.microsoft.com/mappoint/net/. There, you will find the MapPoint SDK. Microsoft has provided extensive documentation, including a number of examples in both Visual Basic and Visual C# showing how to work with the service. Being a Microsoft product, the documentation and interfaces are heavily centered around the .NET development framework. As such, it is recommended that you use .NET to build any systems that you want to hook into the MapPoint API. This doesn't mean that it's impossible to use other toolkits and languages, only that it will be more difficult because of the lack of direct documentation and support.

The MapPoint SDK includes support for four Web services:

- **Common Service**—A group of classes that provide common support for the other three services.
- **Find Service**—Locates addresses, points of interest, latitude and longitude coordinates, and so on.
- **Render Service**—Draws out maps of locations and routes.
- **Route Service**—Provides trip routing service capabilities. Can calculate driving directions and work with either waypoints or locations.

With these services, it is possible to create complex tools for finding addresses, planning trips, providing personalized driving directions and maps, and a host of other activities.

The services are provided on both development and production hosting environments. Use of the development (or staging) environment is free, but has limitations on the number of interactions that can be performed over a period of time. The production environment is a pay service, based on usage, but it does not have the same limitations and can scale much better than the staging environment. For your own personal development, use the staging environment. Only move to the production environment if you are building a system for commercial use and will be able to pay the usage charges!

The WSDL schema for the staging server can be found at http://staging.mappoint.net/standard-30/mappoint.wsdl.

Merrill Lynch

Financial powerhouse Merrill Lynch has recently turned to Web services as a way to reduce its internal development costs and increase reusability of its internal systems. Although not a publicly available service, Merrill Lynch has seen internal benefits in the Web services approach.

Being a large company with a history in IT stretching back to the early days of computing, Merrill Lynch is probably the best example of where Web services can help with integration. Owning many systems, created over various generations of IT methodologies, Merrill Lynch, and other companies like it, have found it difficult to integrate and reuse features of one system inside of another. By embracing Web services as an interface to all of its systems, Merrill Lynch is able to reuse features of its existing systems when building new ones. In one case, this new paradigm took the company from an $800,000 estimated solution built using traditional methods to one costing $30,000 using the Web services approach.

The Web services paradigm has also allowed Merrill Lynch to provide more services to its partners by exposing some of these interfaces directly to them in an easy-to-understand manner. Gone are the days of partners needing special knowledge of the company's systems in order to integrate. Now, it's just a WSDL address and a few accounts that are generated, and that's it.

The Home Depot

Leading do-it-yourself home improvement retailer The Home Depot ran into a dilemma. It had been using a point-of-sale system that was homegrown, monolithic, and very hard to extend and modify. The system was client/server in nature and used UDP for communications between the terminals and the local server in each store. The system worked, but it wasn't ideal. Although the terminal software was compact and fast, it also structured data into silos, restricting information in one area from being used in another. The information being passed from the client to the server was also being encoded in its own format. The company found the solution to have several problems, including

- Not all the store systems had easy access to the data messages that were transferred between the client and the server. This data was often cryptic and proprietary. This made the sharing of the data between different applications very difficult to achieve.

- There was no real contract or schema to describe the message sets in a standard fashion.

- Internationalization meant changing code that parsed the byte streams and client code that created the byte streams.

- Because the program was monolithic (one executable with many threads), regression testing of all functionality had to be performed by QA prior to release, requiring great time and expense, in addition to added complexity.

In the quest to find a better solution that would be more modular in design and allow for more reusability, The Home Depot decided to go with a phased approach to replace its system.

In the first phase, the proprietary data streams over UDP were replaced with XML data sent over TCP. Although this wasn't a full change to Web services, it allowed for a gradual transition to SOAP and the more accepted Web services standards. With more than 1,500 terminals to be upgraded, a full cut over from the old mechanism to the new would not be prudent nor feasible. The decision to go to this phase was made at a time when Web services technologies were just starting to evolve, and their direction was still in doubt. By taking this interim step, The Home Depot was able to fix many of its existing problems by evolving its software to a halfway phase and waiting for the standards to catch up. Evolution, rather than revolution, is often more advisable when dealing with business systems.

In the second phase, The Home Depot is rolling out not only the system from phase 1, but also a number of new applications that will all tie into each other through the Web services mechanisms. Whereas old systems used to run on Novera and JRun Java application servers, the new applications will be hosted on IBM WebSphere and make extensive use of the Web services paradigm through Microsoft's .NET offerings and Apache Axis for the Java-based systems.

The Home Depot has also found the switch to Web services beneficial—teams that previously were not able to share capabilities because of differing technologies (Visual Basic, Java, COBOL, and so on) now have the ability to leverage each other's work. The Home Depot has found the ability to use WSDL to generate code for .NET bindings, and the generation of Java code for .NET servers to be an ideal solution. This synergy of technologies is allowing the company to speed up deployment of new applications and share capabilities among all teams, not just the ones using the same technologies. At the time of this writing, the company has just started its conversion of the systems in the store.

Providence Health System

As a large provider of healthcare services in the United States and Canada, Providence faced a dilemma. It had a large number of dissimilar IT systems that needed to be linked together not only for company use, but also to provide access and interfaces for vendors and suppliers.

In an effort to help tie all of these systems together, a new project was launched. The goal was to pull together all of these numerous systems, provide secure and robust interconnection, and make all new systems comply with the federal HIPAA (Health Insurance Portability and Accountability Act) standards. This was no easy task.

Providence had already been a primarily Microsoft-based shop, so the company chose to use the .NET framework for building its solution. Visual Studio provided its developers with all the tools for quickly building Web services applications.

The Web services architecture also needed to run alongside and tie into the company's existing Enterprise Application Integration (EAI) framework (rather than replace it). In this case, the fact that Web services are built on XML and are cross platform and language independent proved to be a large help to Providence because most of the EAI was developed in other systems such as Java.

One of the first steps Providence took was to develop a systemwide, profile-based authorization and authentication system. This would allow all applications to be able to verify who a user was and what he could do. This tool was written in Java, but it was easily accessible via Web services. Doing this allowed all new applications to share this common concept of a user and the user's security capabilities rather than each system creating its own. This alone has saved Providence large amounts of time in developing new systems.

In order to handle Web services management and provide the necessary monitoring and accountability, Providence turned to a product by Infravio. This product acts as a middleman to monitor the Web services infrastructure and report any problem. This has allowed Providence to handle many of its HIPAA requirements that would have been very difficult to do without a Web services architecture.

Figure 23.1 shows the architecture Providence is using at a high level.

23

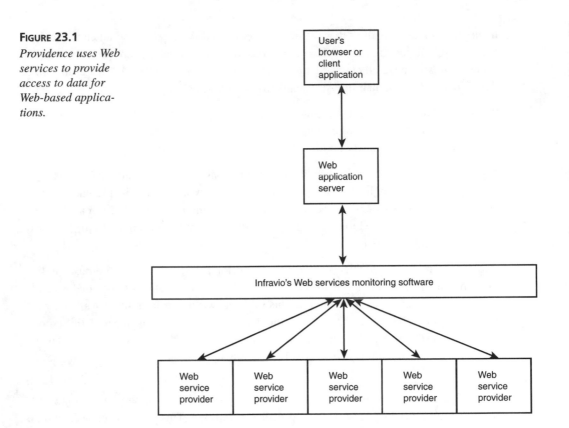

FIGURE 23.1

Providence uses Web services to provide access to data for Web-based applications.

Web Services Directories on the Web

Now that you've seen how others have used Web services to build successful real-world solutions, we'll examine where you can go to find services that others have provided for use. Many of these sites also allow you to list your own services for use by others. Some are strictly for listing free services, whereas others provide a framework for charging for your service. By looking through these sites, you should get a better understanding of what services are available to tap into across the Web and possibly find services that will provide capabilities that you might be looking for.

www.xmethods.com

One of the more popular free Web services directories is run by xmethods.com. One of the best features of this site is that it lists the available services not only by name and function, but it also explains what style (document or RPC) and what tool the service was implemented in. So, for instance, in the case that you're using Apache Axis as your interface technology and want to find services that also use Axis, you can simply look through the list to find them. Of course, with Web services and the SOAP/WSDL/UDDI standards, you can use any toolset to access a service built with any other toolset.

All services found at the xmethods site are free of charge and for noncommercial use. Although this means that you shouldn't use them for commercial systems, you can still utilize the services found here for experimentation and learning or personal-use systems.

Some of the services available on the xmethods directory range from stock quote engines to FedEx package tracking services to services that calculate the distance in miles between two ZIP Codes.

To access the services found at the xmethods site, a UDDI interface has been provided. Depending on the toolset you use, the process will be different, but simply point the toolset to the URL `http://uddi.xmethods.net/inquire` to get to the UDDI listing. (Note: This URL will *not* work in a browser.) From there, follow the process for your toolset to look through the index and build the client-side interface to the service you want, utilizing the WSDL interface provided.

The xmethods site also has a relatively good mailing list in which members of the site can communicate and discuss problems and solutions. Free registration to the site is required for posting any new service to the site and can be accomplished by clicking the Register link on the main page.

www.salcentral.com

The salcentral site acts as a Web services brokerage system. Much like xmethods.com, Web services are listed and categorized for visitors to see and use. Salcentral is different, however, in that it provides a pricing system by which you can easily charge for access to any service you post to its index. This is nice in that it eliminates the need for you to build these features yourself, and also puts your service into a centralized high-traffic clearinghouse environment in which more people are likely to see your service and pay to use it.

Salcentral also has a large variety of services listed on its site. At the time of this writing, its index included more than 600 services. Users are able to provide reviews and ratings on the various services as well.

In order to use any of the services on this site, a free registration must be filled out and completed. Once registered, simply select the service and click on the schema link to get the WSDL interface. From that WSDL, the toolset of your choice can build the necessary interface components for your client.

23

For services that you want to provide and charge for through the salcentral system, a special set of steps must be performed. The instructions for doing this can be found at `http://www.salcentral.com/salnet/wpsubws.htm`. Basically, it involves adding a few parameters to your services to capture username and password information so that users can be identified by the system.

In all, the salcentral site provides a great way to find and stay up-to-date on the Web services out there. The reviews, user-provided scores, and notes sections for each service can be a real help in choosing the one that is right for you and can be instrumental in providing a good interfacing experience for users of your services.

www.remotemethods.com

The remotemethods.com site also acts as a clearinghouse of Web services. The developers of this site have attempted to provide access to available Web services in a categorized manner, similar to the categories found on Yahoo and other top Web search engine sites. The classification system is multitiered and fairly extensive, which should help in finding the right service for your needs. Again, the services found here run the full spectrum from simple calculation engines to message-of-the-day joke servers to graphics charting systems.

Much like salcentral, remotemethods provides a mechanism for users to post reviews of the services for others to see and evaluate as well as a site-ranking system. Services found either in a category or via a search can be listed according to various criteria such as price, popularity, ranking, and date.

uddi.microsoft.com

If you're using the Microsoft .NET framework for building your Web services, one of the best sites to go to for finding other such services is the Microsoft UDDI server at `http://uddi.microsoft.com`. In order to use the services on this site, registration is required using the MS Passport system. Once registered, finding the services available on the site can be a bit of a daunting task because of the way in which MS has organized the information.

To get started, click on the search link on the left side of the screen. This will bring up the first page of the search criteria system.

It is recommended that you make use of the Quick Help-Searching UDDI option in the upper right corner in order to better understand how to use this system.

For example, in order to bring up a list of all RPC-style services currently listed, follow these steps:

1. From the main search screen, click on the Services tab.
2. Click on the Add Category button.
3. Click on uddi-org:types.
4. Click on These Types Are Used for tModels.
5. Click on Specification for a Web Service.
6. Click on Specification for a Web Service Described in WSDL.
7. Press the Add Category button.
8. In the Service Name field, enter % (the wildcard character).
9. Then press the Search button.

If you've followed these steps, a listing of all matching services in the UDDI directory will show up in the left frame on the page, along with brief write ups on each. Clicking on one of the services listed will display information, including the WSDL address to reach the schema for this service. Simply point the Web services toolkit of your choice to that address to find the WSDL specification for that service and generate the needed client-side files to access it.

Summary

In this hour, we looked at how Web services are being used in the real world. We first examined a number of case studies documenting how real businesses have used Web services to achieve greater return on investments (ROI) and lowered their development costs.

Next, we examined a number of the publicly accessible Web services directories found on the Web. We saw how to find what Web services were available and briefly discussed how to get your own service posted to these indexes. We saw that there are already a large number of freely accessible Web services for use, and that number will certainly continue to grow rapidly as the technology matures.

With the information you have, you should now have a much better idea how to take your work and share it with others or find Web services that others have developed and use them yourself.

Q&A

Q **What's an example of a useful system that could be built using a number of the Web services that we looked at in this hour?**

A How about a Web site in which the users could search the Amazon store for a listing of all the cameras sold there via the Amazon API? In a side panel, a list of links to pages containing reviews about that camera could be displayed from the Google API. And finally, FedEx tracking information for the package or stock prices for the camera company could be seen in another area utilizing services found on xmethods.com.

Q **Why should I list my service on one of the service directories discussed in this hour?**

A If you have a Web service that you aim to make publicly available, you probably want somebody to actually use it. These are some of the most popular sites that developers go to when looking for a Web service to suit their needs. Therefore, listing your service on one of these directories will help to draw users to your solution.

Q **Should I bother listing my service on more than one site?**

A Absolutely! Similar to Web sites, the more indexes your service is listed on, the more likely somebody will be able to find and use it.

Q **Should I charge users to access my service?**

A This is entirely up to you. As we've seen, some of the directory services provide tools for making this possible. Standards in this area are still lacking though, so at this time, most public Web services are free.

Q **Should I link to these services using UDDI or just the browser to find the service I want through the Web?**

A Again, this is up to you. If you're looking for something very specific, it is usually easier to manually find the service you want through the Web interface. However, if you want to use the UDDI interface, nearly all the directory sites we examined in this hour provide one.

Workshop

This section is designed to help you anticipate possible questions, review what you've learned, and begin learning how to put your knowledge into practice.

Quiz

1. Why did The Home Depot use a phased approach to switching its systems to Web services?

2. What advantage is Amazon seeing by releasing its Web services package?

3. What limitations are there on the Google API?

Quiz Answers

23

1. The Home Depot was a very early adopter and wanted to wait for the technology to mature, as well as needing to provide a gradual transition from its old solution to the new one.

2. It has become easier for affiliates to sell products through Amazon. This drives more traffic to Amazon, thus increasing sales, helping both Amazon and the affiliate.

3. The major limitation currently is the 1,000 query per day limit.

Activity

1. Download the Google API package. Create a Web client that will accept a list of five search queries and return a list of sites that show up in the results of all five searches. Obviously, the queries should be related in some way for this to work. For instance, a workable set of queries might be: motorcycle racing, AMA, Superbike, Nicky Hayden, and birthday. Such a search should yield only sites that talk about the AMA Superbike motorcycle racer Nicky Hayden, and that mention his birthday. Such a search will probably provide many fewer hits than a single search that includes all the terms. Experiment with possible uses for such a tool.

HOUR **24**

The Future of Web Services

This is the hour in which your humble authors get to play futurist. Predicting the future in any technology is always a risky venture. Although it is true that predictions are very often wrong, there doesn't seem to be any lasting punishment for the erroneous predictor. With this in mind, we will cover what appears to be the direction of Web services for the near future.

When reading about these topics, it is important to remember that there is no centralized leadership in the world of computing. Every individual writer, thinker, company, standards body, and governmental organization that gets involved possesses some degree of self-interest. Many good ideas die on the vine because they conflicted with a few people's or companies' interests. Other weak trends get more attention than they deserve because of powerful backers.

In some ways, we are fortunate that the decision making process is so fragmented. In spite of the financial clout of several software and hardware companies in the recent past, they have been spectacularly unsuccessful at dictating terms to the rest of us. Their only successes have come by working to achieve consensus among the sometimes cantankerous factions that compose our world. This is the fundamental reason that all the predictions in this hour should be taken with the proverbial "grain of salt." All of them might indeed come to pass, but it is more likely that some of them will not.

We will start by talking about other uses of the Web services standards that are already beginning to appear. Following that, we will talk about new versions of the existing standards, followed by a discussion of the new standards that are likely to be adopted.

In this hour you will learn about

- Non-Web services uses of UDDI, SOAP, and WSDL
- New versions of the existing standards
- Wireless Web services
- W3C's Web services architecture
- WS-Coordination and WS-Transaction
- Business Process Execution Language

Nontraditional Uses

As stated throughout this book, Web services are built using a suite of standards. These standards have their own set of followers and are governed, in near independence, by their own standards bodies. Although these bodies monitor the directions that the other groups are taking and take care to avoid incompatibilities, each charts its own course. This will become increasingly true as more standards are added to the Web services suite.

Nearly every invention finds uses that are far outside the vision of its inventors. Could the ancient inventors of gunpowder have foreseen the machine gun, or could the creators of networked computers have foreseen e-commerce?

The standards created for Web services have already begun to be used for other purposes. We predict that every one of the current standards associated with Web services will find a strong following in at least one area not normally thought of as related to Web services at all.

Using UDDI As a Software Reuse Catalog

If you look at the features of UDDI apart from its role in Web services, you will see that it possesses a number of interesting characteristics:

- **Language independence**—The only language that UDDI is required to conform to is XML.

- **Human readable**—The information in the UDDI is in ASCII-character format, which can be read using a simple text editor such as Notepad or any one of a number of more sophisticated approaches.

- **Hardware independence**—A UDDI registry can be created on any platform using any programming language or tool.

- **Universal**—UDDI is capable of describing any piece of software regardless of its platform, origin, language, and so on.

- **Comprehensive**—A UDDI registry can contain a wide variety of information about a piece of software. This includes information about its purpose, its owners, the standards that it is built on, its locations, and its cost per access, if any. In addition, the UDDI registry normally contains the Internet addresses of other resources that describe the service, such as its WSDL description and the phone numbers of support personnel.

- **Standards based**—Standards take some of the politics out of decision making. The UDDI registry specification has brought some measure of peace to the software industry, so it might find acceptance within your organization also.

These characteristics make it a great candidate for maintaining an inventory of all the software systems in a large organization, company, or university. Having a central registry like this is essential to any software reuse strategy. All these organizations have systems that run on a variety of hardware and software platforms and that are written in a variety of computer languages.

In order to reuse a piece of software, you have to know where it is, who owns it, what language it is written in, its purpose, and so on. In short, you must have the kind of information that is normally stored in a UDDI description.

In addition, you also must have a contact person to provide support and advice. Look for organizations to purchase or create UDDI-compliant software to serve as a repository for their software inventory and reuse catalog. Figure 24.1 shows a UDDI-based reuse catalog.

The communication, up to and including the inquiry of the UDDI registry, is identical to the way it would be done to find a Web service. From that point forward, it would be a traditional phone call followed up by email communication.

24

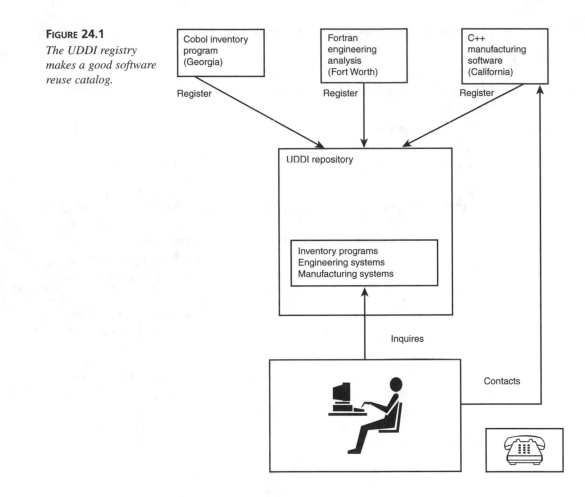

FIGURE 24.1
The UDDI registry makes a good software reuse catalog.

Using WSDL as a Design Document

If you look at the features of WSDL apart from its role in Web services, you will also see that it possesses a number of useful characteristics:

- **Language independence**—The only language that WSDL is required to conform to is XML.

- **Human readable**—The information in the WSDL is in ASCII-character format, which can be read using a simple text editor such as Notepad, or any one of a number of more sophisticated approaches.

- **Machine readable**—Enough information in the WSDL exists that can be used to generate code.

- **Hardware independence**—A WSDL can be created on any platform using any tool.

- **Universal**—WSDL is capable of describing any piece of software regardless of its platform, origin, language, and so on.

- **Comprehensive**—A WSDL document contains a wide variety of information about a piece of software. This includes both a logical view of the services that it provides as well as one or more descriptions of how you would bind to it.

- **Standards based**—Documents written to the WSDL standard can be understood by any person or software system that understands the standard. This makes it possible to share code across organizational boundaries.

These features combine to make WSDL a universal Application Programming Interface (API). The WSDL can be used as the design view of a service or system, regardless of how the actual code that implements it is created. This is true whether or not SOAP is used to provide the message protocol.

This idea is far reaching because a COBOL programmer who knows how to describe his systems in WSDL format can now communicate with a Java programmer in a meaningful way—without either of them having to understand too much about the other's world. In addition, a framework programmer could use the WSDL to generate the code needed to connect the Java front end to the COBOL back end.

In the future, expect to see the WSDL move outside of its current Web services role and find uses in the Enterprise Application Integration world—in many cases, without SOAP.

Using SOAP as an EAI Language

One of the weaknesses of XML is that it is a noun-oriented language. An XML tag represents an entity such as a paycheck or a machine. It can also contain adjectives (attributes), but where do you place verbs? One solution that we and others have used was to use message queues to transfer XML documents. If a document arrived on one queue, it was treated as an order; if a document arrived on a different queue, it was treated as a request to return defective merchandise. Responses were sent using yet a third queue. Figure 24.2 shows this approach graphically.

This approach provided the verbs or method calls implicitly by the choice of queues. This approach was serviceable within a single company or between companies that communicated using messaging, but beyond that it was very limiting.

24

FIGURE 24.2

Multiple message queues provide implicit method calls in a messaging system.

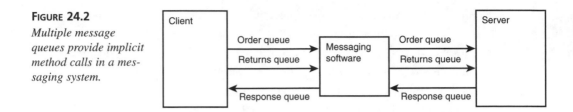

A better approach is to define verbs (method calls) in XML itself. This provides the advantage of having explicit calls instead of implied calls in the messaging software. In addition, this approach would allow you to remove the requirement that expensive messaging software be used. The only thing lacking is the syntax of the XML to be used. SOAP provides that syntax in a standardized fashion. SOAP has the following qualities:

- **XML based**—SOAP is a dialect of XML, and it can be parsed by any XML parser.
- **Standard**—The W3C regulates the contents of a SOAP message, which means that any SOAP engine can be used on any SOAP message. It also means that every programmer trained to use SOAP can understand the format being used by every other SOAP programmer.
- **Easy**—SOAP messages are not complicated, and they can be written by hand using a text editor.
- **Generated**—Your code can generate SOAP messages on-the-fly, just as it can create any other XML document.

These features allow us to redraw Figure 24.2 using this new approach. Figure 24.3 shows this approach.

FIGURE 24.3

SOAP messages allow us to make method calls across the network.

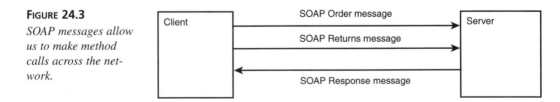

Notice the simplicity of this approach. In addition, note that there is no middleware to buy with SOAP (though a vendor's product might perform better). Each computer can communicate with another directly. This approach is practical any time you want to implement a system in which one computer needs to make method calls on another. This is true regardless of whether you have a WSDL defined for the server or whether you are using a Web services platform such as Apache Axis. It is a useful approach even if all you are doing is opening a socket between one program and another. In addition, if you hire a new programmer who knows SOAP, he might be able to understand your code better.

In the future, expect to see SOAP move outside of its current Web services role and find uses all over your company as a dialect of XML to send and receive method calls. However, SOAP and Web services are getting a reputation for being "slow." They will have to overcome this to move past their current role of "outside the firewall integration" and into the realm of general purpose RPC.

A New Version of UDDI

When standards are in their formative years, they are constantly undergoing changes. The reason for this is that they have been accepted in general, but deficiencies have been identified that must be remedied before they can be declared truly useful.

24

One of the three current Web services standards, UDDI, is still in its formative years. As a result, you can expect new versions of it from time to time. The other ones, SOAP and WSDL, have stabilized, and newer versions of them tend to contain only maintenance-type changes.

UDDI Version 3

In July 2002, a new version of the UDDI was released. It builds on the previous releases and adds the following features:

- **Support for multiregistry environments**—Before version 3, UDDI registries had no way of expressing relationships to one another. Version 3 introduces the concepts of a root and affiliate registries. The root acts as the authority for the registry. It can delegate key partitions so that other registries can interact with the root without having to get unique keys for their entries from it.

- **Subscription**—Before version 3, you had to make an inquiry to learn if the registry contents had changed. As of version 3, your registry can subscribe to be notified whenever an entry that it has an interest in has been modified.

- **Separation of policy from implementation**—Version 3 addresses the issues of permissions and policy by using policy abstractions, rules, decisions, decision points, and enforcement points. All these entities describe who is allowed to do what to the registry.

- **Security features**—The ability to determine the truthfulness of the data in the registry has been lacking until version 3. This version adds the ability to digitally sign all the core data in the registry. It does this by supporting the new XML-Signature standard. As the name implies, XML Signature is a set of XML tags. These tags are designed to contain sufficient information to allow a client to be verified using the public/private key pair that he must possess to participate in a signed transaction. Hour 22, "Web Service Security," covers digital signatures in more detail.

- **Enhanced inquiry**—Version 3 provides significant improvements to the Inquiry API. New qualifiers allow you to perform both case sensitive and not case sensitive matches, sorts, as well as sorts using accents (non-English alphabets). In addition, it now supports approximate matching, binary sorting, and exact matching. Finally, it allows you to search only where a signature is present.

- **Chunked retrieval**—You may now inquire about services and receive the data back in chunks of an appropriate size. This is similar to cursoring through a database, except that each chunk can be retrieved at a slightly different time, allowing some updates in the mean time.

Of the three standards, UDDI is the one that lags behind in adoption by the user community. Its fans hope that this new version will provide solutions to issues that have held it back in the past. It is interesting to note that UDDI has now pulled WS Signature into the Web services standards, albeit in a second-hand way.

Understanding W3C's Web Services Architecture

One of the curious things about Web services is that it hasn't been formally defined. It is generally considered to consist of UDDI, WSDL, and SOAP—all of which are governed by one standards body or another. Until late 2002, however, the formal definition of the architecture was missing.

NEW TERM   In November 2002, the W3C published the first working draft of a document called "*Web Services Architecture*." According to this document, which can be found at www.w3.org/TR/ws-arch,

> "The Web services reference architecture identifies the functional components, defines the relationships among these components, and establishes a set of constraints upon each to effect the desired properties of the overall architecture."

Before you get too excited though, this version of the document contains a disclaimer that the document doesn't reflect the consensus of the W3C Web Services Architecture WG that created it. It was published to stimulate discussion of the topics in which there is still no widespread agreement.

Hopeful signs exist in the document that some of the problems that have held Web services back, such as security and choreography, are going to get some attention.

NEW TERM This document is divided into two parts: basic and extended architecture. The basic architecture describes a Web services *stack*, or completely functional implementation. The extended architecture describes how messages are combined into higher-level interactions. It provides details on support for security, transactions, orchestration, privacy, and business-level transactions.

The document defines messages and intermediaries, as well as operations. It makes a draft attempt at defining many terms, including the following:

- Asynchronous messaging
- Attachment
- Caching
- Correlation
- Long running transaction
- Management messages
- Message authentication
- Message confidentiality
- Message exchange pattern
- Message integrity
- Message routing
- Reliable message
- Session

Finally, this document defines a Wire stack that is composed of three layers as shown in Figure 24.4.

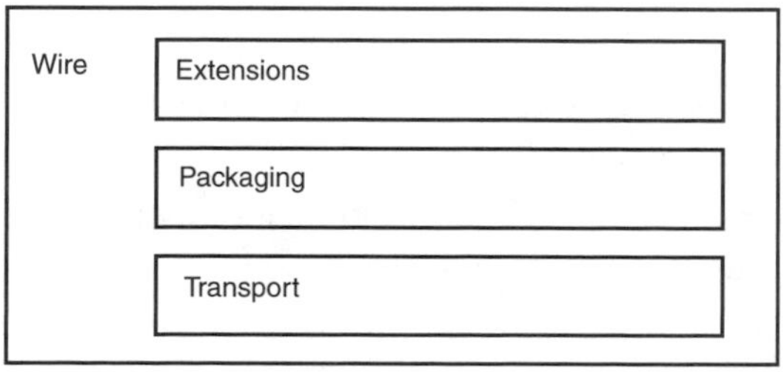

24

FIGURE 24.4

The Wire stack defines how messages travel from one computer to another.

Wire

Extensions
Packaging
Transport

NEW TERM The *transport* is the actual protocol, such as HTTP, or SMTP. In addition, it can be a vendor protocol such as MQSeries. The packaging layer represents the technology that packages information for exchange. XML and SOAP fit into this layer.

Extensions represents the frontier of Web services. It defines the information such as context, routing, policy, authentication, and other technologies that are likely to be implemented in the SOAP header.

WS-Transaction

NEW TERM One of the oft-mentioned deficiencies of Web services is the lack of a *transaction model*. A logical transaction is a set of activities that compose one complete operation from the user's point of view. For example, a deduction of $20 from your savings without a corresponding deposit of $20 to your checking account would invalidate a transfer. Even worse, it would leave you $20 poorer. Logically, the transaction begins before the deduction and ends after a successful deposit into checking.

Database management systems (DBMSs) often provide a way of beginning and ending (committing) a transaction. In the world of Web services, a similar need exists. However, a single DBMS vendor cannot supply this functionality because all the parts of the transactions don't take place in his software. A single transaction might take place over several days and involve a dozen or more computers.

Recognizing this deficiency, BEA, Microsoft, and IBM have begun work on a standard way of handling Web services transactions called WS-Transaction.

At the time of this writing, this paper has not yet been submitted to any standards body. It is still in its formative stage in which ideas are incorporated on a regular basis. You can find a copy of the WS-Transaction document at `www-106.ibm.com/developerworks/library/ws-transpec/`.

The document defines two very different types of transactions:

- **The Atomic Transaction**—This is the class type of transaction similar to the bank account example explained previously. The transaction is an all-or-nothing proposition. If it fails at any time, all parts of the transaction are to be rolled back as if this transaction never started.

- **The Business Activity**—This is a different type of transaction based on the fact that long transactions exist in the real world. Many business activities take weeks to complete and involve dozens of people and computer systems. An example of this would be an order for a jet airplane. If you begin the transaction just after signing the contract, you would commit the transaction after you fly the jet off. In this scenario, you couldn't roll back to the beginning. Parts have been fabricated, money advanced, people hired, and so on. When this type of transaction fails, and it does sometimes, you have to be very sophisticated in your approach to cleaning up. Everyone involved must be "made whole" to the best of your ability.

This specification is designed to fit into the WS-Coordination proposed standard. Both of these specifications must be accepted by the W3C for inclusion into the SOAP header file standards before you can assume that every SOAP engine supports it. That doesn't stop you from using these features today, however, if the other party in the transaction is aware of them and knows how to handle the extra tags that he will find in the SOAP header.

Business Process Execution Language for Web Services

Another area in which specifications are needed is in the area of choreography. Modern business transactions are very complex. If you consider the number of different computer systems used when you are purchasing a house, you will get a feel for this complexity.

If a sufficiently powerful business-process language existed, the level of automation possible would increase, thereby decreasing costs. Imagine being given the task to automate the house-closing process. You would have to create a Web service on every computer that needs to know about the purchase. This includes at least two mortgage banks, insurance companies, title search firms, and a host of governmental agencies, including federal, state, and local. In effect, you would need to create a Web service for every piece of paper that you normally sign at a closing.

That is daunting enough, but after you had completed programming all these Web services, you would need to create a SOAP message that provides instructions on what to do at each stage. You would have a chain of intermediaries that would stretch on for pages. In addition, you would need exception handling for cases in which one of the services doesn't behave the way that you were hoping. The definition of this path is the subject of business-process execution.

Fortunately, IBM, BEA, and Microsoft have joined together and produced a specification to start the process of defining exactly what is needed. Although this effort is far from mature, it does serve to get the ball rolling. They call this proposed standard the Business Process Execution Language for Web Services (BPELWS).

When you consider the complexity of designing the process needed to automate a complex business transaction, you are reminded of a third-generation programming language such as Java. You will need `if...then...else` processing, `do...while`, `catch` exception, and just about every other conditional operation that you need in a programming language.

24

BPELWS provides this type of processing in an XML format. A few of the tags that it uses are

- `<assign>`
- `<invoke>`
- `<source>`
- `<switch>`
- `<terminate>`
- `<while>`

There are so many more that it would be difficult to list them all in the space that we have here. If BPELWS's tags aren't sufficient, you can extend these with the `<extension>` tag that has a namespace attribute.

It is hard to say what will come of this effort. At the time of this writing, the BPEL4WS specification was in its initial draft release. If you study it, however, your time will not be wasted because the need surely exists for some specification to fill this niche. In all likelihood, some part of this specification, small or large, will find its way into the Web service that you will be working on 10 years from now. The URL for this proposal is `http://www-106.ibm.com/developerworks/webservices/library/ws-bpel/`.

Summary

In this hour, we covered some of the developments that are coming up on the Web services horizon. We first covered the use of UDDI, WSDL, and SOAP for other purposes. Next, we discussed the new features of UDDI 3.0. Following that, you learned about the new Web Services Architecture draft specification that has been circulated for review.

Next, we looked at a number of specifications that are well thought of at the present time. Finally, we looked at WS-Transaction and BPELWS as two specifications that fill import needs in the future development of Web services.

Q&A

Q Is the Web services architecture standard necessary?

A Not strictly, but it is very important. Without it, or something like it, the individual standards have no formal relationship to each other.

Q Isn't the BPEL proposal too broad to be useful?

A It is broad and open, but only time will tell whether it is too broad. Many of these standards tend to be conversation pieces that lead us to better solutions by starting the discussion.

Workshop

The Workshop is designed to help you review what you've learned and begin learning how to put your knowledge into practice.

Quiz

1. Why is UDDI changing faster than WSDL or SOAP?
2. Why do we need a formal description of Web services?
3. What are the two types of transactions that WS-Transaction covers?
4. What need is BPELWS trying to address?

Quiz Answers

1. UDDI is newer, and therefore less mature, than the other two standards. In addition, UDDI is performing a function that is very new and not nearly as defined as schemas and message protocols.

2. As long as there is no formal description of what is and isn't a part of Web services, conflicts will always be arising. Without a recognized specification, there is no way to settle the differences.

3. The two types are the Atomic transaction and the Business Activity transaction.

4. BPELWS is trying to add logic to the chaining together of Web services sites as components in a long transaction.

Activities

1. List the types of transactions that you will need to support in the systems that you envision. Categorize them as either Atomic or Business Activities.

2. Discuss one or more of the trends and developments covered in this hour with your co-workers. Declare whether or not you think that each of them will come to pass. Write down your responses and save them for the future.

24

PART V
Appendixes

APPENDIX A

Installing Apache Tomcat and Axis

Hour 13, "Creating Web Services with Apache Axis," shows you how to use Axis. If you want to try the example in the hour for yourself, you will need to follow these directions to install Tomcat and Axis.

Tomcat

Jakarta Tomcat is available at no cost from the Apache Web site at `http://jakarta.apache.org/`.

At the time of this writing, the most current stable release is version 4.0.6. The link for Tomcat 4.0.6 is

`http://jakarta.apache.org/builds/jakarta-tomcat-4.0/release/v4.0.6/bin/`

The actual release that you choose is not that important. We normally install the most recent, stable release that is listed on the Web site. Choose a release that is right for your needs. If you are running Java 1.4 on a Windows environment, the following self-extracting .exe file will work for you.

```
jakarta-tomcat-4.0.6-LE-jdk14.exe
```

> As new versions of Tomcat are released, the links that lead to them will differ from those shown previously. In these cases, you will need to go to the http://jakarta.apache.org/ Web site and navigate to the newest release.

You will then be prompted to enter the location where you want this .exe file stored. Any directory will do because this is a temporary location. Next, open Windows Explorer and double-click the name of the .exe file. This will open an installation wizard that will guide you through the installation. After you answer a few questions, you will be told that the installation is complete.

If you are running under UNIX, you can download the tar version and follow the instructions on the Apache Web site on how to install Tomcat on your machine.

> Vendor Web sites change from time to time. If the previous steps don't work exactly, look for similar links at each step, and you should be able to succeed in getting Tomcat installed.

Starting Tomcat

You start Tomcat by opening a command window and typing the following command (assuming that you have installed Tomcat in the default location):

```
java -jar -Duser.dir="C:\Program Files\Apache Tomcat 4.0"
"C:\Program Files\Apache Tomcat 4.0\bin\bootstrap.jar" start
```

Tomcat will output several lines of response, like these, which provide feedback that the server is really running:

```
Starting service Tomcat-Standalone
Apache Tomcat/4.0.6
Starting service Tomcat-Apache
Apache Tomcat/4.0.6
```

On some operating systems, the installation script places shortcuts in your file system to make the task of starting Tomcat easier. On our test machine, Windows XP, these shortcuts were placed in a directory called

```
C:\Documents and Settings\Your Name\Start Menu\Programs\Apache Tomcat 4.0
```

Your Name will be replaced by the login name of the machine that you are using.

A local copy of the Tomcat documentation is stored on your local hard drive. After you start Tomcat, the following URL will bring up this document:

`http://localhost:8080/tomcat-docs/index.html`

Figure A.1 shows this page.

FIGURE A.1

The Tomcat documentation provides detailed instructions about how to get the server and keep it running.

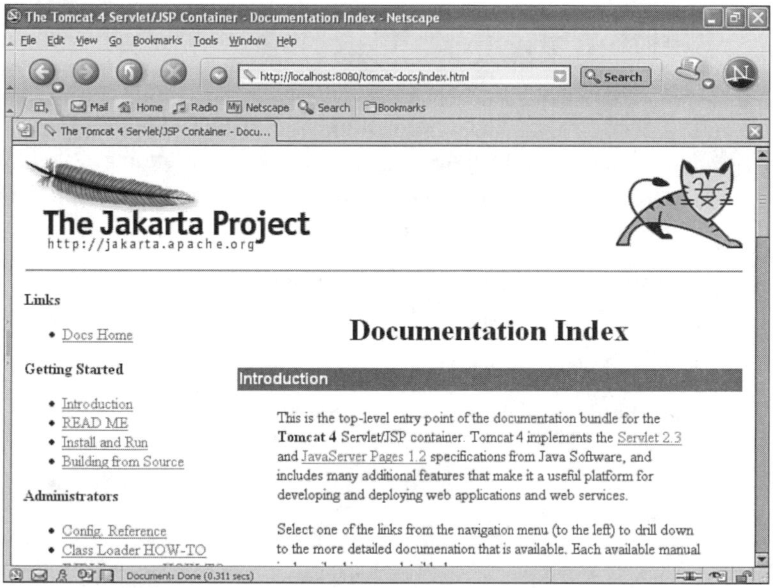

You can find answers to many of your questions with these pages, so it would be a good idea to bookmark the root page in your browser.

Most of the work that you will do with Tomcat will involve four of the directories located under the root Tomcat directory. These directories are

- `C:\Program Files\Apache Tomcat 4.0\bin`—This directory contains scripts to perform functions such as startup, shutdown, and so on. Under Windows, these scripts are .bat files, and under UNIX, they are .sh files.

- `C:\Program Files\Apache Tomcat 4.0\conf`—This directory contains configuration files that control the behavior of the server. Most of these files are in XML format. The most important file in here is called server.xml, which is the main configuration file for the server.

- `C:\Program Files\Apache Tomcat 4.0\logs`—This directory contains the logs that are created by the Tomcat server. You inspect these logs to discover clues about why certain problems are occurring with the installation or your programs.

- `C:\Program Files\Apache Tomcat 4.0\webapps`—This directory is where you put your programs. Web servers don't like to access files all over your computer because of the security risks. They prefer to allow clients to access only files, as well as their subdirectories, that are stored in one place.

Testing the Installation

After you have finished the installation, you will want to test the server using servlets provided by Apache before writing your own. The reason for this is that any problem you have running their servlets is certainly a configuration problem. If you run your own servlets without first verifying that the installation is correct, the problem could be either in the installation or with your servlet.

Testing the installation is easy. First, start Tomcat by following the procedure described previously. Next, type the following command in a browser address box:

`http://localhost:8080`

You should immediately see a screen that looks like Figure A.2.

FIGURE A.2

The Tomcat localhost *home page.*

This page might change slightly with each version of Tomcat. If you do not see this page immediately, the most likely reason is that you have another program listening to port 8080. In that case, edit the file called server.xml in the `c:\Program Files\Apache Tomcat 4.0\conf` directory. Look for The number `8080`. In Tomcat 4.0, it is located here:

```
<!-- Define a non-SSL HTTP/1.1 Connector on port 8080 -->
<Connector
        className="org.apache.catalina.connector.http.HttpConnector"
            port="8080" minProcessors="5" maxProcessors="75"
            enableLookups="true" redirectPort="8443"
            acceptCount="10" debug="0" connectionTimeout="60000"/>
```

Edit the third line and change it to some higher value than `1024`, such as `1776`. It will look like this:

```
<!-- Define a non-SSL HTTP/1.1 Connector on port 8080 -->
 <Connector className=
            "org.apache.catalina.connector.http.HttpConnector"
            port="1776" minProcessors="5" maxProcessors="75"
            enableLookups="true" redirectPort="8443"
            acceptCount="10" debug="0" connectionTimeout="60000"/>
```

Save this file and restart the Tomcat server. Repeat the test by opening a browser, but this time type

http://localhost:1776

If this doesn't open the magic Web page shown in Figure A.2, consult the troubleshooting documentation that Tomcat installed on your hard drive.

A

Axis

Apache Axis is available at no cost from the Apache Web site at `http://xml.apache.org/axis/index.html`.

At the time of this writing, the most current, stable release is version 1.0. The link for downloading Axis is

`http://xml.apache.org/axis/releases.html`

The actual release you choose is not that important. We normally install the most recent, stable release that is listed on the Web site. Choose a release that is right for your needs. The following zip file will work for you, but later releases might be available by the time you read this:

`xml-axis-10.zip`

As new versions of Axis are released, the links that lead to them will differ from those shown here. In these cases, you will need to go to the `http://xml.apache.org/axis` Web site and navigate to the newest release.

Unzip this file somewhere convenient, such as under the c:\ directory. This will produce a directory structure that looks something like this:

```
xml-axis-10
   docs
   lib
   samples
   webapps
      axis
   xmls
```

If you are running under UNIX, you can download the tar version and follow the instructions on the Axis Web site on how to install it on your machine.

Vendor Web sites change from time to time. If the previous steps don't work exactly, look for similar links at each step, and you should be able to succeed in getting Axis installed.

Next, you need to move Axis into your Web server's directory structure. The instructions for installing Axis along with Tomcat 4.0.6 are to copy the Axis directory and all of its contents and subdirectories directly under the `C:\Program Files\Apache Tomcat 4.0\ webapps` directory.

If you are accustomed to working with commercial off-the-shelf (COTS) software, you might find these instructions complicated. All the Apache projects are open source. This means that they are mostly created by and for software engineers like the authors of this book. The project development staff is largely composed of volunteers who produce the code because they love it. Their strength is in programming, however, and not in documentation, ease of use, and so on. In addition, the phone support that we expect from commercial vendors is missing from Apache projects. You can submit questions to forums that are monitored by knowledgeable volunteers, however.

Starting Axis

Before you can start Axis, you must start Tomcat. You don't really start Axis in the same way that you would start a Web server because Axis runs as an application under that server. The server receives requests and forwards them to Axis for processing. When Axis finishes its work, it normally uses the Web server to return the results.

When you have placed the Axis directory in the correct location, you will be able to type in the following URL:

```
http://localhost:8080/axis/index.html
```

Figure A.3 shows this page.

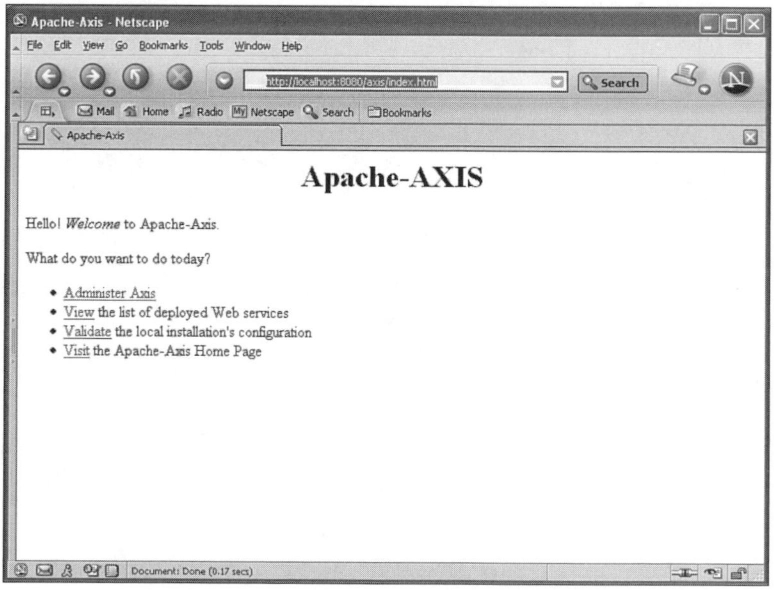

FIGURE A.3

The main Axis Web page.

The successful display of this page doesn't mean that you are really set up correctly, but it indicates that you have placed the main directory in the correct location on your Web server.

In addition, you need two parser files to be in your classpath. The easiest way to get them is to download them as part of the Xerces-J-bin.2.2.1.zip, which we found at `http://xml.apache.org/dist/xerces-j`. When we unzipped this file, we found two files that are required to parse XML, xercesImpl.jar and xmlParserAPIs.jar. Copy them from the `c:\xerces-2_1_1` directory into the `\webapps\axis\WEB-INF\lib` directory in the Tomcat file structure.

Testing the Installation

After you have finished the installation, you will want to test it. This can be done by opening a browser and typing in the following URL:

`http://localhost:8080/axis/index.html`

You should immediately see a screen that looks like Figure A.3.

If you don't get this page, you probably haven't copied the Axis directory and its subdirectories to the correct location under the file structure of your Web server, or you haven't placed the parser files in the right location.

Next, you can validate the installation further by clicking on the Validate hyperlink, which will take you to the following page:

`http://localhost:8080/axis/happyaxis.jsp`

You should immediately see a screen that looks like Figure A.4.

FIGURE A.4

The Axis Happiness page.

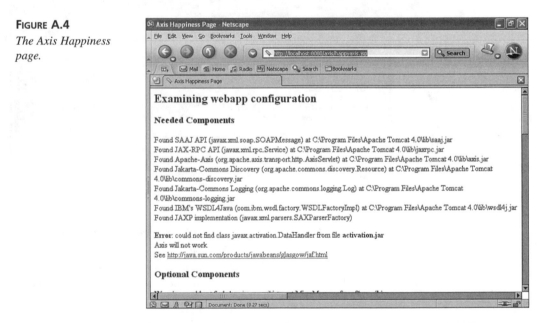

Notice that each needed jar file is listed, along with a status that says where that jar was located. Notice that there is a missing jar at the bottom of the figure. This is the activation.jar, which can be found at

`http://java.sun.com/products/javabeans/glasgow/jaf.html`

Downloading, unzipping, and copying this file to the `\webapps\axis\WEB-INF\lib` directory will get rid of this message.

> You must restart the Tomcat server every time you add a jar file to your lib directory, or Tomcat will not find it.

After you succeed in getting the Happiness page to say that your installation is fine, you can try the other links on the `http://localhost:8080/axis/index.html` page. The most useful of these links is the View link. Clicking on that link will bring up the page shown in Figure A.5.

FIGURE A.5

The Axis servlet page.

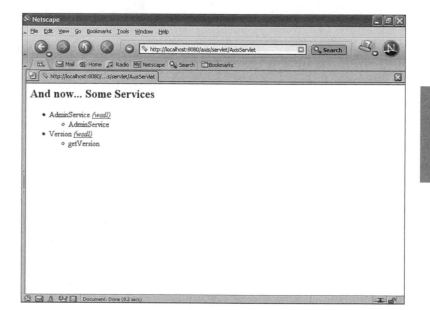

If this page appears, you have installed Axis correctly.

To run a client, you have to set your classpath to point to all the jar files in the Axis download, plus a few others. The classpath that was on our test machine was

```
CLASSPATH=.\;C:\xml-axis-10\lib\axis.jar;C:\xml-axis-10\lib\jaxrpc.jar;
C:\xml-axis-10\lib\saaj.jar;C:\xml-axis-10\lib\commons-logging.jar;
C:\xml-axis-10\lib\commons-discovery.jar;C:\xml-axis-10\lib\wsdl4j.jar;
C:\xerces-2_2_1\xmlParserAPIs.jar;C:\xerces-2_2_1\xercesImpl.jar;
C:\j2sdkee1.3.1\lib\j2ee.jar
```

APPENDIX B

Installing the Java Web Services Developer Pack

The Java Web Services Developer Pack can be downloaded from the Sun Java Web site. You can get to it directly using the following URL:

`http://java.sun.com/webservices/download.html`

A screen will come up with a number of packages that you can download. Select the Web Services Developer Pack. (At the time of this writing, the current version is 1.0_01.)

Before installation, you will need to have a version of the Java 2 Standard Edition Developer's Kit installed. Version 1.3.1 or higher is required. The Java Developer's Kit can also be downloaded from the `http://java.sun.com` Web site in the J2SE section.

After the JDK is installed, download and install the Java Web Services Developer Pack. On Windows-based machines, simply double-click the file that was downloaded for installation.

The pack includes a copy of Tomcat and Ant, as well as a number of jar files and other tools. It is recommended that you install the pack at the root directory (c:\, for instance).

During installation, you'll be prompted to provide a username and password for the Tomcat administrator account. Write these down because you'll need them later for configuring the Ant build scripts.

After the install is complete, go to Start, Programs and find the group named Java Web Services Developer Pack 1_0_01. Inside that group are icons to start and stop Tomcat. Select the Start Tomcat program. You can then verify that Tomcat was installed correctly by opening a browser window and typing the following:

```
http://localhost:8080/admin
```

You should receive a screen containing the Tomcat Administrator's log similar to the one shown in Figure B.1.

FIGURE B.1

The Tomcat Administrator's login screen.

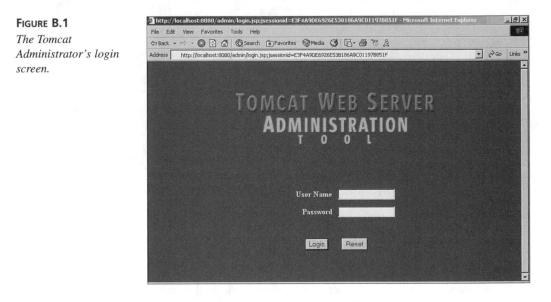

Enter the ID and password that you specified during the installation process and click Login. If everything is correct, you'll get a screen similar to the one shown in Figure B.2.

At this point, you know that Tomcat is installed correctly. Next you need to set some environment variable information. You'll need to include the /bin directory for both your JDK and for the Web Services Developer Kit into your Path environment variable. You should place these entries at the beginning of the path value to eliminate possible problems from other packages.

Figure B.2

The Tomcat Administration tool.

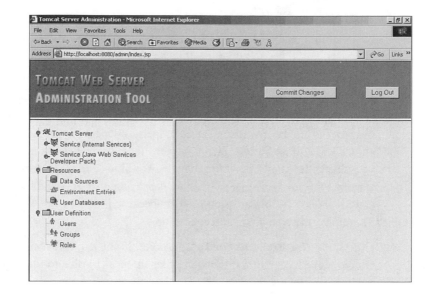

To do this on a Windows machine, right-click the My Computer icon on your desktop, select Properties and then the Advanced tab. (This is for Windows 2000, other versions might vary slightly.) Select Environment Variables. In the lower list box, see whether there is an entry for Path. If so, simply double-click to bring up an edit box and make the changes. If not, you'll need to click the New button to create a new entry for Path.

On our development machine, with JDK1.4_01 and the Web Services Developer Pack both installed in the C:\ directory, our path statement looked like this:

```
C:\jwsdp-1_0_01\bin;C:\j2sdk1.4.0_01\bin;%PATH%...
```

where ... indicated information for other programs that are not important to this book.

You will also need to create a new file in you home directory. On Windows machines, your home directory is usually found in c:\Documents and Settings*your username*\. You'll need to create a file named build.properties. Put the following into that file, replacing the ID and password with the ones you set up for the Tomcat administrator account during installation. Listing B.1 shows a sample build.properties file.

Listing B.1 The Build.properties File in Your Home Account

```
username=tomcatadmin
password=tomcatpassword
```

B

The examples in Hour 14, "Creating Web Services with Java," rely on the ant build tool for compiling and deploying. ant comes with the Web Services Development Pack. However, you'll need to do a few things to get ant to work correctly so that you can build and run the Hour 14 examples.

First, download the sample code from the Sams Web site and unzip the files. Inside the directory that is built, you'll find a subdirectory named common. Inside the common directory is another file named build.properties. Open this file with the text editor of your choice and edit the various directory paths found in that file to match the location where you placed the sample code for Hour 14. You'll need to make these changes to the lines starting with `tut-root`, `clib`, and `elib`. Please note that on Windows machines, the \ character must be used in pairs in these files because java uses \ as an escape sequence. Therefore, use \\ in any paths you set up.

Everything else should be good at this point. If you decide to build your own systems, simply make a copy of the following files in the ch14 directory and place them into another directory at the same level as the common directory. You'll need to modify the copies to match your new project's name, files, and so on.

```
build.properties
build.xml
config.xml
jaxrpc-ri.xml
web.xml
```

Installing and Configuring Other Toolkits

In Hour 19, "Creating Web Services with Other Toolkits," a number of other Web services toolkits are discussed. This appendix will help you install and configure those toolkits. It is recommended that you remove any other Web services toolkits, particularly Java-based ones, before installing any of these in order to minimize versioning issues and compatibility problems. All instructions found in this section assume that you're installing onto a clean system.

The Mind Electric GLUE 3.0

GLUE 3.0 can be fetched from The Mind Electric's Web site at `http://www.themindelectric.com`. From the home page, click on the Products tab and select Download. You will be presented with a screen asking you for your registration ID. You'll need to create an account in order to download the software. Registration is free, as is the software. Below the login prompts is a link to create a new account. Go ahead and do that. After registering, an email will be sent to you containing your ID and password. Save this in a safe place because you'll need it to access the download area in the future.

Once registered, go back into the Download screen and log in using your account. A screen will show up listing all the downloadable versions of GLUE. At the time of this writing, the newest release version is 3.2.3 and the newest beta is 4.0.2. We've chosen to use 4.0B2 Standard. By the time you read this, a full release version of 4.0 should be out and should closely resemble what you find in this book.

> You can use the 4.0B2 Professional version if you'd like, but there might be additional steps for setup that will not be covered here. Refer to the GLUE installation documentation for any problems found during installation of the Professional version.

Select the ZIP link for GLUE Standard 4.0B2. A License Information screen will appear. After reading it, confirm acceptance of the Terms and Conditions. Your browser will then prompt you for a location to store the zip file. Save the file to a location on your machine.

GLUE has the capability to run either as a standalone system, or as part of another application server suite. For the purposes of this book, we're going to be using GLUE in standalone mode.

Once the download is complete, unzip the file using a program such as WinZip. Make sure that you leave the option for Use Folder Names turned on because the zip contains many directories with files in them. You can unzip the contents to any location. On our machine, we're going to place it at the root of the C: drive.

After unzipping, you should find that the following directory structure was built as seen in Listing C.1:

LISTING C.1   Directory Structure of the GLUE System

```
\
  \electric
    \app-template
    \bin
```

LISTING C.1 continued

```
\console
\docs
  \glue
  \exml
\lib
\src
  \electric
  \examples
```

After you have the package unzipped, check the email account you specified during the registration process. A message should have been received containing an attachment named `glue-license.xml`. Save this file in the electric directory that was created during the unzip process. Once saved, you'll need to add this XML file to the GLUE-ALL.jar file found in the \electric\lib directory. The easiest way to do this is to open the GLUE-ALL.jar file with a tool such as WinZip, and then drag and drop the glue-license.xml file into the zip file's contents. This will add the file to the jar.

Next, you will need to modify your system's PATH and CLASSPATH environment variables. To do this on a Windows 2000 machine, go to your system desktop and right-click on My Computer. On the pop-up menu, select Properties. Select the Advanced tab and then click the button labeled Environment Variables. A screen like the one in Figure C.1 will appear.

FIGURE C.1

The Environment Variables dialog screen.

First, look in the lower list box to see if you have a PATH variable set. If not, you'll need to create a new one by clicking the New button. Otherwise, you can simply double-click on the PATH variable entry in the list to bring up its current settings. In either case, you'll need to add *<directory_where_you_unzipped_glue_to>*\electric\bin to the value of the PATH variable, where the first part inside the brackets should be replaced with the drive and location name where you installed the GLUE package. On our test machine, we installed GLUE to the C:\ drive, so our PATH statement looks like this:

```
C:\electric\bin;c:\j2sdk1.4.0_01\bin;
```

You'll need to follow the same procedure for the CLASSPATH variable. Add the following items to the variable's value:

```
C:\electric\lib\GLUE-ALL.jar;C:\electric\lib\GLUE-EXAMPLES.jar
```

We're not going to use JSP in our examples, but if you decide to do so in your setup, also add the tools.jar file from your JDK to the CLASSPATH variable.

Although we have shown the steps for setting up the environment variables on Windows 2000, other versions of Windows will be very similar. Some of the terminology and locations of buttons and tabs might be slightly different. Consult your tech support representative if you cannot find how to do this on your version of Windows.

Make sure that you have a version of the Java 2 Standard Edition Developer's Kit installed. This can be found on the java.sun.com Web site.

Now that you have everything installed, it's a good idea to try to run one of the sample programs that comes with the GLUE package. In this case, we'll run the Invoke example that comes with the GLUE package. To do this, we must first compile the code. Open a DOS prompt and navigate to the electric\src\examples\invoke directory. Once there, execute the following command:

```
javac *.java
```

A few seconds later, you should get a prompt. If you receive any error messages (particularly ones stating that a class cannot be found), double check your PATH and CLASSPATH environment variables. If you receive no messages, everything is set up correctly.

Now that you have the code compiled, navigate back to the \electric\src directory and execute the following command:

```
java examples.invoke.Invoke1
```

If everything is set up correctly, a connection will be made to a Web service running on the xmethods.com site and you will receive the following output (although the actual value might be different depending on current financial market conditions):

```
usa/japan exchange rate = 128.51
```

The GLUE package comes with an excellent set of documentation. If you run into any problems with setup, configuration, or want to learn more about how to do various things with the product, consult the documentation files. The root document will be found at electric\readme.html. Both User's Guides and the GLUE API can be found there as well.

In addition, there is a very active discussion group for GLUE found on Yahoo! at http://groups.yahoo.com/group/MindElectricTechnology/.

PocketSOAP Installation and Configuration

To use PocketSOAP, you'll need to download the latest version, which can be found at http://www.pocketsoap.com/pocketsoap. About halfway down the page is a table containing the links to the various installation versions. (The Win32 version is for Windows95/98/2000/ME/XP/NT.) Select the Win32 link and save the file to your machine.

After the file is downloaded, double-click on the file to start the installer for PocketSOAP. You'll be asked for a directory on which to install the PocketSOAP package. On our test machine, we placed it in the C:\Program Files\PocketSOAP directory.

After the files are installed, you should see a new group in the Window's Start Menu, Programs section named Simon Fell. Inside that directory should be one file named PocketSOAP.

For our example in Hour 19, we chose to use VBScript. If you'd like to use some other language, you'll need to install it at this time as well. VB6 and VC++ are supported, as well as both eVB and eVC++ for PocketPC development.

SOAP::Lite Installation and Configuration

In order to use SOAP::Lite on a Windows-based machine, you first will need a Web server. For this book, we used the Microsoft IIS server, which comes packaged with most versions of Windows including NT, 2000, and XP. If you are using a different operating system, you'll need to find some other Web server software to use. Installation of IIS is

C

beyond the scope of this book; however, many good resources are available online describing how to install it. Before moving on to the next step, check that your Web service software is operating properly.

SOAP::Lite is a Perl-based solution for Web services. Because Windows does not come with Perl support, you'll need to install a Perl package. We have chosen to use ActiveState's ActivePerl package, which is the most common Perl version for Windows. ActivePerl can be freely downloaded at http://www.activestate.com/Products/ ActivePerl/. At the time of this writing, the current version is 5.8.0.

After the package is downloaded, run the installer for ActivePerl. Make sure that you choose to install the examples because we'll use them later to verify your installation. During the installation process, a screen similar to the one found in Figure C.2 will be displayed.

FIGURE C.2

The ActivePerl Install Wizard will allow for setup options for configuring the IIS Plugin.

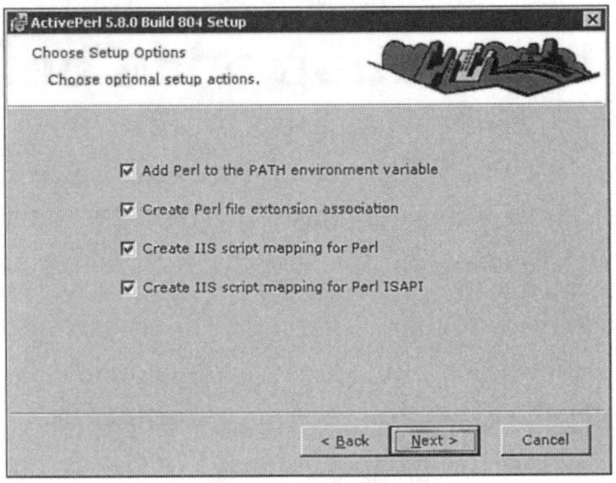

In most cases, you should leave all the options on this screen checked because they will automatically configure both the OS and IIS for using ActivePerl for you.

After the ActivePerl installer is finished, start IIS and then open a browser such as Internet Explorer or Netscape. Attempt to access the default page on the machine running IIS by pointing the browser to an address such as this:

http://127.0.0.1/

If IIS is running, the browser should display the default Web page for that server.

Next, we'll test the ActivePerl integration by making use of the environment variable dump sample script that comes with ActivePerl. Using Windows Explorer, navigate to the directory to which you installed ActivePerl. On our test machine, this was the C:\Perl directory. Move into the eg\cgi subdirectory. In there, you will find a file named env.pl. You'll need to copy this file into your Web server's cgi-bin directory. (Create this directory if it doesn't already exist.) Then, open your browser again and point it to a URL such as the following:

```
http://127.0.0.1/cgi-bin/env.pl
```

You should get back a screen that looks similar to the one in Figure C.3.

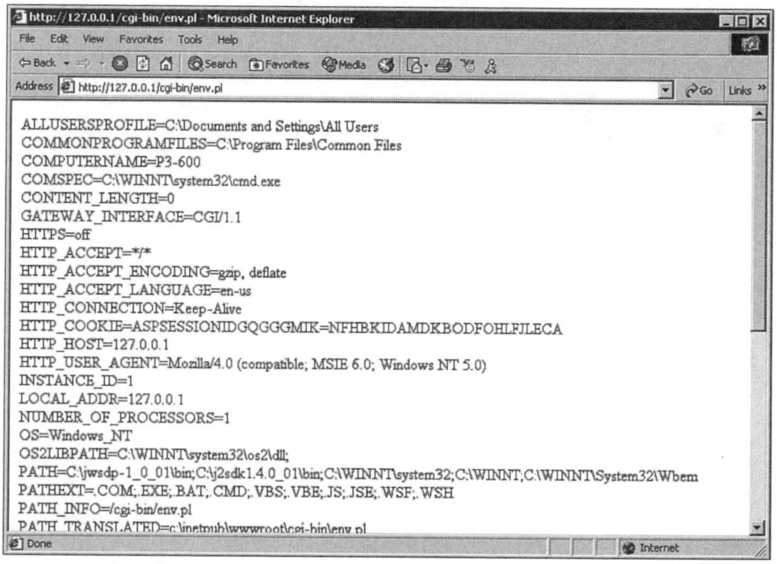

FIGURE C.3

The output of the env.pl Perl script connected to our IIS Web server.

If for some reason you do not get this screen, chances are you didn't select the option to enable the script-mapping option during the ActivePerl installation. To get around this, you can manually enable the script engine inside of IIS. To do this, open IIS. Then right-click on Default Web Site. Choose the Select Properties option from the menu. On the Home Directory tab, click Configuration. Select the tab marked App Mappings. In the list box, find the entry for .pl, highlight it, and then click the Edit button. In the dialog that appears, turn on the check box for Script Engine.

At this point, Perl and our Web server are working correctly. Now you'll need to get and install the SOAP::Lite software. The easiest way to do this is to use the CPAN service, which is a directory of Perl modules. To use CPAN, run the following command:

```
perl -MCPAN -e shell
```

If you don't have CPAN already installed, you'll be prompted through its installation routine. In most cases, you can just use the defaults unless you want to set things up in a special manner. After the install is finished, you'll be presented with a CPAN command line. Next, install SOAP::Lite by typing

```
install SOAP::Lite
```

A few messages will be displayed, and eventually you'll receive a message stating that SOAP::Lite is up-to-date. You can confirm that the package was installed by opening Windows Explorer and navigating to the `C:\Perl\site\lib\SOAP directory`. If that directory exists and contains files, the package is installed.

INDEX

How can we make this index more useful? Email us at indexes@samspublishing.com.

Your Guide to Computer Technology

www.informit.com

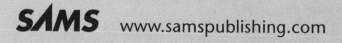

Other Related Titles

Sams Teach Yourself Microsoft Windows Server 2003 in 24 Hours
Joe Habraken
0-672-32494-6
$24.99 US / $37.95 CAN

Sams Teach Yourself Visual C#.NET in 24 Hours
James Foxall
0-672-32538-1
$29.99 US / $44.95 CAN

Sams Teach Yourself Extreme Programming in 24 Hours
Steward Baird
0-672-32441-5
$29.99 US / $44.95 CAN

Sams Teach Yourself ASP.NET in 24 Hours, Complete Starter Kit
Scott Mitchell
0-672-32543-8
$29.99 US / $44.95 CAN

Sams Teach Yourself UML in 24 Hours, 2nd Edition
Joseph Schmuller
0-672-32238-2
$29.99 US / $44.95 CAN

Sams Teach Yourself XML in 24 Hours, 2nd Edition
Michael Morrison
0-672-32213-7
$24.99 US / $37.95 CAN

Sams Teach Yourself Mac OS X in 24 Hours, 2nd Edition
John Ray, Robyn Ness
0-672-32474-1
$24.99 US / $37.95 CAN

Sams Teach Yourself HTML and XHTML in 24 Hours, 6th Edition
Dick Oliver, Michael Morrison
0-672-32520-9
$24.99 US / $37.95 CAN

Sams Teach Yourself Red Hat Linux 8 in 24 Hours
Aron Hsiao
0-672-32475-X
$29.99 US / $44.95 CAN

Sams Teach Yourself Java 2 in 24 Hours, 3rd Edition
Rogers Cadenhead
0-672-32460-1
$24.99 US / $37.95 CAN

Sams Teach Yourself Visual Basic.NET in 24 Hours, 2nd Edition
James Foxall
0-672-32537-3
$29.99 US / $44.95 CAN

SAMS
www.samspublishing.com

All prices are subject to change.